the Unexpected Houseplant

the Unexpected Houseplant

220 EXTRAORDINARY CHOICES
FOR EVERY SPOT IN YOUR HOME

Tovah Martin

Photography by Kindra Clineff

TIMBER PRESS

PORTLAND | LONDON

Published in 2012 by Timber Press, Inc.

The Haseltine Building
133 S.W. Second Avenue, Suite 450
Portland, Oregon 97204-3527
timberpress.com

2 The Quadrant
135 Salusbury Road
London NW6 6RJ
timberpress.co.uk

Printed in China

Book Design by Jeffrey Kurtz

Library of Congress Cataloging-in-Publication Data

Martin, Tovah.
 The unexpected houseplant : 220 extraordinary choices
for every spot in your home / Tovah Martin ;
photography by Kindra Clineff. -- 1st ed.
 p. cm.
 Includes bibliographical references and index.

 ISBN 978-1-60469-243-3

1. Indoor gardening.   2. House plants.   I. Clineff, Kindra.   II. Title.
SB419.M323 2012
635.9'65--dc23
                       2011045164

A catalog record for this book is also available from the British Library.

Many of the plants in this book have toxic ingredients and may cause serious poisoning to people or pets and/or can cause dermatological reactions or eye irritation. Not all toxic plants are noted in the text. For more information on houseplant toxicity in humans, seek the expertise of qualified medical professionals. For cases of suspected poisoning, call 800-222-1222, the national hotline of the American Association of Poison Control Centers. For pets, visit aspca.org for more information on toxic plants. The author and publisher disclaim any liability whatsoever with respect to losses or damages arising out of the information contained in this book.

FRONTISPIECE
A tireless performer of Olympic pro-portions, *Chirita longgangensis* never pauses in its flower production.

OPPOSITE
Anyone can force *Iris histrioides* 'George'; it buds up rapidly after a brief chilling period.

To Dennis and Rob,
for being there

To Einstein,
my research assistant

Autumn 20

Winter 84

Spring

Summer

Love Thwarted

Basics

Contents

ACKNOWLEDGMENTS

This book was a lifetime in the making. So I'm going to delve way back and start by paying homage to my houseplant mentors, Mrs. Bertha Doran and Joy Logee Martin. There were role models along the way, like Elvin McDonald, Mike Kartuz, Peter Loewer, and Thalassa Cruso. I'd like to thank the fellow aficionados who blazed tangential paths, such as my friends at Logee's Greenhouses and greenhouses in towns large and tiny stretching across the country. At Timber Press, I thank Tom Fischer for his enthusiasm and input—he put this book on course. Eve Goodman's insight and guiding hand plus Andrew Beckman's artistic advice aided this book's journey. I'm grateful to Sarah Rutledge Gorman for her skillful, wise, and sensitive editing. My agent, Jane Dystel, worked behind the scenes to make this book happen. My friends Denny Sega, Rob Girard, Peter Wooster, and Naomi Price were touchstones and islands of calm. My mother forfeited several daughterly visits for the sake of this book. Speaking of family, we are indebted to Einstein, the Maine Coon kitten and research assistant, who did the stress and bounce testing. And without the graphic design aid of Tim Preston, the proposal would never have flown. Jody Clineff was her usual bastion of efficiency with the photographic liaison. But most of all, Kindra Clineff deserves all the antiques of her dreams and a bay leaf wreath for the glowing photography in these pages. She put her soul into this book—just as she infuses every project with her sage ingenuity. Without her creativity, ideas, eagerness, patience, acumen, and friendship, this book would be nowhere.

INTRODUCTION

From the road, it looks like any other house. For anyone tooling through town, my home doesn't really stand out, except perhaps for its preponderance of garden beds visible from the street and the fact that it's a tad funkier than the neighboring New England architecture in the center of town. Especially in winter, you'd be prone to roll right on by without giving it so much as a second glance. But if you had reason to nose into the drive-way, knock on the front door, and slip inside, it would be a whole different story.

Just about every sunny or semi-sunny window in my home entertains plants like *Stapelia scitula*, echeveria, *Begonia* 'Zip', and *Euphorbia* 'Peppermint Candy'.

Basically, if you don't like plants, don't bother to enter. Agoraphobics will be just as agri-challenged inside as they are in the field. Because within that unassuming exterior resides a wonderful world of roaming vines and hairy stems. Leaves of all shapes, sizes, textures, scents, and combinations of colors are given free rein. You must brush by them to deliver the FedEx box. It's necessary to engage with the flower spike of the pregnant onion before gaining entry into the converted barn, where the comfy chair awaits. Watch how you angle the groceries around the kalanchoe, because clumsily maneuvered baggage will bring it down. Only dogs with short tails are allowed in.

Wherever it is possible to host plants, my house is wall-to-wall greenery. I didn't bother doing much with decorator colors on the walls; I didn't sweat the window treatments or the framed family portraits—the plants are my decor. At any given moment, I host hundreds of houseplants, give or take a couple of dozen. In autumn, the inventory might swell when I crowd more plants inside than the light venues can comfortably host. In winter, the amaryllis and other holiday cheerfuls hold forth. In spring, the accumulation swells with seedlings that are destined for outdoors. For a few brief months in the depths of summer, the head count decreases while the majority of my indoor plants sojourn outside. But I keep many succulents and all my terrariums close by because the home feels empty without their green presence. I can't live without the jungle of leafy branches and groping vines that I call home.

It's a jungle in here,
with plants sprawling
from the front door
throughout the house.

And it's not as though I don't have green elsewhere in my life. I garden intensively and extensively outdoors in summer. Every weekend, I hop in the car and visit gardens. Then I spend the rest of the year with the enviable job of writing about summer gardens. But I still couldn't live without plants sharing my abode. For me it's all about the plants stretching their limbs, forming their buds, expanding new leaves, and responding to my nurturing (or neglect, if called for). And that sensation—that intimacy with nature—is what I strive to describe in this book. If nothing else, this is the chronicle of a romance between botany and a kid who craves green.

But under that thin veneer is an ill-concealed attempt to convert you. I'm hoping you'll buy into this. I'm doing my best to demonstrate how plants can change your psyche when you welcome them into your life. It's radical. It's the difference between holding nature at arm's length and embracing it into the heart of your home. But don't take my word for it—give plants a chance. Live intimately with them. Let them connect. Experience their cycles and rhythms. Flow them into your agenda. Encourage those tendrils to meander into your everyday experience so they're inextricably woven into your life. Do it with all the style, creativity, and devotion that you lavish on the other aspects of your life. Do it with the fervor you pour on your pets, for example, and you could end up starting a sweet relationship. Here, in the pages that follow, are the tools you'll need to achieve your in-house botanical bond.

BACKGROUND

You're wondering how I got into this pickle, aren't you? How did I get this green gig going deep inside in the first place? Well, it started innocently enough. There's probably a green-oriented child in every bunch of youngsters, and I was that kid. I spent my spare time pestering the old florist down the street who puttered around her greenhouse, and I brought home anything she would give away. That's really how it began—with an ivy, I believe.

I brought it home and I put it proudly on my desk at the end of the room, far from a light source. I was clueless, but it's hard to go wrong with an ivy. That initial positive input probably set me on my future track. My sister had great pictures on her wall on the other side of the room. She had great clothes, great friends, great taste, a great figure—and I had my ivy. It moved me in the right direction.

I grew up (sort of), and somehow ended up working with tropical plants. I thought I wanted to be a farmer, and grew an acre of organic vegetables in my spare time, but ended up in a family greenhouse business, falling in love with one of the sons and also with the collection of tropical plants that three generations of houseplant fanatics had built. Meanwhile, we grew a polite smattering of houseplants in the Victorian home we shared with my mother-in-law. It wasn't as plant-dense or funky as my current domain, but it was in keeping with the ambiance.

That setting leads into the backstory here, because houseplants came of age with the Victorians. Of course, throughout history, gardeners have brought plants indoors out of necessity. No one wanted to leave their favorite rosemary out to freeze during the winter when they desperately needed its savory zing to make the potatoes tasty. But prior to the nineteenth century, most homes were too dark and heating systems too primitive for plants to thrive in the typical dimly lit abode that

Smack dab in the middle of the converted barn, receiving only indirect light, mosses such as *Selaginella kraussiana* 'Aurea' (right) and 'Frosty Fern' (*Selaginella kraussiana* 'Variegata') dwell beside an immense terrarium cradling *Asplenium nidus*.

went below freezing indoors every frigid winter night. Stoic plants survived indoors during the winter, but they weren't the salubrious, ebullient entities I describe in this book.

That changed with technological advances. Heating systems became different, streamlined animals in the nineteenth century, and glass-making processes were perfected, allowing the average homeowner to expand window space. Houseplants followed close on the heels of increased light.

Our Victorian home had a bay window in its back parlor, and this was one offshoot of the trend toward increased light indoors and its influence on gardening. Bay windows really were an architectural response to a generation of gardeners who wanted to bring nature indoors to enjoy close up. Not only did a bay window augment light, but because it was recessed from the main room, it kept plants cool at a time when improved heating systems were making living spaces newly toasty. True to tradition, our bay windows hosted begonias staged in jardinieres. It was a nod in the right direction, but it was much more buttoned down than the jungle that would fill my later living space.

This story really begins when I moved on. That was my initiation into houseplant gardening in earnest. There was no question that plants would infiltrate my new home. But as the plants started marching in, I was surprised at how different this mode of indoor gardening was from my previous tropical experience. Beyond the Victorian house, my new situation offered a more engaging relationship with plants. It was indoor gardening embraced. It was intimate and much more of a lark. Funk found its way into the dialogue. Once I got the hang of it and learned its parameters, there was more potential. That's what led to the wall-to-wall coverage.

Not everything is a long relationship. Some flirtations are brief, such as mine with *Ornithogalum thyrsoides* 'Alaska'. For a few months, it was the first thing I looked at when I woke in the morning. Then it went dormant.

Sending out entangling arms and legs, if ever a plant was bound and determined to gather converts into the houseplant fold, it's *Jasminum polyanthum.*

An attached greenhouse came with this home, and it greets everyone who enters the front door. But the greenhouse bank of glass faces east with a solid wall (not glass) on the west, plus it has buildings cutting off light on three sides. It basically acts like a large window, maybe slightly improved by the light coming in from above. It's crammed with plants. And the rest of the house is equally maxed out by plants. I have only one north window; other windows face east, west, and south, and there are many. But I wouldn't call it a house that is overly endowed with windows. That said, I have conscientiously kept my incoming light unobstructed. Although gardens have sprung up everywhere surrounding the house and beyond, I've never planted a tree that stands (or one day might stand) between potential sunbeams and my houseplants. That's not happenstance—it's a policy.

Plants are everywhere indoors. Literally, I've commandeered any place that can be coaxed to grow any sort of plant. The situation has been edging in that direction since the first day I moved into my house 15 years ago, and the quantity of botanical roommates has increased over the years. Long before I started this book, my life was filled with plants. Just ask the UPS man.

Of course, I have help. The houseplants are Einstein's mission too. Einstein is the nonpedigree Maine Coon shelter kitten I adopted a few months ago to fill the oversize paws of Monk Monk, a much-beloved 20-year-old Maine Coon who passed away last year. Not to be a spoiler, but Einstein figures prominently in these pages. So it seems like a good moment to talk about houseplants and their interaction with the rest of your family. Until he established himself firmly and indisputably as a mauler (of epic proportions), bouncer, and shredder, rather than an ingester, the houseplants and Einstein kept their distance. Some plants are toxic. Do not assume that any plant in this book is edible. To be on the safe side, keep houseplants out of reach. Grow them where children and pets can't possibly tangle with or ingest them. If you think they might be a problem for your family, steer away from plants such as calla lilies, narcissus, ivies, hyacinths, crotons, euphorbias, sansevierias, *Passiflora caerulea*, and others that are particularly toxic. But this is by no means a complete list. For information about animal toxicity, go to aspca. org/pet-care/poison-control/plants/. For questions about human toxicity, call a poison control center and visit aapcc.org. But keep in mind that an allergic reaction to any plant is possible. Dermatological reactions to many plants are also possible. Always wear gloves and protective clothing when working with plants. Several excellent books have been devoted to the subject and they are mentioned in Suggestions for Further Reading. And even though you may garden organically, it is possible that a nursery might have applied pesticides to a plant prior to your purchase. Einstein has learned to live with my collection of plants, but it was an educational process for us both.

The teaching process had plenty of opportunity. The unique factor of this book is that I focus only on the plants that I grow or have grown. This book isn't about all the houseplants in the world—there are too many. This is a chronicle of the highlights of my indoor garden. It's about my very own, overly green, botanically jam-packed home.

So call me a fanatic. I won't even flinch, because it's true. But I like to think I'm a realistic maniac. I'm not going to claim that you can feed yourself on citrus through the winter. I'm not even going to say you can grow an abutilon without whitefly or a gardenia that doesn't look jaundiced. But I am going to share the successes that I've had growing houseplants in a fairly ordinary growing environment. And the successes have been many and glorious.

But I'm a confessed missionary and I'm trying to dangle the lure and offer the tools to rope you in as well. You can easily savor these successes. There's nothing privileged about my situation besides perhaps access to windows; there's nothing vastly different between our circumstances. I want you to give this a try. Tell you what: kick off your shoes, sit back, and imagine a jasmine sending its tendrils meandering toward your comfy chair. Now turn to Spring, and I'll tell you how to make it happen. We'll do it together.

Only have a small pocket of space? *Serissa foetida* 'Mount Fuji' remains miniature to fill that niche.

YOU CAN DO THIS

Absolutely, you can do it. Once you steady your shaky hand, give yourself the pep talk, march into the supermarket, tenderly ease a deserving little plant into your shopping cart, and proceed to the checkout line to make the adoption legal, you stand an excellent chance of securing success. You don't have to go to a specialty nursery (although you can, if you want); you don't have to spend scads of money (although that's certainly an option)—you can just go to the grocery store and start with something safely on the beaten track. Give it a cool container, some care, the right light, and enough water, and you might be on your way to a lasting relationship.

In my opinion, the secret lies in selecting a plant that tugs at your heartstrings. When your Aunt Maude saddles you with her spider plant (notice that I haven't bothered to profile spider plants; I'm boycotting them in this volume and probably in all possible sequels), bring it straight to the dumpster if you share my aversion. Don't even go through the motions of growing it, neglecting it, and watching it gradually suffer a slow and painful death. (Of course, if a spider plant is your heartthrob, my apologies for the slight. And by all means embrace one.) In your home, grow only plants that you find appealing. I know it sounds obvious. But I am also continually blindsided by this issue. Somebody will bestow their favorite plant on me (usually right before moving to a very distant part of the country), and I feel obligated to welcome it into the fold. But not really. I almost always treat it badly. I act like the evil stepmother. And because Cinderella stories don't prevail in the plant world, the poor wee (or not-so-wee) thing begins to fail. Then it gets insects. Before it dies, it takes out all the newly infested plants in close proximity. You see what I mean.

Einstein on a rampage.

There's got to be chemistry. In the back of this book, there's a chapter that reveals all the basics of plant care. Throughout, I offer hints in every chapter to guide your way into houseplant proficiency. Certainly, all this advice will help you reach bingo. But the romance comes first. True, you might learn to adore a houseplant that didn't have "love at first sight" appeal, but only if it survives to become something that might lure you into that sort of affair.

Other than the desire to create something meaningful with a green thing, it doesn't take much. You'll get the hang of it in no time. You can accelerate from total non-greenness to an extremely adroit houseplant grower in a blink. With the right botanical someone, decent potting soil on hand (that's important), the proper light, and an appropriate container, Eden can be yours.

Actually, a little creative imagination might come in handy. Supermarket plants are (alas) inherently unappealing. By and large, they look fairly dowdy in their pathetic plastic pots. But don't let the package stand in the way of a first date. Try to think about what that little plant might look like when dressed for success. The container is key: it's like a picture frame. Give that little plant the shine of a natty container, and it just might glow. I know—sometimes it seems like a stretch. But if you feel the slightest spark, give it a chance.

This book is filled with plants that worked for me. I confess that I jump hoops for certain houseplants. But it doesn't have to be difficult. It really isn't hard. There are moments when it's a challenge to fit watering into my schedule, but I quench my plants' thirst. There are times when fitting a meal into my schedule is a crush. And nonetheless, I have managed to keep myself alive and fed. Not only that, but I've managed to keep Einstein nourished. And I attend to the plants' needs as well. Good things have happened as a result of all this nurturing. Yes, you do have to devote a little effort to growing houseplants. But it's absolutely worthwhile. Don't take my word for it: give houseplants a chance.

No need to search far for appropriate plants; any supermarket will serve up *Cyclamen persicum* when the winter holidays draw near. Your task is to jazz it up.

The scene in the
converted barn is
stolen by a huge
apothecary jar
terrarium. Closer
to the windows
dwell a few *Tillandsia*
spp. on the table
and a flowering kale
'White Peacock'
beside a sansevieria
and kalanchoe.

Other people rend their clothes and mourn the loss of summer, but not me. I'll miss the outdoor garden and fresh air just as much as the next guy, so I'm not actually dancing a jig. Still, there's a quiet comfort that comes in autumn. That's why I'm starting this book in fall, because it really is the beginning of the indoor gardening season. Autumn is all about gathering. It's the time when all my green buddies are herded indoors. All are safe. All are warm. But even more to the point, all are close.

Indoors is a great place to be in autumn. Spaces that seemed lacking suddenly are overflowing with robust growing things. Those few summer months of increased light, open windows, and a porch sojourn do a world of good for plants. But the hunkered sense of intimacy in autumn is everything.

By autumn, plants have added girth. Those that have become too bulky get trimmed. But not many are curtailed, because there's something truly sensual about brushing past branches and stems as I move around the house. It's like all my botanical brethren are giving me the glad hand. It's like we're a team and this is the victory lap.

Simultaneously, there is a lot going on in autumn. Fall is no slouch. In the houseplant calendar, it really is a season worth looking forward to. Some plants missed the summer boat and need a longer season to swing into flowering mode—calla lilies come to mind immediately. Other plants, such as plectranthus, receive a signal from the shortening days to set buds. Even the citrus starts its winter performance with a dribble of precocious blossoms. But flowers aren't the only game in town. In autumn, the foliage on houseplants glows, and the sunbeams coming through the windowpanes train a spotlight on the glory. I don't mean to be smug. But autumn is my proudest moment.

With *Plectranthus oertendahlii* in my east-facing bedroom window, autumn is all promise and few regrets.

It's another clear case of Not In My Backyard. I do it. You do it. We all do it. We've sent our houseplants outside to play for a summer recess, and we're in denial as the temperatures begin to drop. When the weather reports threaten the first touch of frost, it is not going to happen to me. Nope. Frost will smite someone else, maybe. But not here.

Well, in Zone 5 New England, frost always comes eventually. (The USDA has created a Hardiness Zone map to help us match our climate with garden plants outdoors. The average minimum temperature in Zone 5 is −10°F to −15°F.) And one day, I'm going to learn not to let it sneak up on me. I'll gradually march my tender plants back inside from their summer sojourn outdoors and let them acclimate to the changes in light and heat while I'm still throwing windows open during the day. That way, the transition won't be so abrupt. But I'm just as human as everyone else. So there's an eleventh-hour panic when the weatherman lays down the law and everything is rushed inside. Considering the bedlam that ensues, it's amazing that all the houseplants take the mass roundup in their stride. The scene could really be likened to a rodeo, with bleachers being dragged in, plant stands positioned, and piles upon piles of saucers lined up on standby, ready to be matched with a plant partner. As I see it, the trick is to get everything into its permanent position on the first run. You don't want to be lifting and shuffling twice (or more).

And yet, every year the puzzle pieces are thrown up in the air (or at least totally disassembled) and reconfigured. A few plants have permanent stations—especially the largest individuals, such as the massive staghorn fern. Beyond that, every year is different. First and foremost, the plants are arranged according to light needs. The bright south windows receive the sun-lovers. Plants that can tolerate lower light conditions are paraded onto the east- and west-facing sills or plant stands near the sills.

After light, I stage plants as if designing a garden. I think about height, shape, texture, color, and how the containers look with their benchmates. I even factor in the saucers and try to match them. If it weren't such a mad rush, it would be the year's highlight. When all is said and done, it's a several-day affair that I savor. And it also goes without saying that I want to be home for the event. I don't leave home in autumn without keeping tabs on the long-range forecast.

I know it sounds trivial, but I spend a lot of time matching pots with saucers. And in my home, this detail produces the most trading back and forth. When a saucer isn't sufficiently large or deep to handle overflow, my wood floor suffers the consequences. I have no expensive furniture, and pretty much every flat surface is appropriate for plants. Still, even if a table is worth almost nothing in the dollar-and-cents market, I don't want to mar its finish or paint. So everything gets a saucer or is put on a surface that will allow me to water without fear of mildew stains or worse. That's important. But it's also key to have saucers or other bases that befit your home. Doilies and cheap clear plastic saucers don't work for me. Cork or another pad prevents mildew stains if I use a saucer that might sweat.

Some plants come in ahead of the crush. Several in my collection would rather not witness the gradual cooling outdoors, such as begonias. When temperatures dip below 50°F (10°C), they stop growing. Some of the more finicky rex begonias (which I avoid, by the way) start curling their leaves and become susceptible to leaf-spotting diseases and powdery mildew. Don't put them through it. Ditto for gesneriads, which really don't want the stress.

And speaking of temperatures, keep a gap between plants and heating vents when you're placing your green refugees. Nothing confuses a plant as much as suddenly receiving a jet stream of dry, hot air when it just spent the last few months in the Great Outdoors. Actually, any plant (even individuals who haven't been given a summer recess) might react badly to a steady diet of forced hot air. And don't put plants on radiators when the heating season begins, or their soil will dry out irreparably and the roots will become parched.

That brings us to watering. I find myself watering more often in autumn when I first bring plants indoors. It helps ease the transition from outdoors to inside. And I continue to fertilize until Thanksgiving, when light levels dip, although I decrease the dosage and frequency as the days shorten.

Keep in mind that light changes in autumn. The rays stream into windows at a different angle. I've actually scorched jasmines by failing to monitor bright sunlight careening through a west window in fall. Plus, trees are suddenly dropping their leaves, allowing light to penetrate where it wasn't previously a factor. In most cases, plants enjoy the additional light, but not always. Plants that prefer shade can be adversely affected. Keep an eye on things.

Many plants get haircuts when I bring them indoors. Pruning allows me to jam more plants into limited space, but it also reduces the amount of water each plant requires and readies the plant for lower light. Even more important, it holds the line on repotting. Unless a plant is so pot-bound that it's a water guzzler, I prefer not to repot in autumn. Why provide fresh soil when most plants are moving into a season of diminished growth? Instead, I wait until spring.

After the initial re-entry, when everything green is hurled back into your stratosphere and comes solely under your influence again (no more shaking your fist at the Powers That Be and complaining for lack of rain), autumn is for soaking up the vibes again. Enjoy.

ACALYPHAS

I LOVE FLOWERS as much as the next guy. But you can't always bank on them, especially indoors. Instead, you've got to hang your hat on something more stable. Superdeluxe foliage fills that slot. And that's where *Acalypha wilkesiana* and its many cultivars ('Bourbon Street' and 'Beyond Paradise' are personal favorites), with their colorful (but not too over-the-top gaudy) leaves, come in handy for creating the right dynamic in an indoor garden. After all, indoor gardening is all about balance, and acalyphas give height as well as never-ceasing color of the foliar kind.

But let's step back to talk about the flagship member of the acalypha crew. I used to grow red hot cat's tail or chenille plant, *Acalypha hispida*, when I worked at Logee's Greenhouses in Danielson, Connecticut. When I first came, back in the 1970s, an immense specimen monopolized an entire corner of a greenhouse. You had to brush past it to do any potting, which was a nice sensation, given the caterpillar-thick, bright-red, chenille-like streamers that dangle 8 inches (20cm) from the stems. Still a teenager and new to tropicals, I wasn't the least bit apologetic about finding the plant fascinating. It's big and outrageous. And yet, even then I acknowledged that, if you discounted the flowers, *A. hispida* doesn't have a whole lot going for it. In later years, I totally avoided the chenille plant in my home. It lacks the qualities that make it worthwhile over the long haul.

Acalypha hispida illustrates the nexus of my experience with growing houseplants in my cottage. What works in a greenhouse doesn't necessarily translate in your home. It's like the difference between loving the baby elephant at the zoo and bringing him home with you. Plus, growing in a house is totally different than growing in a commercial greenhouse. You follow different practices and make different selections when a plant will become part of your daily life. Meeting the chenille plant at work was mildly amusing. Navigating around it close up and personal was another matter entirely. Plus, cleaning up its continual detritus of brown and deflated catkins is still another reason to give pause.

Although *Acalypha hispida* doesn't tickle me, a slew of close relatives have appeared on the scene, and they raise the bar considerably. The difference is the foliage. Rather than putting their emphasis on the wacky flowers, *A. wilkesiana* and its many cultivars go for ravishing leaves and, as a bonus, throw their production of discrete little incidental furry catkins into the brew. Often, the catkins enhance the foliar pizzazz, but they aren't key (although they also shed shamelessly).

Size-wise, most acalyphas are substantial plants. With the exception of *Acalypha godseffiana*, which has the potential for remaining much more compact but can gain girth with time, the rest quickly become 2 to 3 feet (60–90cm) in diameter. It is space well invested, though, because they pack quite a punch. And because the foliage is performing the stunts, the show is ongoing and uninterrupted. However, pruning is essential to carve the plant into shape; otherwise, it can become gangly. Do the whacking in summer to bask in the results when autumn and winter roll around. A sunny window is also a critical ingredient to keep the plant from becoming gangly. Like poinsettias, which are their relatives, they can tolerate lower light for a week or more while they're on display for an event or family get-together.

Compared to *Acalypha hispida*, the rest of the brood is easy street. They don't need the heavy dose of fertilizer that *A. hispida* demands, and they don't have the same propensity to attract whiteflies. Spider mites can be in the cards if that pest is roving around. But I've never had the problem. All in all, they're great houseplants.

Acalypha wilkesiana

cultivars

ACALYPHA

ALSO CALLED: **beefsteak plant, chenille plant, copperleaf, Jacob's coat, red hot cat's tail, red hot poker**

FLOWERS	**Furry, colorful catkins**
FOLIAGE	**Cultivars have colorful leaves similar to coleus**
SIZE	**2–3 feet (60–90cm) in height**
EXPOSURE	**Sunny**
WATER REQUIREMENTS	**Moderately thirsty**
OPTIMUM NIGHTTIME TEMPERATURE	**55–65°F (12–18°C)**
RATE OF GROWTH	**Fast**
SOIL TYPE	**Humusy potting soil with compost included**
FERTILIZING	**In early spring, summer, and late autumn only**
PROBLEMS	**Spider mites are frequently an issue. Acalyphas are toxic and can cause a severe dermatological reaction.**

CALLA LILIES

With thick, waxy white "pulpits" and arrow-shaped leaves, my calla lily came from the original Victorian collection at Logee's Greenhouses.

There is only one cupboard in my office so tall and solitary that Einstein can't (easily) sail onto it, and that's where *Zantedeschia* 'Mango' sits.

SECRETLY, I DON'T mind if my calla lilies fail to flower in summer. During the growing season, I take them outdoors and position them where they can get the full benefits of fresh air, frequent rain (assuming it's not a drought year), and all the other perks that summer serves up. They respond by sending up their handsome, fleshy, arrow-shaped leaves. That's all I ask in summer. But one of autumn's big moments indoors happens when the calla lily I've hauled back inside sends up flower spikes and begins to unfold. That marks the beginning of a long, slow, seductive unfurling that rivals any ballet. Finally, the gigantic Jack-in-the-Pulpit flower is in full, pearly white splendor, with its little curlicue tip on the end. No wonder artists were enthralled by this sexy seductress.

I primarily grow *Zantedeschia aethiopica*, the traditional white calla lily I brought with me when I moved in. Some plants follow you wherever you go, and *Z. aethiopica* was a keeper. And when I say that this is a traditional plant, my calla lily (originally known as *Richardia aethiopica*) is an heirloom. Each leaf of this majestic plant is 6 to 8 inches (15–20cm) broad and every leaf stretches to stand about 2 feet (60cm) long. After I've schlepped everything in to shelter the caboodle from imminent frost, a flower spike (or two) finally initiates in the pots. Weeks will come and go before they actually open their waxy white sheath, but the prelude is part of the beauty.

The calla lily often gets leggy outdoors over the summer. So I whack it back to the base when I bring it indoors (and the journey inside is a body builder—we're talking a heavy, 12-inch [30cm] wide container to give the tubers space). Without fail, the plant begins to sprout up again immediately after cutting back and the blooming sequence is not dissuaded, although it might be delayed slightly. I give it some fish emulsion (but note that fertilizing heavily will result in weak, floppy stems rather than the strong erect leaves and flower spikes that the calla lily is capable of producing). And I keep it very generously watered—callas are nearly aquatic. There is a downside to *Zantedeschia aethiopica* in a home environment: its leaves exude a sticky substance that forms a teardrop at the point of the arrow-shaped leaf and then drips down. There's not much you can do about it, except perhaps to put something underneath to protect the floor or carpet. Calla lilies are also poisonous, so keep them away from children and pets.

Nowadays, all sorts of *Zantedeschia* cultivars are available, adding *Z. albo-maculata* and others into the brew. Many have intriguing dappled leaves, most are more compact than *Z. aethiopica*, and they are bred to blossom in containers throughout the summer. The waiting period is a thing of the past. And the color range is incredible, from smoldering orange to darkest (nearly black) burgundy. They are all excellent houseplants and survive drought better than my favorite species. I say, go for them. I'm smitten.

Zantedeschia aethiopica
and cultivars

CALLA LILY

FLOWERS	Lovely Jack-in-the-Pulpit blossoms in varying colors
FOLIAGE	Arrow-shaped and dark green; some cultivars have speckles
OTHER ATTRIBUTES	Glorious cut flower
SIZE	2 feet (60cm) in height, depending on cultivar, but many are shorter
EXPOSURE	East or west
WATER REQUIREMENTS	Heavy drinker
OPTIMUM NIGHTTIME TEMPERATURE	55–65°F (12–18°C)
RATE OF GROWTH	Fast
SOIL TYPE	Rich, heavy, humusy soil
FERTILIZING	Between early spring and late autumn
PROBLEMS	Whiteflies, mealy bugs, and spider mites; cut off the foliage before it goes dormant. Calla lilies are highly toxic.

Cissus rhombifolia 'Ellen Danica' doesn't demand direct light from a window.

CISSUS

I LIKE TO think of my indoor garden as a stage. And the plants swarm inside in autumn like actors in a drama. They play the roles, they fill my life, they are my family. It's all woven together, and each plant serves a function. These are the thoughts that run through my head—sometimes subliminally, occasionally coming to the surface—as I parade each pot into the house in autumn. Foremost in my mind is giving these tender guys shelter. The Noah's Ark mentality is definitely a factor. But the house isn't just a refuge. It's my home. It's our home. Beauty is not just a jumble; it must have order. It takes all types to achieve a functional community.

As the houseplants flow in (who am I fooling? as the houseplants are hauled in) to take their stations indoors, everything pivots around a few firmly established sentinels. Although my *Cissus rhombifolia* isn't going to make top billing, it is a constant standby. Sometimes you need old faithfuls to keep the beat rolling. Blossoms aren't in the cards for *C. rhombifolia*. Fireworks are definitely not in its future, nor is glitz. But when it comes to creating the mood of wall-to-wall greenery with zero trouble, where would I be without 'Ellen Danica'?

I gave plain vanilla *Cissus rhombifolia* the cold shoulder a few years ago. Anything that looks identical to poison ivy is not going to get far in my home. I would've been ecstatic if the plant, called the grape ivy, really did resemble a grape leaf. But no. Poison ivy came too readily to mind. Plus, it was prone to leaf diseases. I've read that powdery mildew is a problem, but mine seemed susceptible to a type of unsightly black spot. Anyway, out it went.

'Ellen Danica' is much more graceful, and you can find huge plants for a song. With deeply cut, oak-shaped leaves on climbing stems with tendrils galore, I use mine to camouflage the toilet tank (don't ask what happens when I call a plumber). You laugh. But if you're really with me on this, why not the toilet? I've never met one with soft lines; they all could use a few meandering branches to break the sharp angles. Needless to say, the toilet isn't positioned right in the window, but the cissus does fine with low light. I'm not saying no light, but it definitely does not need to monopolize a window.

Also in the ironclad category is *Cissus antarctica*, with beech-shaped leaves and almost no redeeming qualities whatsoever. It's clumsy, boring, and virtue-free. However, you can't kill it. If survival is your primary criterion, go for it. More interesting is tiny *C. striata*, which basically looks like someone shrank the big grape ivy and made it demure. *Cissus striata* isn't quite as easy, but it's almost up there in the impossible-to-kill department. I grow it in terrariums to look like a miniature grape, and it performs the ruse and tolerates high humidity without batting an eyelash.

Not quite so fail-safe is *Cissus discolor*. Although it is readily available, this cissus can be a challenge in a home environment. Known as the rex begonia vine, the long, pointed foliage is plush velvet with deep purple midrib and veins against cream. The tendrils are reddish, and so is the underside of the leaves.

It's just stunning. But the foliage is rarely in perfect shape and tends to melt away fairly quickly after you remove it from the greenhouse where it was purchased (and where it had high humidity, high light, and all sorts of other unachievable benefits). In other words, it's prone to pouting.

All cissus climb by tendrils and would love a trellis for getting a leg up. Equally effective is letting them dangle down. Either way, they object to being overwatered. During the winter, their growth tends to slow down. At other times of the year, they're full speed ahead, making such fast tracks that keeping ahead of their mass can be a chore. If possible, try to direct their progress onto sanctioned supports. If left to their own devices, the tendrils will enlist anything within grabbing distance including the curtain rod.

Cissus species

CISSUS

ALSO CALLED: **grape ivy**

FLOWERS	**None**
FOLIAGE	**Usually trifoliate, sometimes long and slender; handsome.**
OTHER ATTRIBUTES	**The tendrils are part of the show, great for giving the sense of jungle**
SIZE	**Long trailing**
EXPOSURE	**Whatever you've got, but ideally shady east or west**
WATER REQUIREMENTS	**Moderate; allow to dry out between waterings**
OPTIMUM NIGHTTIME TEMPERATURE	**50–65°F (10–18°C)**
RATE OF GROWTH	**Rapid**
SOIL TYPE	**Will endure almost any soil, but rich, well-drained is best**
FERTILIZING	**Early spring to late autumn**
PROBLEMS	**Mealy bugs, but that's their only foe**

CITRUS

Granted, citrus blossoms aren't ravishing, but their scent is divine.

EVERY HOUSE HAS its own aroma. Open the door, breathe in, and that's the essence of home. Some smell like freshly baked bread; others are perfumed by cologne. Mine is gently flavored by the scent of plants growing. To everyone else, it's an indescribable composition of intermingling aromas, like when the orchestra tunes up. But I can always pick out the components. When the citrus is in blossom, there's no question in my or anybody else's mind—a certain scent is topmost. I can usually follow my nose directly to the soloist.

Growing citrus feels like a privilege. Something about it smacks of aristocracy or indulgence, or perhaps folly. But citrus might well be the "on-ramp" that beckons many newbies to try their hand at attaining a green thumb. I can't say that it really seduced me. But I also

admit there's a heady quality inherent in pointing to the citrus when people close the front door behind them in autumn, take a deep breath, and inquire into the source of the scent. I try not to seem glib as they sample the citrus's wares, but I also drop considerable hints about how easily just about anyone can have that perfume.

A south window is not essential to secure the fragrance. Your citrus will chug along reasonably well in a bright east- or west-facing window (I find that west tends to be brighter in autumn and winter, when citrus need light most). But the more light you give a citrus, the better it will perform. And south offers a stronger chance of increasing the brightness. In autumn, that means a bumper crop of blossoms. We're talking sparkling white flowers that vary in size, depending on the fruit you're growing, but top out at one inch (2.5cm) or so, even if you're hosting a Ponderosa lemon.

Physically, citrus flowers are neither here nor there on the beauty meter. You certainly would never stop in your tracks to gawk. Throw in the fragrance, however, and it is a different story entirely. Even though I harbor an admittedly opinionated nose, citrus passes muster with flying colors. Indeed, my nose is drawn to it. Rather than cleaning house and instead of washing vegetables for dinner, I find myself with my face half-buried in the citrus blossoms, stalled in sensual bliss.

That universal two-thumbs-up aroma happens in autumn. Until winter, the fruit crop won't be ripe or ready or much more than in the early developmental stages. But for me, the flowers are sufficiently rewarding. And, theoretically, fruit will come later.

All citrus plants go into more or less dwarf mode when grown indoors in a container. (In other words, don't worry that you'll be juggling a full-blown tree someday.) However, that's not to say they're tight little nuggets by anyone's definition. With the possible exception of kumquats (*Fortunella hindsii* and *F. margarita* are usually the kumquats available in containers) and their hybrids, citrus tend to make gangly, unstatuesque plants unless you inflict some extremely brutal shearing (I love to prune, but even I don't have the stomach to do the swipes in its formative stages that a citrus needs to become a swan). Without a whole lot of intervention, Ponderosa lemon (*Citrus ponderosa*) can become a fairly good-looking individual. Plus, it tends to fruit early in its lifespan. But dwarf by a Ponderosa lemon's standards is too much of a handful for the average home.

Want a rewarding citrus that remains relatively compact? The Calamondin orange, ×*Citrofortunella microcarpa*, produces fruit indoors.

The drama is slow but savory as the Calamondin orange, ×*Citrofortunella microcarpa*, gradually ripens fruit from autumn through winter.

We're talking about a plant that will rapidly require a 12-inch (30cm) or larger container and 3 to 4 feet (90–122cm) of headroom. After all, it has to shoulder fruits that can tip the scales at five pounds. It should be noted that Ponderosa lemons have an ultra-thick skin and are pithy inside; they are not the best for eating. But if you want something larger than life, this is the baby for you. Most other lemons, limes, and oranges lack grace and tend to drop lower leaves as houseplants.

But if you're dying to grow your own orange juice, I'm not going to be the one to talk you down. So here's the scoop on indoor citrus. Although I am admittedly keeping my citrus more for blossoms than fruit, if my goal was for the table, I'd veer toward a kumquat. I think Roger Swain, host of the PBS series *The Victory Garden* and hands-down expert on growing fruit indoors, would bear me out on this. Without Florida sunshine, most citrus don't make the grade taste-wise. Kumquats are naturally on the sour side anyway, so they don't get demerits for lacking sweetness. They also tend to be compact, productive, and fairly good-looking in a home. A runner-up (and more readily available from your average garden center) would be the Calamondin orange, ×*Citrofortunella microcarpa*, thought to be a hybrid between a kumquat and a tangerine (alias Mandarin orange). Many indoor gardeners feel it is one of the easier citrus to entertain.

When grown in containers, citrus can be bears. They like cool winter temperatures, but very chilly conditions will bind up trace elements and inhibit their absorption. I would say that 50°F (10°C) would be the lowest the thermometer should sink on a regular basis, but most citrus prefer 55°F to 65°F (12–18°C). As far as fertilizing goes, this is a glaring case where the organic approach achieves better results than citrus grown in soilless mix. Citrus plants demand a broad spectrum of trace elements to do their thing. If deprived of iron, copper, zinc, and manganese, the foliage will yellow and become misshapen or the fruit will be lacking or deformed. Throwing on the trace elements can lead to overload, which is equally counterproductive. Organic commercial growers generally add compost to the soil and use seaweed fertilizer. This is worth a try indoors, as well. Considering that gardening remains a competitive sport for some, citrus is an excellent forum for trumping your friends and neighbors. As for me, a blissful nose is enough.

Citrus species

CITRUS

ALSO CALLED: kumquat, lemon, lime, orange

FLOWERS	White and small, but outrageously fragrant
FOLIAGE	Glossy deep green
OTHER ATTRIBUTES	Edible fruit
SIZE	Depends on the citrus, but generally 30 inches (76cm) and up in height
EXPOSURE	Sunny south or bright east or west
WATER REQUIREMENTS	Moderate; do not overwater
OPTIMUM NIGHTTIME TEMPERATURE	55–65°F (12–18°C)
RATE OF GROWTH	Slow
SOIL TYPE	Rich organic potting soil with compost included
FERTILIZING	In early spring, summer, and late autumn, but also as needed in winter to keep foliage green
PROBLEMS	Yellowing foliage, mealy bugs, aphids, spider mites

COLEUS

Coleus make surprisingly easy houseplants. The old standby *Coleus* 'Lava Rose' does just fine in an east-facing window beside *Juniperus* ×*pfitzeriana* 'MonSan'.

IT HAPPENED. The weatherman predicted frost last night. What followed was a frenzy of pot hauling, saucer finding, plant-stand positioning, and plant ditching. There was the triage scene.

"Throw it out."

"But it's been loyal. Brave. Trustworthy…"

"Just throw it out."

When the dust settled, the tears were dried, and the 21-shovel salute to the fallen botanicals at the compost heap was just an aching memory, I woke up to a house filled with plants. All the mixed containers were jettisoned. And, I confess, most of the coleus didn't make the cut.

By coleus, I really mean cultivars of *Solenostemon scutellarioides*. If you're not familiar with that name, join the crowd. Few gardeners know it, and most nurseries stubbornly stick with the familiar name of coleus (for good reason—they're trying to earn a living). Every summer, I can't resist tucking a few coleus in containers to jazz up the display spilling out my front door onto the Belgian brick "patio" in front. I go for the usual suspects— 'Sedona', 'Alabama Sunset', 'Tilt-a-Whirl', 'Inky Fingers', and 'India Frills'. But in autumn, some tough decisions must be made, and that's when they get dumped. It's not that I don't love them. They simply monopolize too much space and get leggy over the winter. Instead, I give some of the small-leaf varieties safe harbor. 'Inky Fingers' and 'India Frills' both make laudable houseplants, remain compact, and remind me of the outdoors when the garden is merely a snow-blanketed rendition of its former self.

Coleus are one of the great mysteries of life. Most prefer shade outdoors, especially the lime-green cultivars. But inside over the winter, the larger-leaf versions tend to become leggy if they don't get good light. And nothing is sadder than a stretching coleus. Not only are the smaller cultivars, such as 'Inky Fingers' and 'India Frills', easier to accommodate indoors size-wise, they don't readily show the earmarks of light deprivation.

Of course, if you don't want to devote windowsill space to something as common as a coleus, it's simple enough to take cuttings and keep a sprig of a favorite cultivar going year after year. They root in a blink. The traditional method is to put a cutting in a glass of water. I find it easier to simply stick a cutting directly into a tiny clay pot and skip the glass-to-pot repotting sequence. Either way, you'll have a rooted plant in three to four weeks. Then you just have to do some "pinching," and you've got fodder for next summer's outdoor display.

Pinching and pruning are critical for coleus. Without some nips and tucks, they're going to get leggy or deteriorate into blossom spikes. And most gardeners agree the blossoms on coleus detract from the show. They're mauve, small, and blah, and they divert the focus from those fantastic leaves, which come in some fairly snappy colors. 'India Frills' is magenta with yellow edges. 'Inky Fingers' is burgundy with a lime-green hem. Both have irregularly notched edges on their thumbnail-size leaves.

Other than the light requirements and pruning admonition, there's not much else to warn with coleus. The succulent stems break easily when you shuffle them around, it's true, so I select a permanent location for my plant and leave it there. Einstein's continual leaping and batting sprees take their toll. But then that's more cuttings for summer fare.

Solenostemon scutellarioides

cultivars

COLEUS

FLOWERS	Boring, blah, and should be dissuaded
FOLIAGE	Handsome, with wonderful colors and markings
OTHER ATTRIBUTES	Easily rooted, great for containers outdoors
SIZE	12–30 inches (30–76cm) in height, depending on cultivar
EXPOSURE	Bright east, or west
WATER REQUIREMENTS	Moderate
OPTIMUM NIGHTTIME TEMPERATURE	55–65°F (12–18°C)
RATE OF GROWTH	Medium
SOIL TYPE	Light, humusy soil mixture
FERTILIZING	Between early spring and late autumn
PROBLEMS	Aphids are a major issue; whiteflies can also happen

CONIFERS

Traditionally, we bring evergreens in for the holidays. But why not enjoy the company of conifers such as *Chamaecyparis obtusa* 'Blue Feathers' all autumn and winter long?

The rugged good looks and quirky posture of *Juniperus squamata* 'Chinese Silver' are more poignant inside.

OUTDOORS THE LEAVES are ablaze with color. But every day, another tree or shrub goes naked. And every morning, I wake up to the squawking of Canada geese hysterically announcing their takeoff, arrival, or intention of making yet another reconnaissance mission to check out the pond at my property's farthest point. That's not the only morning music—there's also the reassuring hum of the furnace firing up to warn me that the path down to the goat barn will be slippery with frost when I venture out to do the morning chores. Sure enough, when I slip out of bed, find my slippers, and make my way through a hallway booby-trapped by mangled kitten toys, I look out the window to confirm what I suspected—it frosted again last night. Almost every houseplant I pad past seems grateful that it was chosen to be shepherded back into the fold. But sometimes I wonder about the conifers. Would they have preferred to remain outside? It's one of those instances where I need them more than they need me.

Mornings run like clockwork around here. Exercises, shower, breakfast. For breakfast, the traditional morning yogurt is consumed on the table surveying the entire Great Room from the far end of the converted barn. Most of the meal is spent shuffling aimlessly through the stack of magazines and newspapers on the table. But between the letters to the editor and the obituaries, I occasionally glance up. And when I do, the potted conifers come into my field of vision. There's something infinitely comforting in that view. As much as conifers slip into the background outdoors, they stand out inside. A few years ago, I began framing my windows by bringing a few potted conifers indoors, and now they've become a fixture.

Originally, it was just a stopgap measure. On a whim, I bought *Cupressus arizonica* 'Blue Ice', and then discovered it is only marginally hardy in my unpredictable region. Rather than putting it in the ground, I placed it in a massive long tom–shaped container. Over the summer, I became rather fond of the blue-green fellow as it stood sentinel beside the front door. Meanwhile, it showed its grit by surmounting the challenges of low light thanks to the massive maple that shades the front of the house. Come fall, the obvious solution to the "what now?" quandary might have been to plant it and throw caution to the wind. Instead, I procrastinated. And procrastinated. When the window of safe transplanting opportunity outdoors slammed shut, it was marched indoors—with a little help from my (muscular) friends. And it changed my world. That started a whole spate of experimentation with conifers.

Stately trees indoors, such as *Cupressus arizonica* 'Blue Ice' standing tall beside *Kalanchoe thyrsiflora* 'Flapjack' and *Juniperus squamata* 'Chinese Silver', blur the lines between inside and outside.

The secret to conifers like *Juniperus procumbens* 'Nana' is to let their roots sink into a deep container.

Next came a juniper, purchased at slashed prices at an autumn nursery sale. In the fall leaf-raking, bulb-planting rush, I failed to get it into the ground (are we noticing a trend here?). To be specific, it was *Juniperus procumbens* 'Nana', and I began to like the way it spread out at right angles from its nursery container, like a teased-out bouffant. So it was given an industrial metal cylinder container and brought inside. *Chamaecyparis pisifera* 'Boulevard' followed suit (by that time, the conifers no longer needed justification). Although the chamaecyparis gave the strongest silhouette and went furthest toward establishing the mood of a forest indoors, it was not the easiest conifer to care for inside. The juniper, on the other hand, never let out a whimper.

The critical secret to success with conifers lies in their containers. They demand something deep, with plenty of root room to plunge down,

but also a sufficiently broad base so that the root ball isn't cramped. You need to be able to water easily and effectively. The main cause of death for conifers inside is drying out because of lack of water. Problem is, they are not whiners; a conifer will rarely, if ever, wilt. So check the soil and water generously, keeping in mind that you are quenching a large mass of roots. Skip fertilizer. For the duration the conifers remain inside, they receive no nourishment beyond the compost in the organic soil where their roots are plunging.

Practically speaking, trees of any sort work best in the periphery of a room. Junipers, in particular, tend to be prickly (and can irritate the skin on some people), so you wouldn't want to collide with one in the dark. Off the beaten track, they take the same position they usually assume outside: they're the strong-

Cupressus macrocarpa 'Lemon Yellow' isn't hardy in my region, but placing it in a window box bedded with *Selaginella kraussiana* 'Variegata' helps it reach hedge-like proportions.

and-silent types standing on the sidelines. It's one of those delicious moments when design and necessity merge.

Plus, conifers need a light source. Mine dote on their eastern exposure and do just fine, even though the sun is not strong during the winter. Rather than placing them on the floor, I raise them up— they sit on an inverted antique rain barrel or straddle a metal stool. This keeps the wooden floor from harm. The elevation adds to their stature (and conifers make great exclamation points indoors), and the raised height puts them squarely in the window, delivering the dosage of light the foliage craves.

As soon as temperatures moderate sufficiently to keep their containers from cracking, out the conifers go. I don't wait for danger of frost to pass entirely. At the maximum, they're inside for five months. After that, they need the fresh air and I need the space to start seedlings.

Various conifers

ALSO CALLED: **false cypress, juniper**

FLOWERS	**None**
FOLIAGE	**Lots of texture, can be golden or blue-green**
OTHER ATTRIBUTES	**Great vertical elements in a home**
SIZE	**Tree size; groundcovering conifers are also apropos**
EXPOSURE	**Shady east or west; will survive in south**
WATER REQUIREMENTS	**Lightly moist, do not allow to dry out**
OPTIMUM NIGHTTIME TEMPERATURE	**50–55°F (10–12°C)**
RATE OF GROWTH	**Slow**
SOIL TYPE	**Rich, well-drained, humusy soil**
FERTILIZING	**I don't fertilize mine**
PROBLEMS	**Mealy bugs, but that's their only foe.**

GESNERIADS

IF THERE WAS a time when members of the African violet family struck me as frumpy, I left the association with doilies and teacups in the dust long ago. The only thing standing between members of *Gesneriaceae* species and me is temperature. Most of the growing spaces in my home are just too chilly for the tender sensibilities of some members of the African violet family. I try to make them comfortable, but I don't always succeed. In general, my policy is that any gesneriad that will live with me is welcome into the corps. After all, autumn needs promise, and several gesneriads are all about hope. In autumn, they are gearing up to blossom.

When I think of gesneriads, I can't say my mind goes immediately to riveting foliage. There are some definite exceptions, but leaves are a secondary show for most members of the African violet clan. Flowers are their strong suit. Some members of the family, such as chiritas and codonanthes, blossom all year. But with autumn, the blossoms really venture out in droves, especially on aeschynanthus and columneas. Gesneriads stage an annual reaffirmation, reminding me why I just brought all these plants indoors. It's like they all stand up and cheer. It's not calamitous, but more of a subtle glad hand. Part of the beauty of gesneriads is that they are sufficiently compact to be discreet. A touch of color here, a little trumpet there—they sprinkle sparks around. Mine don't have the saturated color mass that, say, the columneas achieve in a greenhouse environment. The whole production is not as dense in a home situation.

There are some gesneriads that I can't grow. Given my cool temperatures, Cape primrose (streptocarpus), with velvety leaves that spring from the base and colorful

Gesneriads go far beyond what you can find in a supermarket. Take this refreshingly funky *Sinningia* species, for example.

snapdragon-like flowers, are out of my league entirely. As soon as the heating season kicks in and the house starts seeing temperatures below 60°F (15°C), they are goners. And when a streptocarpus is gone, it's gone. Ditto for many of the columneas and episcias. They won't withstand it. Chiritas do great, blossoming blithely away. So do aeschynanthus, codonanthes, most *Sinningia* species (with the exception of miniature *Sinningia pusilla* hybrids), and African violets (saintpaulias).

Yes, I grow African violets. Knowing they are sometimes seen as frumpy, I go out of my way to give them a tony presentation. I steer clear of the frilly double versions (only because I'm not keen on them, not because I care what anyone thinks). But they all deserve liberation. And a face lift is a snap to achieve.

They all would love warmer temperatures and most will tolerate indirect light, but that's where the familial similarities end. Members of the African violet family come in all shapes and sizes; there are versions that grow as upright plants, while others are danglers. On aeschynanthus, the blossoms form elongated tubes, resembling gaping dragons, with highly ornamental bracts that herald the actual blossoms and linger after the bona fide flowers have faded, extending the show. Saintpaulias really do look more like violets. The color range encompasses reds, oranges, blues, whites, and yellows. Achimenes are the exception to the autumn rule: they grow from tiny, pinecone-shaped rhizomes that send up growth and form blossoms in summer before going dormant in late autumn. I can usually bring them indoors to enjoy on the windowsill before they slip into slumber.

Perhaps because they were once so popular, there are all sorts of admonitions surrounding the cultivation of African violets and their clan. Although most are the epitome of low-maintenance houseguests (hence their popularity), the rumors circulating about their requirements are enough to sour anyone. First, to shatter the foremost myth, African violets don't demand water only from below. Sure, you can serve drinks via their saucer, if that fits into your lifestyle. But a well-directed stream of water from the spout of a watering can is equally effective. Avoid chilly water from the tap whenever possible. But then again, in the summer I put my gesneriads outdoors where the rains always come from above, and I'm sure the raindrops are

Aeschynanthus 'Laura' isn't the most prolific bloomer— other aeschynanthus have it beat in that category—but it has a nice, tight, tidy habit and a smattering of red blooms.

Summer-growing *Achimenes* 'Santa Claus' doesn't make it to the holidays for me, but I can enjoy it in the windowsill for a while in autumn before it goes dormant.

sometimes chilly. The plants are fine. As for fertilizer, they enjoy my fish emulsion menu. I feed them once every three weeks or so, diluted according to the manufacturer's directions. I withhold food from November until March, when light levels are low.

If you see a handsome little gesneriad performing its heart out in a supermarket, go for it. My suggestion is to find a smart container (hint: they hate to swim in an over-size pot) and welcome them into the clan. They provide a ray of hope when things are otherwise winding down. And they bestow their goods without fuss or bother. Let them work their magic.

Members of the *Gesneriad* clan

GESNERIADS

ALSO CALLED: **African violets**

FLOWERS	Usually tubular in a broad array of colors; some are violet-like
FOLIAGE	Some have felted leaves; others are smooth
OTHER ATTRIBUTES	Profuse bloomers and readily available
SIZE	Varies from minute to large, depending on the species, but most are easily windowsill size; some are prostrate
EXPOSURE	East or west; they dislike bright, direct sun
WATER REQUIREMENTS	Moderate, do not overwater. Keep the foliage dry, if possible, and avoid chilly water.
OPTIMUM NIGHTTIME TEMPERATURE	60–65°F (15–18°C)
RATE OF GROWTH	Medium
SOIL TYPE	A light, humusy mix; African-violet soil mediums are available
FERTILIZING	Early spring to late autumn
PROBLEMS	Mealy bugs, but that's their only foe, and it isn't a pressing problem

IVIES

Not your typical ivy, *Hedera helix* 'Oak Leaf' has tiny, three-pointed leaves on vining stems that can be part of mini woodland scenes. Play with your plants.

NOT EVERY HOUSEPLANT is going to head up the marquee; somebody's got to get the congeniality prize. That's where ivies come in. Because of lack of space and a slight bias toward sensationalism (or, at least, a penchant for plants that actually do perform in one way or another, even if it's snappy leaves), my plant collection isn't big on ivies. Most are just too, shall we say, uneventful for me. But ivies are undeniably great workhorses. And there are a few I couldn't live without.

First, let's talk about the congeniality issue. Few indoor plants are as versatile as an ivy. Only have a north-facing window? No problem. Got low humidity? No sweat. Forget to water occasionally? They can cope. Forget to water constantly? Maybe not. Ivies can withstand heavy artillery, but if you drop the total-neglect bomb, it's going to get ugly.

The only time I've killed ivies was when they were completely out of sight and mind and subjected to a steady diet of abuse. Otherwise, they were okay with pretty much anything.

Ivies will grow in some very dark conditions. However, very low light won't earn the same results as an east or west window. An ivy grown in dense shade will be leggier, with longer spaces between leaves. It won't be on top of its game. If good-looking is what you're after, try to summon up a slightly brighter exposure.

I lean toward the minis. Other indoor gardeners use ivies for their big mass of foliage, but not me. I'd rather go for tiny leaves and an interesting growth habit. High up on my list of favorites are 'Oak Leaf' (with pinky nail–size three-lobed leaves) and 'Erecta' (with foliage tightly stacked along the stem). I tend to play with my ivies, winding them into shapes and prodding them to do tricks. Acrobatics is another

talent on a hedera helix's list of credentials. Among vines, this one does yoga positions like you won't believe. Weave it into pretzels if you want, and it holds that posture. Larger versions will do the same thing, and variegated ivies wound into wreath shapes are all the rage for the holidays. So it should surprise no one to learn that more than one florist has come up with the idea of weaving *Hedera helix* 'Heartleaf' into a heart for Valentine's Day (if you thought this was your brainstorm, sorry).

Above and beyond my darlings, there's an army of ivies with various spins on shape and variegation. One of my first memories of gardening indoors involves a variegated ivy and my frustration when it failed to flower. Although you can occasionally get mature ivies to bloom and make berries outdoors, it isn't likely to happen inside—at least, not in your lifetime. I finally gave up waiting and stuck it in a terrarium for kicks, and it did fine. Notice that I didn't hold the ivy's lack of performance against it, despite the fact that it just chugged along doing little or nothing—I still got deep into houseplants. But that brings me to another character trait of *Hedera helix*. Most don't break any speed records, growth-wise. Although they can survive inclement situations, they don't move quickly.

Thanks to their leathery leaf texture, ivies aren't prone to pests. That's a fortunate state of affairs, because spraying a plant with such dense foliage can be a challenge. If stressed, they can easily come down with mealy bugs. But that's the full extent of their woes. These plants are the Golden Retrievers of the plant world.

Hedera helix
cultivars

HEDERA HELIX

ALSO CALLED: **common ivy, English ivy**

FLOWERS	**Not in the cards**
FOLIAGE	**A variety of intriguing leaf shapes and sizes. Usually deep-green, but variegated and chartreuse versions are available.**
OTHER ATTRIBUTES	**Very easily grown, and vines can be trained onto supports**
SIZE	**Vining; size depends on cultivar**
EXPOSURE	**East or west; will tolerate north**
WATER REQUIREMENTS	**Light, but will tolerate anything but constant drought**
OPTIMUM NIGHTTIME TEMPERATURE	**50–65°F (10–18°C); will tolerate colder conditions**
RATE OF GROWTH	**Slow**
SOIL TYPE	**Not finicky; will tolerate most soil types**
FERTILIZING	**Would appreciate some food**
PROBLEMS	**Mealy bugs, scale. Ivies are toxic. Ivies are particularly toxic and can cause a severe dermatological reaction.**

MARANTAS, CTENANTHES, AND CALATHEAS

Probably the flashiest member of this group of plants is *Ctenanthe oppenheimiana* 'Tricolor', especially when sunbeams hit the leaves.

THE SUN HITS at rakish angles in autumn, training the spotlight on backstage plants that suddenly shine in the glimmerglow. There's that moment in the early morning when I pad downstairs to find the light hitting the recesses of a dark corner where sunbeams rarely strike. For that one occasion (if I had awoken half an hour later, I would have missed it), *Ctenanthe oppenheimiana* 'Tricolor' is ignited in a conflagration of smoldering shades. I navigate the gnaw-hole-pierced electric-blue feathered birds, octopus-legged mice, and stuffed veterinarian-effigies in my path. I sidestep the furry ambush ("I don't suppose that tail swishing behind the staghorn fern belongs to you, Einstein?") en route to the arrow-shaped leaves on fire by a stray sunbeam at the far end of my attached, generally poorly lit greenhouse. Because it rarely blossoms in a home environment, the ctenanthe might be overlooked most of the time. But this morning, it's a stunner.

The kitten's hobby is shredding. He takes out orchids at regular intervals and has such a vendetta against the lavender that the hapless plant has been surrendered as sacrificial. The cissus is spaghetti. If his wrath was unleashed on

Although it's not one of the most entertaining plants to sit next to at dinner, *Ctenanthe oppenheimiana* 'Tricolor' is elegant and colorful, especially in front of *Callisia fragrans* in the background.

the members of the genus *Marantaceae* in residence, there would be no justification for letting those plants linger. A marred leaf on a maranta is enough to blemish the overall picture. And most take their time sending up a replacement crop of foliage. Mercifully, Einstein is not the least bit interested in marantas. Yet.

Einstein might not agree (thankfully), but there's something truly enthralling about this group of plants. They run the gamut from incredibly easy (I'm thinking of the prayer plant, *Maranta leuconeura* var. *kerchoviana*, with its little rabbit-track markings running down the center of oval leaves, which is featured at supermarkets far and wide) to devilishly difficult (*Calathea makoyana*, the humidity-demanding peacock plant, comes to mind). The middle ground is populated by plenty of truly lovely, house-worthy individuals that add to the tapestry of color in a home.

Marantas, ctenanthes, and calatheas are the best-dressed plants around. Compared to some of the other foliage standbys, like dracaenas and aglaonemas, marantas have an unparalleled sophistication. Interior designers wouldn't hesitate to upholster a sofa with the patterns on their leaves. Most members of this family are native to tropical America; many hail from Brazil and thereabouts. Their coloration reflects that heritage.

Their native environments explain why some members of this group are tricky in our humidity-deprived, seriously not-tropical homes. Even with my menagerie of houseplants increasing the overall humidity in their close proximity, calatheas are a challenge. I consider *Calathea roseapicta*,

Maranta leuconeura 'Massangeana' (in watering can) and *Ctenanthe lubbersiana* 'Brazilian Snow' are both gorgeous and ultra-easy to grow, unless you tend to forget to water.

For such an exotic-
looking plant,
Calathea lancifolia
is mercifully
low maintenance.

C. musaica, and *C. undulata*
to be terrarium fare only,
although you can occasionally
find them in garden centers
(with no warning signage
about their difficulty for houseplant applications). Marantas
of all stripes are easier,
however. And ctenanthes are
somewhere in the middle.
Although identification
sometimes feels like splitting
hairs and is classified on
the basis of flower traits, I can
usually tell the difference
from the foliage. Marantas
are all slightly different spins
on the same theme of broad,
paper-thin leaves with jagged,
lightning bolt–like markings
on their surface. They generally remain less than a foot
in height. Occasionally, they
have little wispy flowering
spires that don't amount to
much and could be accused
of distracting. Ctenanthes are
taller, blossom infrequently,
and bear their beautiful

Maranta, Ctenanthe, and Calathea

ALSO CALLED: never-never plant (Ctenanthe), peacock plant (Calathea), prayer plant (Maranta), ten commandments (Maranta)

leaves on branching stems. And those little snobs, the difficult-to-grow calatheas, are hauntingly otherworldly, with designer-quality patterns on their thick, glossy leaves that initiate from the ground. They rarely bloom.

If my home was very dry, I would be limited to (yawn) *Maranta leuconeura* var. *kerchoviana*. But thanks to all the resident plants raising the humidity levels, I can support everything but fussy calatheas. As for cultivation, I go for a light, fluffy growing medium with plenty of leaf mold included. I've noticed that ctenanthes are heavy drinkers. Most of my early morning visits are followed immediately by a return with the watering can. Let a ctenanthe dry out, and in no time it will retaliate with shriveled, browning leaves. Fortunately, the whole shebang never goes sour all at once. Instead, ctenanthes signal their displeasure with a few token pleas for help in the form of leaf-edge browning.

Although it's true that mealy bugs pester lots of plants, I find that they are drawn to marantas with almost the same sadistic vehemence as bougainvilleas. It takes a while for mealy bugs to undermine a plant, so keep a vigilant eye out for these varmints and take action quickly (while simultaneously segregating the plant). They are worth the trouble.

FLOWERS	Insignificant; could be accused of being distracting
FOLIAGE	The main attraction, with colorful, artistic markings
OTHER ATTRIBUTES	Foliage can curl after dark
SIZE	Depending on species, 1–3 feet (30–90cm) in height
EXPOSURE	East or west
WATER REQUIREMENTS	Heavy, but don't overwater. Fluoride in water can cause browning leaf edges in calatheas.
OPTIMUM NIGHTTIME TEMPERATURE	60–65°F (15–18°C)
RATE OF GROWTH	Slow
SOIL TYPE	Light, humusy potting soil
FERTILIZING	Early spring to late autumn
PROBLEMS	Mealy bugs

Phormium, the grass lookalike, can be easily wintered indoors. Equally low-maintenance is *Festuca glauca* 'Boulder Blue', partnered in a window box with *Sedum* 'Angelina'.

ORNAMENTAL GRASSES

KITTENS HAVE PRESCRIBED play times. Nine times out of 10, I will be attacked by a pounce first thing in the morning and then suffer another ambush before dinner. Around noon, I'm safe. And so is the blue fescue.

Certain plants are placed (with a prayer) out of Einstein's reach. But the blue fescue is his designated play toy. Before he was born and while his predecessor was still reigning, I planted the fescue in a window box for my edification. The senior cat could not have cared less. Einstein is a different story entirely. He is still sufficiently compact to crouch on the whole thing (which vies for comfort with your average bed of nails) and roost there for hours. When he isn't flattening it, he takes on the role of hairdresser from hell and rearranges its coiffure. Amazingly, the fescue takes all the abuse in stride.

The fescue is *Festuca glauca* 'Boulder Blue', and it's become the go-to plant for trendy garden designers working outdoors. Granted, it looks fine in the ground. But it's even more fetching when given a sense of importance in a container. Grasses might not seem like exciting roommates indoors. They might not even strike you as worth the bother. I disagree: they add a nice touch.

You've probably run into those trays of lawn grass that were circulating the flower markets not so long ago. Or maybe you have had a brush with cat grass (generally *Avena sativa*, otherwise known as oats), grown from seed. But I wouldn't really call those ornamental grasses. I'm thinking more along the lines of carex, festuca, pennisetum, and similar performers.

Really, lawn and cat grasses don't last more than a few weeks before they start to yellow. The grasses I'm recommending have a longer-lasting glory. In my home, it started with *Pennisetum setaceum* 'Rubrum'. Stingy gardener that I am, I dug it out of its container and tried to winter this tender annual over in a shady window so I could get another season of splendor from it outdoors the following year. What ensued was an entire winter of intrigue. Honestly, people would come into the house, sidestep all the more classic houseplants, and swoon over the pennisetum. Although sheared back to a stubble when I brought it in, it quickly revitalized. Then it began to blossom, producing those bunnytail-like, soft, blushing pink heads—the same blooms that won it a focal point place in the garden. I let the flowers

Festuca glauca 'Boulder Blue' was an easy target for Einstein to maul in a window box, partnered with *Sedum* 'Angelina'.

linger too long, I admit. After a while it began to shatter all over the place and for weeks I was chasing little fluffballs with the vacuum. But that was my fault.

Fescue doesn't do much indoors as far as flowers are concerned (although the blue-green foliage is cute), but many of the carexes oblige. Plus, several carex tend to boast great foliar color and markings. With the exception of the pennisetum, I go for grasses that remain dwarf because they perform best in containers. They also serve the same function as they do in a garden—they lend texture and a sense of quiet to the scene. Plus, there's nothing like an ornamental grass to impart the feeling of nature indoors.

More conventional and typically sold as a houseplant, we might as well group cyperus in this category. I've grown *Cyperus albostriatus*, umbrella plant (*C. alternifolius*), *C. alternifolius* 'Gracilis', and Egyptian paper reed (*C. papyrus*). My favorite is *C. alternifolius* for its bold, plump, stark-straight stems crowned by a fireworks-like topknot of foliage and insignificant flowers. If you keep its roots crammed, it will remain about 2 to 3 feet (60–90cm) in height. The more root room you give it, the more space it will rapidly expand to fill. In my experience, the more slender *C. alternifolius* 'Gracilis' tends to flop and bend, whereas *C. alternifolius* stands bolt upright, strong and proud.

Grasses tend to be ultra-low maintenance. The only caveat is their drinking habit. Keeping up with a grass's thirst can be a time drain, especially during the heating season. And several of the ornamental grasses begin to brown if you aren't continually serving drinks. Aside from that, you are home free. Fertilizer would be appreciated, but isn't essential. I would keep it to a minimum—once every month or so—to prevent weak growth, which results in floppy foliage. And for the same reason, withhold food completely during the short days of the year (early autumn to late spring).

My grasses are staged where the kitten can enjoy their company, often conveniently on the floor. This means they never get bright light. I suppose they might perform better in a south window, but they don't seem to care. In fact, I am absolutely certain their life would be 100 percent happier without periodic mauling. But that doesn't seem to be their plight.

The fact that *Festuca glauca* 'Boulder Blue' is no bed of roses doesn't deter Einstein from his roost.

Grown in an Industrial Era metal rectangle without drainage, *Cyperus alternifolius* loves the soggy soil underfoot.

Carex, Cyperus, Pennisetum, Festuca

ALSO CALLED: ornamental grasses

FLOWERS	Insignificant on carex and festuca, bunnytails on pennisetum
FOLIAGE	Can be red, bluish, or variegated
OTHER ATTRIBUTES	Can be transplanted into the summer garden easily
SIZE	Depending on species, 6–30 inches (15–70cm) in height
EXPOSURE	South, east, or west
WATER REQUIREMENTS	Heavy
OPTIMUM NIGHTTIME TEMPERATURE	45–65°F (7–18°C)
RATE OF GROWTH	Slow, except cyperus, which rapidly becomes a hulk
SOIL TYPE	Heavy, rich potting soil
FERTILIZING	I have never bothered to feed the grasses in pots, but once a month will do it
PROBLEMS	Can get spider mites; plants dry out easily

OXALIS

With a little shaping, the blushing golden leaves of *Oxalis vulcanicola* 'Molten Lava' form a tight, comely mound.

JUST LIKE ALL gardeners (right?), I can't resist pulling together a few containers specifically for summer. I know, I know, the house is surrounded by plants—why do I imagine I need more? Because it's fun, and I have all of outdoors to fill. Inevitably, at least one container has an oxalis in the brew. Generally, it's *Oxalis vulcanicola* (now also available as the fiery cultivar 'Molten Lava', with yellow and peach leaves). And eventually, the day arrives in autumn when the outdoor plants need to come back inside. Not all make the cut. But no matter what configuration the oxalis is a part of, it always ends up being broken apart from its bulkier companions and brought in to safety.

This might be a good place to mention that I never bring in a mixed container as a whole unit. With assistance from Mother Nature and the elements outdoors, mixed containers thrive. In a windowsill setting with inherent diminished light, the competition between bedfellows is just too nasty in a combined container. The "every plant for itself" slug-out leads to stress for the individual plants. Usually, the whole crew doesn't go down with the ship, but only the strongest survive. And the survivor isn't always a favorite. So I partition off those that are worthy houseplants and focus my salvage efforts in their direction. *Oxalis vulcanicola* rates.

If your only encounters with oxalis are limited to that noxious weed, yellow wood sorrel (*Oxalis corniculata*), capable of sowing itself indiscriminately hither and yon, you are probably wondering what on earth I'm talking about. But oxalis come in many guises, and some of those manifestations are truly gorgeous and notable houseplants.

Oxalis can be divided into two categories: those with stems and those that come from bulbs or rhizomes. For oxalis with stems, flowers are pretty much an after-thought—the foliage really seals the deal. Most oxalis hold their leaflets in group-ings of three, making them dead ringers for shamrocks and infinitely marketable around Saint Patrick's Day. The foliar configurations are where similarities end, however. When the bright yellow–leaved, almost succulent stemmed *Oxalis vulcanicola* is not in bloom, you would be hard pressed to identify it as related to the equally charming but totally dissimilar *O. ortgiesii*, with purple and burgundy triangular leaves on woody stems. And *O. herrerae*, with minute pea-green shamrock-like leaves initiating from woody stems, is also totally different. All three, however, share yellow, buttercup-like blossoms. And all are trouble-free, infinitely rewarding houseplants. With small, satiny burgundy leaves against profuse yellow blossoms, firefern oxalis (*O. hedysaroides* 'Rubra') fits this rewarding description, but it's a pill to grow. All oxalis prefer a sunny south-facing sill, but without extremely bright light and toasty temperatures, the firefern fizzles out.

After some nips and tucks, the woody stems of *Oxalis herrerae* can take on a bonsai-like appearance.

With small tufts of blue-green, split leaves on reddish stems and crowned by lavender-colored flowers, *Oxalis adenophylla* is an easy, handsome package.

Some of the bulbous oxalis get stretchy if not given ultra-bright light. And blazing sun doesn't describe autumn—at least, not in New England or most of the United States or Europe. An exception is *Oxalis adenophylla*. Even without blossoms, it is intriguing with its umbrella-like, bluish, folded leaves on red stems. It will stretch toward the window for light during a shady spate, but it doesn't suffer. And if luck (and sun) are on your side, it will be covered with a crown of violet-colored blossoms throughout late winter and early spring. It's gorgeous, and easily acquired from mail-order bulb sources. *Oxalis adenophylla* is supposedly hardy to Zone 5, although I've never wintered it successfully outdoors (and yes, I've tried).

Oxalis species

OXALIS

ALSO CALLED: shamrock, wood sorrel

FLOWERS	Usually yellow buttercup-like blossoms, but lilac, white, and pink versions are available
FOLIAGE	Generally shamrock-shaped, but not always— usually intriguing
OTHER ATTRIBUTES	Bulbous types can be groundcovers for potted trees
SIZE	2 inches (5cm) to 3 feet (90cm) in height, depending on species
EXPOSURE	Sunny south
WATER REQUIREMENTS	Allow to dry out between waterings; dislike overwatering
OPTIMUM NIGHTTIME TEMPERATURE	50–55°F (10–12°C) (possibly colder for the bulbous types)
RATE OF GROWTH	Rapid
SOIL TYPE	Well-drained and rich
FERTILIZING	Moderately early spring to late autumn
PROBLEMS	Fungus gnats; aphids might also be an issue

The easily grown *Oxalis regnellii* cultivars are currently the buzz on the market. The plain vanilla *O. regnellii* is rhizomatous and has green, sharply deltoid leaves and profuse white flowers. But even more exciting is *O. regnelli* 'Atropurpurea', with deep velvety purple foliage and pink flowers. Then along came *O. regnellii* 'Triangularis', with a magenta triangle-within-a-triangle marking on the leaves. A little leggier, but with a similar refrain, is *O. tetraphylla*, with a jagged burgundy V marking on each triangular leaflet and peachy pink blossoms. 'Iron Cross' is a spin-off with a burgundy marking in the center. Without intense light, it begins to go floppy.

Beyond their demand for bright light, oxalis are troupers indoors. They keep their composure when you forget to water, but soggy doesn't sit well with them. Give them a well-drained soil mix, don't overpot, and don't rush to give them graduations in container size. They all do just fine with organic fertilizer, but be sure to cut off the feedings from Thanksgiving to March. Don't panic when oxalis leaves fold downward after dark; this family trait just means they have closed shop for the evening. The next morning they will be back to their normal rise-and-shine mode.

PLECTRANTHUS

One of autumn's little pleasures comes when *Plectranthus oertendahlii* begins its lacy flowering spree.

AUTUMN HAS ITS perks. Take plectranthus, for example. I've always had an affinity for plectranthus. Although some people might simply see plectranthus as texturally tricked-out close cousins to coleus (solenostemon), I've always stood in awe of their finery (if you discount Swedish ivy, *Plectranthus verticillatus*, which is devoid of any redeeming qualities whatsoever). Otherwise, these plants have great foliage, are easy to cultivate, and burst into flower in autumn when most bloomers are winding down. Compared to other houseplants with fewer virtues, plectranthus are quite a promising package.

I was going to say that the curtain rises for plectranthus in autumn, but I stopped myself short. After all, most plectranthus do a valiant job of entertaining throughout the year. *Plectranthus amboinicus* is a case in point. We're talking 2- to 3-inch (5–8cm) wide, rounded leaves covered in soft, strokeable velveteen. Each leaf is thick, like a succulent (which might account for the plant's ability to endure long periods without water) and the pea-green color of the species is pleasant enough to look upon, but all sorts of gold, cream, and darker green variegated cultivars exist to add intrigue. As it turns out, the flowers are nothing to applaud and are best removed, but other *Plectranthus* species put more emphasis in their blossoms, which often gear up when the days begin to shorten.

A stellar example is *Plectranthus oertendahlii*. Where would I be without this plant? I tuck it in the base of potted trees, I use it as "socks and shoes" (I believe Brent and Becky Heath of Brent and Becky's Bulbs in Gloucester, Virginia, coined that phrase) beneath all sorts of plants that are all stem and lack

With *Plectranthus* 'Mona Lavender', you need not wait until autumn— this cultivar starts blooming precociously in summer.

interest down below. Unlike *P. amboinicus*, which grows upright, *P. oertendahlii* swoops down on graceful arching stems. Although there is some diversity in this species from nursery to nursery, I opt for versions that have silver-marked veins on each forest-green leaf and deep-burgundy undersides. After the initial investment, no need to spend again. I break off a stem and propagate my own for more of a good thing. As if all that wasn't enough, *P. oertendahlii* adds long sprays of little off-white, guppy-like blossoms in the fall. It sort of puts autumn on the map.

Even more impressive is *Plectranthus hilliardiae*, a handsome plant throughout the year with plush, deep-green, serrated-edged leaves accented by dark purple undersides. With only minimal pinching, you can achieve a chubby silhouette (and the ability to form a nicely rounded specimen without a whole lot of effort is a trait of this genus). In *P. hilliardiae*'s case, you wouldn't want to pinch past midsummer, because you'd curtail flower production—and that's really what *P. hilliardiae* throws its strength into. Long, bluish-purple, oboe-shaped blossoms with speckles in the throat begin to develop as the days shorten. However, Kirstenbosch National Botanical Garden in South Africa did some complex hybridizing on this species and achieved a cultivar called 'Mona Lavender' that blooms through summer and spends its days smothered in flower spires.

There are other species around, and most are worth enlisting into your indoor arena. Whether you're adopting the velvety silver-leaved *Plectranthus argentatus* or the wonderfully pungent-smelling Vick's plant, you can't really go wrong. Unfortunately, the nomenclature is a disaster for this genus, but what's in a name? Go with whatever

package you find attractive. Most plectranthus grow rapidly, are trouble free, tolerate low light and drought, and look stunning. There is one sticky wicket in the group, and it is *P. thyrsoideus*. It is crowned by ravishing spires of sailor-blue blossoms in the dead of winter, making it infinitely tempting. However, it is a stinker to grow (and speaking of smell, the foliage is also unpleasantly scented—moldy comes to mind). Without bright light (of the intensity you are not likely to secure in winter), this plant melts into a fungus-riddled mush. Plus, whiteflies are attracted like magnets. Most other members of the genus are just the opposite. Sure, they might be slightly more compact with bright light, but they don't demand it. And all make stellar, low-maintenance container foliage plants when summer rolls around.

Plectranthus species

PLECTRANTHUS

ALSO CALLED: **Mexican mint, Spanish thyme**

FLOWERS	**Tubular white or bluish blossoms in spires**
FOLIAGE	**Often felted, usually handsome**
OTHER ATTRIBUTES	**Often used in summer containers**
SIZE	**12–30 inches (30–76cm) in height, depending on species**
EXPOSURE	**East, west, or south**
WATER REQUIREMENTS	**Medium to low**
OPTIMUM NIGHTTIME TEMPERATURE	**50–65°F (10–18°C)**
RATE OF GROWTH	**Fast**
SOIL TYPE	**Heavy, rich potting soil with compost included**
FERTILIZING	**Early spring to late autumn**
PROBLEMS	**Prone to whiteflies; aphids can be an issue**

SANSEVIERIAS

It's not the most exciting plant in the house, but stick a few cuttings of *Sansevieria cylindrica* in a pot and you can achieve a package that looks amusingly similar to a jester's hat (with barbs on the end). Grow them where nothing but knick-knacks will survive.

I NEVER THOUGHT I'd be devoting a book chapter to sansevierias. Through most of my life, these plants went right below my radar screen. I wouldn't even bother to stifle a yawn on the subject besides chuckling over the plant's mildly entertaining common name of mother-in-law's tongue. If I haven't exactly become a devotee, at least I realize that sansevierias have a certain charm for folks who need something bulletproof in their bedroom.

No one purchases a sansevieria, including me. These are pass-along plants because they make prolific pups. Most often, you're saddled with your great-grandmother's *Sansevieria trifasciata*, a plant that was all the rage when it was introduced to Europe in 1731, and subsequently earned its nickname, which is particularly apt because this species is long, sharp, and infinitely boring. It never dies. Plus, I've never seen blossoms on this species. It merely sits around in a permanent state of stasis, giving houseplants a bad name.

Slightly more interesting is *Sansevieria cylindrica*, a species from Angola with wonderfully rounded, tube-like stems ending in a sharp barb. Mine remained a foot (30cm) tall and had four canes springing from the container, giving it a jaunty jester's-hat look. The fact that it is the only plant that will live on my mantel was a definite plus.

For entirely different reasons, I'm rather fond of *Sansevieria trifasciata* 'Golden Hahnii' and its brethren. Unlike the taller species from whence it came, 'Golden Hahnii' is dwarf, standing merely 6 inches (15cm) at maturity. It forms a lovely plump rosette of foliage, like a rosebud composed of leaves. And the foliage has fields of mottled silver accenting the center with bold golden streaks running up each edge. It's a handsome plant. Other variations on the theme abound, and they make a nod toward nature possible where you might not be able to host anything more exciting.

Dim light would be sansevierias' druthers. Direct beams cause them to bleach and brown. A north-facing window would probably work just fine, but I'm a generous soul and give mine east or west. Besides burning from direct sun, sansevierias show no signs of distress in any situation. They look just about the same in low humidity, lack of light, minimal water, a deluge of rain, or whatever you or nature hand out. And they even make abundant and continual little pups to share with other folks who might be deserving, but also apt to neglect their houseplants.

Sansevieria species

SANSEVIERIA

ALSO CALLED: **mother-in-law's tongue, snake plant**

FLOWERS	**Not a major element, except the fragrant *Sansevieria gracilis*, which has a delightful, intensely sweet scent**
FOLIAGE	**Dark green and thick, with various markings**
OTHER ATTRIBUTES	**Tolerant of less-than-ideal growing conditions; easily divided to share**
SIZE	**6–24 inches (15–61cm) in height, depending on species or cultivar**
EXPOSURE	**North, east, or west**
WATER REQUIREMENTS	**Light**
OPTIMUM NIGHTTIME TEMPERATURE	**55–65°F (12–18°C)**
RATE OF GROWTH	**Slow**
SOIL TYPE	**Almost any potting soil will suffice**
FERTILIZING	**Not critical, but would enjoy feeding between early spring and late autumn**
PROBLEMS	**Sansevierias are particularly toxic.**

SEMPERVIVUMS

In spring, *Sempervivum arachnoideum* emerges its chicks with cobwebs intact. (Just what you need in your home.) Mercifully, the cottony film disappears by summer —no dusting needed.

ONE OF MY earliest memories of the garden involves hens and chicks. My mom used to read us poetry on the porch after lunch, and my childhood kitten (I've always had cats) would hang around to keep us from rudely falling asleep between verses. The kitten did what kittens do best—pawed around in the garden beds. By the time my mother was just two or three pages into *A Child's Garden of Verses*, he had invariably teased out a few sempervivums, leaving them stranded on the cement and begging to be replanted.

So sempervivums and I go way back—they were quite possibly my first brush with a trowel—and no garden of mine is complete without a few. That includes the garden indoors. If part of houseplants' purpose is to keep the embers of summer symbolically burning throughout the dormant season, sempervivums are a critical element of the scene. Considering that another common name is house leeks, I suspect other folks feel exactly the same way.

Fact is, there's no houseplant on earth as easy as a sempervivum. Yes, they do best in bright light. But they're as tough as nails. I forgot one in a dark corner, and it looks pretty identical to the version I pampered in sun. Use them around the base of a tree-like plant to add interest on the ground level. Or give them a funky container of their own. Granted, they just tread water and don't generally do stunts (like making multiple chicks or sending up their arching flower spires) in autumn or winter. But they are worth bringing in just for summer sentimentality's sake.

Unless you're an expert, the various sempervivums look pretty similar, with a few minor diverse details. When the foliage isn't highly defined in autumn and winter, it is particularly difficult to distinguish one from the other. They all make little rosettes of succulent leaves that cluster along the ground in configurations of larger hens surrounded by flocks of chicks. Without any other bells or whistles, it's totally heartwarming (or is it just me?). In spring, *Sempervivum arachnoideum* adds a "fur" of cobweb-like cotton to the center of each rosette. And several varieties blush red or burnish blue-gray, but the diversity isn't so apparent indoors. The flowers are truly intriguing perks, though. In summer, the center of the hen begins to elongate and form an arching plume of intricately bizarre, star-shaped pink flowers with green raised "buttons" in the center. Even in the bud stage, they could qualify as visitors from another galaxy.

But the true beauty of hens and chicks is their invincible spirit. They fail to bat an eyelash when faced with any sort of abuse. However, in the best of all worlds, they prefer bright light, and you should water only when their soil mix is dry. Too much humidity might be a killer, but I've never been able to test them on that point. They would prefer a sandy, well-drained potting mix in a shallow container. But really, those accommodations are just icing on the cake. They will persist regardless.

However, I have found that sempervivums are frequently plagued by root mealy bugs, so much so that I think nothing of checking plants' root systems at the nursery for the telltale cottony masses before buying. If they pass the test, it's a straight path back to memories of my childhood, poetry, and kittens. Can you think of a more soothing association?

Sempervivum species

SEMPERVIVUM

ALSO CALLED: **hens and chicks, house leeks**

FLOWERS	**Arching spires with little white to strawberry-red buttons**
FOLIAGE	**Rosettes of pointed, succulent leaves**
OTHER ATTRIBUTES	**Form colonies of rosettes; can be groundcovers for potted trees**
SIZE	**2 inches (5cm) in height**
EXPOSURE	**Sunny south**
WATER REQUIREMENTS	**Allow to dry out between waterings; dislike overwatering**
OPTIMUM NIGHTTIME TEMPERATURE	**40–55°F (4–12°C) (most are hardy to Zone 5 outdoors)**
RATE OF GROWTH	**Slow**
SOIL TYPE	**Well-drained**
FERTILIZING	**Probably best omitted**
PROBLEMS	**Root mealy bugs**

I hunker down with houseplants in my bedroom during the long nights and snowy days of winter. In addition to a *Paphiopedilum*, *Stephanotis floribunda*, and *Polypodium formosanum*, plus a begonia and maranta in the Wardian case, even parsley comes into play.

Wind is gusting at 40 miles per hour, snow is piled 3 feet high, and the highways are closed. Meanwhile, two bright blue blossoms are bursting on the thunbergia, there are some baby blue flowers bouncing on the chirita when the wind jiggles the windows, and the paphiopedilum is still lingering in the bathroom after its debut several weeks ago. Countless amaryllis (hippeastrum) are trumpeting their wares, the leaves of a kalanchoe are buried behind its clouds of sizzling orange blossoms, and the citrus has sent its perfume roaming throughout my office all morning. This is why I garden indoors.

I've never had the opportunity to explore whether I am prone to Seasonal Affective Disorder. With all this greenery around, I never feel the full brunt of winter. Sure, my back aches from shoveling snow and my fingers are swollen from chilblains. But my spirit is warmed by all the growing things performing around me. Forced bulbs are pushing their noses through the soil, vines are climbing around, grasses are bristling in little tufts only to be flattened and stomped into oblivion by kitten paws. It's a happening place.

And I shuffle around, carrying watering pots to and fro, dousing the soil with silver streams arching from spouts, removing a brown leaf here and tucking a flower spike in front of a leaf there. In the darkest hours of winter—and we count plenty—I feel every inch a gardener. All my nurturing instincts are put to the test; all my horticultural talents are unleashed. Right here, right now. Not in a few months, not when the ice melts or the snow run off rushes into my basement. I need not wait for a thaw or the sun to shine. This is why I grow houseplants.

For a different spin on an old chestnut, substitute *Crassula ovata* 'Minima' rather than the humdrum jade plant.

It might be
winter outside,
but in my bedroom
there's parsley,
a paphiopedilum
orchid, and
a stephanotis
huddled around the
window, soaking
up the sunbeams.

Everything slows down in winter. Even the blossoms that open seem to linger longer. Plants grow lethargically and require water less frequently, and I move around at a more leisurely pace—snail is an appropriate description—to service their needs.

When light levels are low, plants do not grow by leaps and bounds. As a result, they do not slurp up water as rapidly as they did in summer. However, when the furnace is running full tilt, plants in the direct line of fire (also near woodstoves and close to hot-air vents) feel the drying effect. And when you combine the atmospheric dryness with sun reflected off snow, you might occasionally find yourself serving up drinks nearly as often as you did during other seasons. But never assume that because it's Friday, drinks are on the schedule. Instead, monitor each plant for its watering needs. Of course, that's the way you should run the ship throughout the year, but in winter, it's critical. Overwatering is the primary cause of untimely death for most houseplants, and winter is when overzealousness with the watering can tends to occur. Blame it on sheer boredom, but we spoil our houseplants to death in winter.

The best way to avoid this capital offense is to use a hand-in-glove approach to matching root systems with pot sizes. When a plant is potted in a plus-size container, excess soil remains soggy, rotting the roots. I avoid that pitfall by graduating only one pot size at a time. Furthermore, I never transplant in autumn or winter unless a plant is continually thirsty and has become a nuisance factor. Otherwise, I bide my time until I see spring coming around the corner.

Because light levels are low, I rarely fertilize in winter. Of course, if a plant has that pale and hungry look, I pull out the fish emulsion. But that's definitely the exception, and I think twice before doling out food at a time of year when incoming light levels won't be prompting vigorous growth. Don't assume that the remedy for a plant's problems lies in repotting or feeding. That's usually the worst solution, especially in winter. Instead, just hold steady.

Meanwhile, I find myself constantly wielding the pruning shears in winter. This is the time when plants make spindly, leggy growth that won't compare favorably with the tight, sinuous limbs that develop when more light streams in. I just whack those stretching branches right off. In fact, some plants, such as angel wing begonias, get clipped right down to the base in expectation of tighter shoots as the days lengthen.

Winter is when we're all starved for greenery. But no need to settle for the first green thing that crosses your path. No need to act out of desperation. Don't feel you must give a permanent home and precious window space to every poinsettia that throws itself at your mercy. Instead, I focus my energy (and windows) on plants that are trouble free, truly glam, and worth the room and care. That's not to say I don't have plants on my holiday wish list. Plenty of friends lavish me with green gifts, and I'm grateful. You can never have enough orchids, amaryllis, camellias, ferns, or newly sprouting bulbs in your life. Winter is when you need them the most.

ASPARAGUS

Can you blame me
for the falling-in-love
aspect of my love-hate
relationship with
Asparagus retrofractus?

MY HOME IS a fluid affair. Like any other fickle gardener, I play favorites for a few years and then turn my attention elsewhere. For a very long time, I carried on a hot relationship with *Asparagus retrofractus*, but we had to break up. Actually, it didn't end well.

First of all, notice that I didn't commit the usual lapse of lumping asparagus into the fern category. Granted, the lacy asparagus species that we grow indoors do look somewhat like ferns and definitely act a lot like ferns, but asparagus are in the *Liliaceae* family. Unlike ferns, they produce insignificant little flowers often followed by berry-like red fruit. For years, mine grew happily in the bathroom, where it remained winter and summer because it became obese and I could no longer cart it around.

Left in position, it acted like a vine and sent an occasional groping stem up the trellis behind the toilet. Problem was, it kept expanding. The more it grew, the more I had to distance myself. Although its tufts of green leaves were soft to the touch, its woody brown stems brandished thorns. All of this would be fine at arm's length, but up close and intimate (we're talking the toilet, after all), it wasn't a comfortable living situation. It was a constant tug of war. Then there was another problem: the soft, fine, needle-like leaves had a habit of shedding all over the place.

The time eventually came when the asparagus was cut back and extracted from the bathroom and brought into the shadiest end of the greenhouse instead. I relocated it not because it needed additional light, but because its swollen roots demanded a huge pot and I simply couldn't accommodate it elsewhere. It delighted in its new digs, to the point that it outgrew several pot promotions. Finally I had to call things to a halt. Because it was pot-bound, it required constant watering. So I decided to end the relationship.

But the story doesn't stop there. Stupidly, I gave the asparagus one of my favorite glazed containers. As of this writing, it still persists in holding onto that pot for dear life. I can't seem to extract the root system, and the custody battle is getting ugly. Meanwhile, it keeps desperately sending up signs of life. The asparagus is a plant that will not say die.

This has been the ongoing saga of *Asparagus retrofractus*. You are undoubtedly wondering about the more commonly grown *A. densiflorus*. I'm here to tell you that it would not be permitted to set its foot in the door. (Here's where the opinionated indoor gardener rears her ugly head.) Compared to the poetic tufts of *A. retrofractus*, *A. densiflorus* is coarse, with a blob-like growth habit and leaves like pine needles, which shed worse than the plant I entertained for so long. Much worse. It has all the same bad habits, plus more. At least my *A. retrofractus* and I have many happy memories. And I am sure we'll work this out.

If, after all this bad-mouthing, you still want to host an asparagus, it is one of the easiest plants on earth to grow. I would not recommend a dark north window because your asparagus will become leggy and sparsely foliated. But it will tolerate just about every other situation and still look great. It's a water guzzler, so be prepared. Expect to hand out frequent container promotions. And, most important, don't give it your favorite container—you may never be able to wrench it free.

Asparagus retrofractus

ASPARAGUS

ALSO CALLED: asparagus fern

FLOWERS	Tiny white blossoms; red berries sometimes follow
FOLIAGE	Needle-like on barbed stems
OTHER ATTRIBUTES	Can be used in flower arranging
SIZE	30 inches (76cm) in height, with plus-size girth
EXPOSURE	East or west
WATER REQUIREMENTS	A guzzler
OPTIMUM NIGHTTIME TEMPERATURE	55–65°F (12–18°C)
RATE OF GROWTH	Lightning fast
SOIL TYPE	Any good, well-drained potting soil
FERTILIZING	I don't suggest encouraging this plant with food
PROBLEMS	Obesity, shedding

BURBIDGEA

After *Burbidgea schizocheila*'s blossoms emerge from their fiery ball, they linger long, topping plants that stand only slightly taller than a foot, which is compact compared to most members of the ginger family.

FOR THE MOST part, I don't hunt for my houseplants in obscure places. I find them where most people look for green roommates—at my local garden center, in super-markets, and at little green-house businesses that I spy when I'm tooling around the countryside. When traveling, I make inquiries. Sensitive hosts know of my proclivity and take me on junkets. But a few of my plants did come from specialty nurseries. *Burbidgea schizocheila* hails from Logee's Greenhouses.

This is one of the best houseplants in my ever-expanding collection. It's a member of the ginger fam-ily, so it grows by creeping rhizomes that expand to give the plant girth. Some gingers are fussy or fail to blossom until they reach a ripe old age, thus testing your patience. So *Burbidgea schizocheila* is a blessed relief. It can't be accused of either fussiness or tardiness. It tends to begin blossoming in its first autumn as a small division. From then on, all the rest is gravy: it hap-pily chugs along, expanding to send up new growth from the base, and it blossoms throughout autumn and early winter to beat the band.

There's dance movement in these blossoms. From the little topknot that promises to swell into blossoms onward, the show is like watching choreography. The flowers are orange toward the center of their little yellow whorl and then expand like sea urchins to open like orchids. The whole performance continues for weeks, until the flowers gracefully fall. When the plant matures into multiple heads, it's quite the scene.

But the beauty of the show is that it isn't difficult to achieve. The deep-green foliage juts out at right angles on either side of a stem that stands no taller than 15 inches (38cm), so you can fit this into your house with no problems. And it snuggles all its shoots fairly close together, giving it a tidy, compact presentation. Really, it's like a flower arrangement growing in soil. If you bruise the stem, it emits the slightest ghost of a gingery scent. Give it an east or west window. The plant asks almost nothing except an occasional repotting to accommodate its expanding growth. Fertilizer every three weeks or so will keep its foliage deep green and luscious. And flowers will follow at the appointed hour. Can you tell I'm fond of this plant?

Burbidgea schizocheila

BURBIDGEA

ALSO CALLED: **golden brush**

FLOWERS	**Fiery orange-yellow, orchid-like blossoms in whorls**
FOLIAGE	**Pointed, dark-green leaves against a brown stem**
OTHER ATTRIBUTES	**Very slight ginger scent when the stem is bruised**
SIZE	**15 inches (38cm) in height**
EXPOSURE	**East or west**
WATER REQUIREMENTS	**Does not dry out often**
OPTIMUM NIGHTTIME TEMPERATURE	**55–65°F (12–18°C)**
RATE OF GROWTH	**Medium**
SOIL TYPE	**Well-drained, humusy potting soil with compost included**
FERTILIZING	**Early spring to late autumn only**
PROBLEMS	**None; this is the perfect houseplant (at least, so far)**

CAMELLIA

Although *Camellia japonica* cultivars can elude me, *C. sasanqua* 'Fragrant Pink' entertains willingly. Potted in a deep container with *Dichondra micrantha* as a groundcover, its roots can plunge to their hearts' content.

IF YOU RATED the windows in my converted barn, the designations would be cold, colder, and coldest. And the closer you get to the panes, the chillier the reception. So it was easy to select where to station a certain blooming shrub. Coldest is fine for a camellia.

In that way, camellias and I get along just great. In a house that hovers around 55°F (12°C) at night and never seems to go above 60°F (15°C) during the day, camellias blossom vigorously. With no heat vents nearby, the upstairs loft is particularly chilly, and camellias do not mind. Facing west, with good light in the winter when the sugar maple sheds its clothes, the camellia dotes on this unique state of affairs.

I'm currently growing *Camellia sasanqua* 'Fragrant Pink' up there. Although I've dabbled in the larger, flashier *C. japonica* cultivars, I confess I haven't had similar success with them. Somewhere in the growing cycle, I either forget to water or indulge in cranking up the thermostat a little too high (it doesn't take much; 65°F [18°C] will do it), and boom—the unopened buds go tumbling down to the floor. In addition, I just can't seem to keep abreast of *C. japonica*'s repotting requirements. The plant races into tree form too rapidly, and I struggle—and fail—to keep up with the promotions. If I manage to achieve one or two flowers by midwinter on *C. japonica*, I go into celebratory mode.

Just the opposite occurs with *Camellia sasanqua* hybrids. We get along famously. They start blooming in late autumn, not long after I bring the plants inside, and keep right on happening through most of the winter. They rarely drop buds, no matter what the temperatures do indoors. Flowers on *C. sasanqua* cultivars tend to be about half the size (or smaller) of japonica blossoms. But the good news is that they nestle into a bush of smaller (and more statuesque) stature with downsized leaves. *Camellia sasanqua* is a better fit for the average home. I think you could even get away with a coolish corner in a normally heated house and still secure blossoms. Not only are the flowers of sasanquas within your reach, but they are fragrant. Granted, you have to apply your nose to the blossom to discover its wares, but the scent is light, candy sweet, and totally agreeable. That's another improvement over the japonica hybrids, which generally have no scent.

I spent a great deal of time talking with Tasha Tudor, the famed illustrator, Yankee icon, and unparalleled gardener, while she was alive, and one of her favorite topics was camellias. She grew several *Camellia japonica* cultivars in her cool greenhouse and could talk about them by the hour. "Now tell me the secrets," she'd prompt. First, camellias prefer a slightly acidic soil. Furthermore, the usual fish emulsion regimen can be too potent when a camellia is not in full growth. Instead, some growers recommend applying cottonseed meal according to the label specifications in summer when camellias are adding foliage (I haven't tried this). I provide any camellia as much root room as possible. In general, I grow woody indoor plants in deep cylindrical containers to allow roots to plunge down rather than graduating to increasingly wide pots that hoard a massive footprint in cramped conditions where every square inch of light is prime real estate. A friend shared the knowledge that the japonicas want to face the same orientation no matter where they are moved. For example, when being relocated, they supposedly would love to keep their east side facing east. I try not to shift camellias around much because they tend to weigh a ton. Also, the buds drop readily when the plant is bopped around. And they love profuse water, especially when setting buds. Pampered camellias dote on all the perks mentioned. But my 'Fragrant Pink' persists with some water and a promise. It blossoms valiantly nonetheless.

Camellia japonica and *C. sasanqua*

CAMELLIA

FLOWERS	Depending on the cultivar, white, pink, or red rose-like blossoms, either single or double
FOLIAGE	Glossy green leaves; quite handsome
OTHER ATTRIBUTES	*Camellia sasanqua* hybrids are often pleasingly fragrant
SIZE	48 inches (122cm) and up in height
EXPOSURE	East or west
WATER REQUIREMENTS	Prefers regular water when in bud
OPTIMUM NIGHTTIME TEMPERATURE	50–60°F (10–15°C)
RATE OF GROWTH	A slow-growing tree
SOIL TYPE	Acidic, well-drained potting soil with compost included
FERTILIZING	They prefer fertilizer while in active growth in spring and summer
PROBLEMS	Prone to scale, tend to drop buds easily

CLIVIAS

I go to my neighbor's greenhouse to pay visits to *Clivia miniata* rather than take up precious window space with its bulky presence.

I USED TO be a clivia fanatic. I was right alongside all those crazies who ferret out slight color variations and send for seed from South Africa. But no more. I really cannot explain it, but clivias just do not send me into palpitations. They are still moderately thrilling, but not transformational enough to justify allocating such a huge footprint in the cramped spaces appropriate for plants in my home. (Don't misunderstand—I have plenty of spaces to grow plants in my house. It's because of total green overindulgence that they're overcrowded.) My friend Peter Wooster has a clivia in his greenhouse down the street, and visiting it every few weeks is sufficient exposure to its charms, even in the dead of winter.

Everyone goes gaga over *Clivia miniata*, the big, round-flowered, fiery-orange-verging-on-molten-red species that looks like someone clustered a crowd of tulips together and nestled them in a fan of tidy, deep-green foliage. This culprit seduced me into spending long evenings trying to find color variants with the promise of yellow in their spectrum. When butter-yellow *C. miniata* var. *citrina* was auctioned off at a fundraiser for $500, I was not among those who frowned in disbelief. I was in the "only $500?" contingent.

Based on that auction, *Clivia miniata* var. *citrina* became the Rolls-Royce of houseplants. Everybody who could afford one flocked to plunk down money on a seedling that would not flower for several years. Most had estate gardeners poised and ready to handle any connoisseur plant that might come into the collection. But in this case, the gardeners' talents were not challenged. Nothing could be easier than growing a clivia of any color. Back in

the 1850s, when clivias first came to Europe, they gained cult status. The Victorians hailed as a hero any plant that sends up flowers despite very low light, produces blossoms that linger for several months at a time, and requires almost no special care. For the very same reasons, it is also a friend of mine.

I still harbor a soft spot for clivias, but their size gives me pause. A mature clivia with several fans planted in a container will take up a hefty chunk of real estate in your home. Granted, it can monopolize a low-light corner of your world, but it also spends two-thirds of the year (longer, for some people) doing nothing. In fact, the complaint about clivias is that they sometimes skip a year. Plus, some years the flowers are nearly hidden deep in their fan of long, strap-like leaves, whereas other years they totter way above the foliage. However, it's likely that temperatures control the floral stem length (cooler will shorten the flower stem). Clivias tolerate temperatures of 50°F (10°C), but do not insist on cool conditions.

Some say that clivias should be given a dormancy period. They have it pinned down from October to November, when you withhold water and minimize light. Few people remember to inflict deprivation, and clivias generally forgive the lack of the torture sequence.

It's true that clivias blossom best when pot-bound. And a healthy clivia will keep sending up pups and producing roots to fill a container in no time. At some point, you will need to repot. The roots are nearly as wide as your finger, so they will eventually fill and possibly break terra-cotta. Dividing is a contact sport that will challenge your average wrestler. Be careful.

Clivia species
CLIVIA

FLOWERS	Brightly colored and very showy
FOLIAGE	Long, strap-like leaves jutting from a fan
OTHER ATTRIBUTES	Foliage is handsome when it's not in blossom
SIZE	12–24 inches (30–61cm) in height
EXPOSURE	East or west
WATER REQUIREMENTS	Not a particularly thirsty plant
OPTIMUM NIGHTTIME TEMPERATURE	50–60°F (10–15°C)
RATE OF GROWTH	Slow
SOIL TYPE	Well-drained, fertile soil
FERTILIZING	Early spring to late autumn
PROBLEMS	Can fail to blossom in certain years. Clivias are toxic. Keep all members of the *Liliaceae* family away from pets who are prone to ingest, especially cats.

EUPHORBIA

Euphorbia amygdaloides 'Efanthia' isn't your ordinary houseplant. But if what you need in winter is a hint of spring, it's your man. Here it's standing beside several amaryllis.

WHAT DO WE want out of winter? From the standpoint of someone who has been stuck inside for approximately four weeks with towering monoliths of snow facing her from all sides, we want spring. We don't just want spring; we would commit just about any desperate act to attain spring, including buying spring-blooming perennials in the hope they will give us a sneak preview.

I must admit, *Euphorbia amygdaloides* 'Efanthia' was a gamble. I was really just hoping to enjoy its rigid, dark burgundy leaves surrounding the stem like bristles on a cleaning utensil. The plant seemed to have a nice strong form when I saw it stuffed in the corner of a garden center chock-full of poinsettias and similar holiday junk for pushovers. But a few weeks ago the euphorbia began to bud, and there has been rejoicing ever since (as much as is possible muffled beneath 3 feet of snow).

So, I fooled you. If you turned to this section thinking I would extol the virtues of *Euphorbia fulgens*, the nonsucculent member of the spurge family sometimes sold during the winter, I'm sorry to disappoint you. Although *E. fulgens* is undeniably cute, with its long, slender, pointed leaves and wands of small, bright scarlet, midwinter flowers, I have no luck whatsoever with it. Neither the regular green form nor the purple-leaved variety works for me in a home setting. They just need too much light for the average home.

The bracts of *Euphorbia amygdaloides* 'Efanthia' are primarily responsible for the show. The flowers are the yellow knots within.

On the other hand, *Euphorbia amygdaloides* 'Efanthia' (and probably all the other *E. amygdaloides* hybrids as well) has far surpassed my greatest expectations. Absolutely trouble-free, this summer perennial is worth adopting indoors. Insects are not an issue; other woes have not hindered its progress. The plant I obtained in early winter was already well branched, but an autumn whack with the pruners would produce the same result. Get it when your nursery is in the throes of its autumn sellout, or dig one from your garden (some of the *E. amygdaloides* hybrids have not proved equal to our spring thaws in Zone 5) and sequester it inside. Rather than a light, fluffy, peat moss–based soil medium, I went for a heavier potting mix with compost. A cacti-succulent soil mix would be just the ticket (add some compost if it seems lean). I gave it a deep, but not wide, container. Mine is a heavy drinker, so I water it frequently to prevent wilting. Euphorbias detest overwatering, though, so do not smother them with gratuities.

Until the flowers started forming, 'Efanthia' kept its tight shape in a bright spot indoors. Then the plant started to form those wonderful leprechaun-green buds. They eventually expanded into the green bracts and flowers for which spurges are famed. Granted, they are not the tight little topknots that spring brings in the garden, but beggars cannot be choosy.

This is my first investment of the year in my garden outdoors. As soon as spring arrives, I plan to plant 'Efanthia' out in the perennial border. My idea is to cut it back to a nub again and make it sprout out in the hopes of a second blooming. It's worth a try. And next year, I can start over for the winter follies.

Euphorbia amygdaloides 'Efanthia'
and other cultivars

EUPHORBIA

ALSO CALLED: **wood spurge**

FLOWERS	Billowing masses of tiny, bright green, cup-like bracts holding yellow blooms
FOLIAGE	Long slender leaves are burgundy in 'Efanthia', but variegated versions are also available
OTHER ATTRIBUTES	Hardy in the garden, so you can plant it out in the summer.
SIZE	1 foot (30cm) in height not in blossom; 2 feet (61cm) in height in bloom
EXPOSURE	South or bright west
WATER REQUIREMENTS	Heavy drinker when in blossom
OPTIMUM NIGHTTIME TEMPERATURE	50–65°F (10–15°C)
RATE OF GROWTH	Medium, but quick to flower
SOIL TYPE	Heavy cactus soil with compost added, or just good, rich container soil
FERTILIZING	Between early spring and late autumn
PROBLEMS	No insect or disease problems. Euphorbias are toxic and can cause a dermatological reaction.

FERNS

I NEED FLOWERS in winter. When it comes to rewards, I'm right alongside everyone who craves flowers when the garden refuses to comply. But I also need a respite; preferably a green oasis. And that's where ferns come in.

Ferns are soothing. They have a certain inherent sophistication. Within your indoor garden, ferns are crowd control. Too many flowers jammed together, and the place begins to bear a disquieting resemblance to a bordello. You laugh, but you don't want your home to look like a carnival scene. I prefer something quieter, so I balance out the bloomers with ferns.

Ferns have a hushed sort of splendor. They possess staying power. Their silhouette is architectural and sculptured; their fronds and fiddleheads display subtle innuendos of green, gray, smoky blue, chartreuse, and other variations in hue. Want a place where your eyes can fall and rest? Hire a fern.

Plus, ferns can fill a niche that might otherwise remain bereft of nature. Here's a plant that will suffer your north-facing exposure and live to tell the tale. Sure, some ferns are a bear. Interestingly, I find that although Boston or sword ferns (nephrolepis) are omnipresent in nurseries, they are among the trickiest to grow in the average home. Without high humidity, they brown. Forget to water them once or twice, they get browner. Neglect them over a protracted period of time, and they go permanently into the wild brown yonder. It's amazing that such a finicky fern has attained superstardom.

An exception in the group is *Nephrolepis cordifolia* 'Duffii', a downsized version with tiny round pinnae (a fern's substitute for leaves) lining the rachis (a fern frond's midrib). Not only does it survive for me, but it tolerates occasional dryness and other abuse. Give the larger *Nephrolepis* cultivars plenty of root room. Keeping any fern from becoming root bound is a step in the right direction. Also on the "trouble" list in an indoor setting are all maidenhair ferns (adiantums), *Hemionitis arifolia*, and doodias, which I've tried and failed with innumerable times.

But the horticultural world is full of ferns that work brilliantly in a home. A personal favorite is the caterpillar fern, *Polypodium formosanum*. With sci-fi monster–green, caterpillar-size rhizomes that crawl over the top of the soil and chartreuse segmented fronds that shoot up, it gives some gardeners the creeps. But if you can't handle nature's sense of humor, you're not going to find my home particularly amusing. Plus, *P. formosanum* is forgiving, which is an important requisite in a houseplant. Repeated water neglect will cause the fronds to brown and the rhizomes to shrivel, but the rhizomes recover admirably and send up new fiddleheads when the breach is rectified. The caterpillar fern is just one possibility in this clan; other polypodiums are equally accommodating if you give them ample root-roaming room.

Along the same tangent but adding fur to the rhizomes, *Humata tyermannii* is another home workhorse. Some people make the association with tarantula legs when they encounter humata's furry feet, but I prefer to think of squirrel paws. Impeccably tidy, low-growing, dark green fronds jut above the network of gray furred, creeping rhizomes. It's a rapid grower and readily available.

Several aspleniums work for me. The bird's nest fern, *Asplenium nidus*, with its flattened, ribbon-like fronds, verges on indomitable. A close second in the ironclad division is the bird's nest's cousin, *A. bulbiferum*, which holds its family of piggyback plantlets on lacy fronds. Not only does *A. bulbiferum* make multiple divisions, but you can just pull off the plantlets and tuck them into loose, humusy soil, and they will send out roots. It's great for sharing with children.

Years ago, I planted my staghorn fern, *Platycerium* species, in a wire frame, which it completely engulfed. I carry it outdoors to be watered once or twice a week.

Some folks get the creepy-crawlies from footed ferns (which sprout their fronds from slinking, above-the-ground rhizomes), but I love them. *Humata tyermannii* wins the congeniality award and is the most compact.

All these ferns are well and good. But my pride and joy is a staghorn fern. Allow me to boast. It's been a member of the family for so many years that I've lost count. Originally, I planted it in a wicker basket with a little built-in wire pedestal. Since then, my platycerium (I admit that I do not know the platycerium's pedigree and it appears to be a bit of a mutt) has proceeded to send out flat plates around the outside of its basket as well as fertile staghorns jutting out in all directions. It has completely engulfed its container beyond recognition. Believe it or not, I drag it outside whenever the weather goes above freezing in winter

Pteridophyta

FERNS

FLOWERS	Not a factor
FOLIAGE	Various intriguing combinations of subtle shades of green
OTHER ATTRIBUTES	Rather than the perk of flowers, ferns always look great
SIZE	Usually from 6 to 24 inches (15–61cm) in height
EXPOSURE	East or west preferable if pulled away from direct sunbeams; north also works
WATER REQUIREMENTS	Ferns don't like to dry out
OPTIMUM NIGHTTIME TEMPERATURE	55–65°F (12–18°C)
RATE OF GROWTH	Slow
SOIL TYPE	Light, fluffy, humusy soil mix with a lot of organic matter
FERTILIZING	Early spring to late autumn
PROBLEMS	Prone to scale; tend to be sensitive to oil-based sprays

and pour water through what remains of its container. During most winters (remember, I'm in New England), I can find an hour or so that is above freezing to run it outside once a week. If this sort of Olympic feat has you nervous, go the bathtub route and shower it down.

In the fear that someday my old staghorn buddy might bite the dust, I have a younger version in training. It is displayed with the more typical treatment of lashing the plant with fishing line to some sphagnum moss against a slab of wood. In summer, I hang it on my front door where normal people have their knockers. It never fails to impress first-time visitors and (hopefully) dissuade solicitors.

FORCED SPRING BULBS

Rather than accusing them of flopping, I prefer to say that species tulips, such as *Tulipa clusiana*, have a graceful arch.

NORMALLY, *Tulipa clusiana* 'Cynthia' does not make my heart race. For sure, it's nice enough. With alternating whisper-pink and white petals on slender 2-inch (5cm) flowers, 'Cynthia' would not be rated as a showstopper when it unfolds in the garden outdoors. Bring that little baby onto your windowsill in winter, though, and you'll be singing the hosannas with a whole different fervor. Proof again that a few tulip flowers in winter are worth a whole bulb meadow in spring.

It's been a long time since I tried to survive winter without bulbs. Many years ago, I learned it was possible to coax spring bulbs to perform prematurely indoors. Ever since, I've enjoyed orchestrating that sneak peek at the growing season on my windowsill. Did I say enjoyed? What I really mean is that bulbs serve up salvation. I would not miss this opportunity for the world.

You've undoubtedly caught wind of the phenomenon. By pre-chilling bulbs, waiting patiently (or not so patiently) for several weeks, you can prod narcissus, tulips, muscari, puschkinias, fritillarias, and other harbingers of spring to blossom precociously in your home. You don't really skip their dormant sequence, but you cut it short. You cheat. And it's golden to have a few little bulbs happening in the warm, cozy recesses of your home when everything outside is still locked in the Big Chill.

Most spring bulbs are capable of serving as lifesavers. I've had resounding success with potted narcissus of all sorts (but the dwarfs and the cyclamineus types, in particular, lend themselves to forcing because they blossom earliest), tulips (especially species tulips and their kin, such as

If you're going for a spring prelude, why not pair a forced *Tulipa* 'Henry Hudson' with something equally outdoorsy, like Jill-over-the-ground?

Tulipa bakeri 'Lilac Wonder', *T. batalinii* 'Bronze Charm', *T.* 'Lady Jane', *T. linifolia*, and *T. marjolettii* because they perform after a particularly brief chilling sequence), scillas, puschkinias, *Iris cristata*, fritillarias (crown imperials are within the realm of possibility, but smell distinctly skunky—a trait that can be vexing in close quarters; I go with the guinea hens, *Fritillaria meleagris*), and *Allium karataviense*, to mention only my most tried-and-true favorites. Hyacinths are a mainstay as well, partly because they're so simple. Most of the early blooming hyacinths perform without refrigeration after arrival. Apparently, the pre-chilling they received from my vendors is sufficient (and I always obtain my bulbs through the mail to ensure the highest quality and proper storage treatment). Grape hyacinths (muscari) and cro-

cus also perform when put in expedited mode, but the flowers come and go so rapidly, the payback is too brief. And you can often find growing, budded, or even blooming muscari at the supermarket, effectively skipping all the prep work and going straight to the glittering prize.

The prep work that I refer to is the pre-chilling sequence. You can cheat nature only to a certain degree; you have to play her game. Every year, right after we clear Thanksgiving, you can find me at my potting bench (which is just a standard-issue flea-market worktable). This moment is like Christmas, my birthday, Independence Day, and all other celebratory junctures rolled into one. In preparation, I amass an arsenal of forcing containers that far exceeds my horde of bulbs. (There is no need to go for the traditional shallow, glazed forcing pots. Any container will do the trick. But on a practical level, containers must fit into the refrigerator, leaving some space for food.)

I tuck as many bulbs of the same type as possible cheek to jowl in each container, placing them an inch or two below soil level using an organic potting mix with compost included. Combos can be tricky. My advice is, don't bother. Those happy jumbles of hyacinths, scillas, muscari, tulips, and daffodils all thrown into one container and touted as synchronizing perfectly in blossom rarely (if ever) perform in unison as advertised. I've given up on the mixed bag in favor of one cultivar per container. When two pots of bulbs coincide in blossom, I display them side by side. It works for me.

What the cherry-red species *Tulipa linifolia* lacks in flower size it gains in willingness to perform easily.

A single flower on *Ipheion uniflorum* 'Rolf Fiedler' might not read as much in the garden, but indoors it's everything in late winter.

If you've come to the conclusion that houseplants have railroaded my home, you should see the refrigerator. When the bulbs first arrive, I stash them unplanted in the salad-crisper drawers. After they are potted into containers, they pretty much monopolize the refrigerator for the duration of the chilling period, until signs of growth begin to sprout (when in doubt, leave them in the refrigerator—removing too early will result in foliage, but no flowers). And if you prefer to reserve your fridge for food, other options are the cellar, garage, barn, barely heated mudroom, or any place that remains around 40°F to 45°F (4–7°C) and does not freeze. In the refrigerator, the planted bulbs are monitored to make sure the soil hasn't dried out during the 8- to 12-week cold treatment (tulip hybrids can take 15 to 18 weeks). After

chilling, they come out as needed to brighten what could be a dangerously boring blip in time. I put mine in a bright window while they start to send up growth. The hope is that the winter sun (especially reflected on the snow) will be sufficiently bright to keep the stems from stretching. The fact that I keep my house quite cool also helps to prevent legginess, while also keeping my mother in the steady business of knitting sweaters. As another perk, the chilly environment also prolongs the flowers when they come. Blossoms are the big payoff. So, to make them linger longer, I usually move the bulbs away from direct

Purchased at the market and repotted, *Muscari* 'Valerie Finnis' is a lighter shade of blue than other grape hyacinths.

sun while they're performing.

And there you have it. A few simple steps that mark the difference between abject, unmitigated ennui and a long stint of anticipation and enthralling performance. Sure, the flower colors might not be as radiant as they would be outdoors. Absolutely, the stems might stretch a little longer than they would in the garden. But you will not be disappointed. If winter is your malady, forced bulbs are the cure.

Narcissus cultivars

(I focus on daffodils, because they are the easiest)

DAFFODILS

FLOWERS	The usual yellow, orange, and white trumpets we adore in spring
FOLIAGE	Grasslike—not remarkable
OTHER ATTRIBUTES	Some have wonderful fragrances.
SIZE	Most are 1–2 feet (30–60cm) in height
EXPOSURE	Bright east or west
WATER REQUIREMENTS	Medium
OPTIMUM NIGHTTIME TEMPERATURE	50–55°F (10–12°C) when they begin to grow
RATE OF GROWTH	Fast after the chilling sequence
SOIL TYPE	Heavy fertile soil
FERTILIZING	None
PROBLEMS	Remove from house after performance so they don't attract pests. You can plant forced daffodils outside without a problem. Narcissus and hyacinths are particularly toxic and can cause a severe dermatological reaction; check toxicity of other bulbs individually.

FRAGRANT PLANTS

If ever there was a ventriloquist of a plant, it's *Osmanthus fragrans*, capable of throwing its scent across the room.

MY HOME ALWAYS smells like plants. In winter, the dense, humid smell of moist soil tends to permeate the place. My living space is a little like an oversize terrarium in that way. That's the underlying theme, but various flowers layer their top note above that constant voice. That's what visitors notice when they arrive, but sometimes it all settles into a generic smell of home for me. I notice the aroma of newbies when they first come into blossom, and then it all shifts into the steady beat of the place. And not all flowers throw their wares into the room. I actually prefer the blossoms that keep their scents to themselves until you zero in to sample the goods. Touch your nose to *Stephanotis floribunda* and you are bound to get a delightful surprise. It's like your own secret garden, and you can hoard the experience, if you're inclined. Walk into a room with paperwhites (all it takes is one) and, like it or not, you are exposed to the smell it is spewing forth. Which brings me to another salient issue: not all floral smells are happy marriages with your personal set of sensory prejudices.

The plants listed aren't a full roster of all the fragrant plants available for indoor gardeners; they are my personal picks for growing indoors in winter. Not only is winter when you need good scents the most, but it is also when floral essences have their greatest impact. During the rest of the year, you throw the windows open and dilute your own home-grown perfume. In winter, the ecosystem is closed. The combined brew is undiluted by outdoors. It's a heady and individual affair.

Hermannia verticillata

HONEYBELLS

FLOWERS	Masses of tiny, lily-of-the-valley-like, yellow blooms
FOLIAGE	Small, notched, and ferny
OTHER ATTRIBUTES	A honey-sweet fragrance
SIZE	Dangling
EXPOSURE	South
WATER REQUIREMENTS	Medium; try not to moisten the leaves
OPTIMUM NIGHTTIME TEMPERATURE	50–60°F (10–15°C)
RATE OF GROWTH	Medium
SOIL TYPE	Humusy and well-drained
FERTILIZING	Early spring to late autumn, but continue fertilizing in autumn if the foliage pales
PROBLEMS	Can get aphids

HERMANNIA VERTICILLATA

You would think that honey would be a common floral scent, wouldn't you? Not the case. Few flowers go that route. But honeybells, *Hermannia verticillata*, is the essence of pure clover honey. However, if you don't touch your nose to the blossoms, you will never know.

Even without sampling the wares, the flowers are absolutely adorable. We're talking small, furled, nodding, canary-yellow flowers about the size of lily-of-the-valley blossoms on trailing stems clad in slender, notched leaves. The flowers occur only in midwinter. Although the plant can be tidy (with pruning to encourage branching) throughout the year, quite frankly, you will never give it a second glance without the flowers.

Bright light is essential for honeybells. A hanging basket might seem to be the obvious route, given the plant's lax habit, but who has room to hang a plant? I go with a tall pedestal pot or long tom, making sure to rotate and expose the plant to balanced light on all sides. Without sufficient light, you're apt to court brown spots.

In general, I'm not a fan of paperwhites because of their smell, but *Narcissus tazetta* 'Grand Soleil d'Or' is an olfactory improvement.

Narcissus papyraceus and *N. tazetta*

PAPERWHITES

FLOWERS	White or yellow open stars in umbels
FOLIAGE	Long, thin, grass-like
OTHER ATTRIBUTES	If you like a musky scent, you'll like paperwhites
SIZE	1–2 feet (30–60cm) in height
EXPOSURE	East or west
WATER REQUIREMENTS	When dry
OPTIMUM NIGHTTIME TEMPERATURE	50–60°F (10–15°C)
RATE OF GROWTH	Very fast
SOIL TYPE	They will tolerate any soil; pebbles will do
FERTILIZING	No need for food during their brief moment in the sun
PROBLEMS	Not everyone likes the scent. Throw paperwhites onto the compost before they die back and attract aphids. Narcissus are particularly toxic.

PAPERWHITES

Paperwhites are ridiculously easy to grow. Stick the bulb in just about any sort of growing medium, including plain old pebbles (driveway grit will do), and it will sprout. No chilling session is needed (or wanted) for this Mediterranean native. And in no time, green shoots begin to appear. Before you know it, those green shoots have grown long and lanky and are beginning to flop. I have a few solutions. Pack them into the bottom of a deep glass vase and let the rim serve as a support. I also found a chicken-wire cage that was formerly a baffle to protect plants outdoors—the stalks threaded through and stood tall. Those stalks hold buds that swell and pop into snowy clusters of star-shaped blossoms that are quite compelling. The smell of the typical *Narcissus papyraceus*, however, can be musky (or worse) and not everyone's favorite. Always in search of a paperwhite that will prove livable, I tried 'Inbal' and 'Ariel'. When only a few buds were open, the scent was mildly pleasant, but it became overpowering in an unpleasant way. As I write this, both plants have been escorted outdoors. There is one golden exception. Also sold as a paperwhite, *N. tazetta* 'Grand Soleil d'Or' stems from different parentage to give it lovely mustard-yellow petals surrounding a small, light orange tube. The scent that comes from that tube is sweet and spicy compared to the heavy, cloying scent of the traditional *N. papyraceus* clan. It sits only footsteps away, and we're on extremely friendly terms.

What *Osmanthus fragrans* lacks in looks, it compensates with fragrance. Think high-pitched, spicy, and heady.

Osmanthus fragrans

OSMANTHUS

ALSO CALLED: fragrant olive, sweet olive

FLOWERS	Tiny, indistinct white flowers
FOLIAGE	Glossy green, bay-like leaves
OTHER ATTRIBUTES	A memorably heady fragrance
SIZE	Prune to 2–3 feet (60–90cm) in height
EXPOSURE	East or west
WATER REQUIREMENTS	Water regularly; the thick root mass tends to dry out often
OPTIMUM NIGHTTIME TEMPERATURE	50–60°F (10–15°C)
RATE OF GROWTH	Slow to medium
SOIL TYPE	Rich, well-drained soil mix
FERTILIZING	I start in late winter and continue to late autumn
PROBLEMS	Prone to scale

OSMANTHUS FRAGRANS

On the surface, sweet olive (*Osmanthus fragrans*) is a wholly unremarkable plant with woody stems and glossy green leaves that resemble a sweet bay's foliage. Don't misunderstand—it isn't ugly. But physically, it's not engaging. The flowers are off-white and so nondescript that you would definitely overlook them if their scent didn't grab your attention.

There is no fragrance that compares with the aroma of a sweet olive. It's like someone sprinkled sugar on the air. It floats gently into your nose, high-pitched and sweet, with perhaps just a hint of spice. You could inhale it all day and never tire of it. When you leave the room, the fragrance calls you back. It's heaven. Generally in blossom from September through early winter, it eases the liaison between outdoor and indoor gardening.

I used to insist that *Osmanthus fragrans* was finicky. I used to harp on the special soil it required underfoot and the dangers of fertilizing. Bull. Someone dropped off their plant before moving and I gave it no preferential treatment whatsoever. It thrived. Provide even water and good organic soil, don't let it get pot-bound, and dose it with fish emulsion, and it will perform beautifully to perfume your home.

The solution for anyone uncomfortable with an athletic vine is to wrap *Stephanotis floribunda* in a wreath.

Stephanotis floribunda

STEPHANOTIS

ALSO CALLED: Madagascar jasmine, waxflower

FLOWERS	Clusters of long, white tubes
FOLIAGE	Oval, deep-green, thick leaves
OTHER ATTRIBUTES	Intensely fragrant; also blooms for the winter holidays
SIZE	Rope-like vine is best wound around a loose support or trained in a circle
EXPOSURE	South, bright east or west
WATER REQUIREMENTS	Medium
OPTIMUM NIGHTTIME TEMPERATURE	55–65°F (12–18°C)
RATE OF GROWTH	Medium
SOIL TYPE	Rich, humusy, well-drained soil
FERTILIZING	Early spring to late autumn; may need additional fertilizer in winter
PROBLEMS	Mealy bugs and scale

STEPHANOTIS FLORIBUNDA

I am an unabashed cheerleader for this vine. Point the finger at the fact that my plant has been in bloom steadily for the last few months or blame it on the tidy, dark green, impeccable leaves—for those reasons and the flower's fragrance, everyone owes themselves a stephanotis.

If the long, tubular, white flowers didn't clue you in that this is a member of the milkweed family, *Asclepiadaceae*, then the fragrance might drop the hint. Stephanotis flowers don't send their scent roaming; you discover it only when you touch your nose to a flower cluster. That intimacy yields some tantalizing rewards. The scent is full-bodied and deep, but pleasant in a baby powder sort of way. And the flowers linger over the long haul. Without the stephanotis close up and in constant blossom during winter, my mood would be a whole lot worse.

Most vines are energetic forces to be contended with, but *Trachelospermum asiaticum* is compact and thoroughly windowsill size.

TRACHELOSPERMUM ASIATICUM

You are probably familiar with the far more readily available Confederate jasmine or pinwheel jasmine, *Trachelospermum jasminoides*. It is not a jasmine, actually, but its vining habit and star-shaped flowers gave it the nickname. *Trachelospermum jasminoides* is commonly sold at garden centers as a summer porch plant. Rapidly reaching focal-point proportions (3 to 4 feet [90–122cm]) and holding a smattering of flowers with furled petals (like a pinwheel) through most of the summer, it has earned mainstay status as far as nurseries are concerned. Throw in the soapy scent that the flowers emit, and the pinwheel jasmine gives you yet another reason to become a fan.

Not many people are familiar with my personal heartthrob, *Trachelospermum asiaticum*, a demure version of its more prevalent cousin. Its foliage is also dark green and it also wends around as a vine. But in spring, summer, and autumn, it bears creamy yellow blossoms that fill the air with a captivating cinnamony scent. True, it doesn't blossom in winter, but size-wise it is an easier vine to host over the winter months. And as soon as light levels rev up, the buds will form.

I find that trachelospermums love to be fed. Throw on a little fish emulsion, and they respond by producing buds. They also send up energetic growth, but it's not a problem. Just wind those vining arms and legs around a trellis. *Trachelospermum jasminoides* needs a larger container and a sturdier support than *T. asiaticum*, but both are trouble free.

Trachelospermum asiaticum and *T. jasminoides*

ALSO CALLED: pinwheel jasmine, star jasmine

FLOWERS	Stars with furled petals, white to cinnamon-colored
FOLIAGE	Tidy, glossy green leaves
OTHER ATTRIBUTES	The fragrance is a delight
SIZE	Smaller vine for *Trachelospermum asiaticum*, larger vine for *T. jasminoides*
EXPOSURE	East or west
WATER REQUIREMENTS	Medium
OPTIMUM NIGHTTIME TEMPERATURE	50–60°F (10–15°C)
RATE OF GROWTH	Medium to fast-growing vine
SOIL TYPE	Rich, humusy, well-drained soil mix
FERTILIZING	Early spring to late autumn
PROBLEMS	Scale can be an issue

HERBS

Herbs such as *Origanum majorana* 'Compacta', *Satureja montana*, *Foeniculum vulgare*, and *Thymus vulgaris* make meals a little more savory in summer. But in winter, they spell the difference between scrumptious and blah.

ANYBODY CAN GROW an herb during the summer. I habitually season my outdoor garden with parsley, sage, rosemary, thyme, and a long list of other savory plants. Because I'm perennially in a rush (especially around mealtime), I also host herbs in containers just footsteps from the back door, which is, in turn, just a brief commute to the kitchen. In those containers, I slap together various combinations of thymes. 'Silver Posie' is a favorite for its white-rimmed leaves and durability when I've forgotten to water, but plain old *Thymus vulgaris* tastes better. Meanwhile, marjoram is a mainstay. They do their job (making summer squash edible and even quasi-interesting), and they revive despite serial wilting. In summer, herbs are a cinch.

Not so in winter. First of all, your roster of applicable herbs is diminished considerably. Right now, if you came to visit, you'd pay call to several pots of *Thymus vulgaris* (I'm a heavy user), a winter savory (*Satureja montana*), marjoram (*Origanum majorana*; I found a cultivar called 'Compacta' that remains midget making it perfect for pots), *Origanum* 'Silver Anniversary', cardamom (*Elettaria cardamomum*), salad burnet (*Sanguisorba minor*), and *Lavandula* 'Goodwin Creek Gray' in various windows. I had a fennel (*Foeniculum vulgare*), but someone admired it so excessively that I had no choice but to send it home in her car (it was the holidays, after all). Although I don't have a single ounce of Puritan blood, each of these herbs is a workhorse. Some are plucked within an inch of their lives to rescue lentil soup from

terminal blandness. Others are simply grown for their aromatherapy, loosely applied. And I'm not the only one who indulges. When Einstein was the new kitten on the block, he quickly learned that playing with the herbs didn't elicit loud or demonstrative rebukes.

Notice that rosemary isn't in my lineup of herbs. I wish I could include it, but rosemary refuses to survive the winter here. And I'm not alone. I have been told that rosemary prefers cool temperatures, regular watering, bright light, and basically all the other conditions that herbs in general hold dear. Cool, bright, and even-handed is a fairly accurate assessment of the state of affairs here. However, rosemary invariably comes down with a nasty (lethal) case of the snivels (symptoms being rot and general leaf collapse, followed by stem disintegration) or powdery mildew. Both of these afflictions make the plant look gross enough to squelch any thoughts of consumption. I love rosemary, but I leave it outdoors, sacrifice it to cold weather, and grow it fresh every year.

Lots of herbs don't translate indoors. Basil is a good example. Its light demands are too high. In basil's desperate attempt to seek more sun, it stretches, forms few leaves, and goes to flower in a blink. And what's basil without leaves? Worthless. Ditto for cilantro. I veer away from sweet bay (*Laurus nobilis*) because where am I going to host a massive shrub that needs full sun? I like the theory of lovage (*Levisticum officinale*), but it bolts into flower too rapidly. Sage (*Salvia officinalis*) is lovely, but it tends to rot without mega-bright sunbeams. The same sorry fate befalls

Lavandula 'Goodwin Creek Gray' is the only lavender that survives winter in my windows. *Origanum* 'Silver Anniversary' is more of an ornamental oregano, rather than the culinary sort, but it still tingles your sense of smell.

Although not in the mainstream with the herbal superstars such as parsley, sage, rosemary, and thyme, salad burnet (*Sanguisorba minor*) windowsill worthy.

sweet herb (*Stevia rebaudiana*). I have to skip summer savory (*Satureja hortensis*) indoors even though it is a vast improvement, taste-wise, over winter savory (*Satureja montana*, which I do grow quite successfully on my windowsill). As the name implies, summer savory grows best as an annual.

Beyond the inventory that I've chosen based on space limitations and culinary taste choices, other herbs would do just fine in my home. The mints, for example, would undoubtedly thrive indoors. Even if they go into a snit and lose leaves, they will soon regrow from the underground rhizomes. I am wild about horehound (*Marrubium vulgare*) for its deep, throaty, menthol-scented leaves, but I leave it outdoors in the garden where it is nearly evergreen (when not buried in snow). Curly parsley makes a splendid

houseplant, and I have entertained it for several winters. Eventually, it will act like a biennial and bolt up into blossom, but not before its leaves have improved many meals for several months. Patchouli (*Pogostemon heyneanus*) makes a great indoor herb. But it would either be the patchouli or me, because we can't live in the same house, scent-wise.

What growing conditions do most plants like? As much sun as possible, cool temperatures, a brief dry soil lull between waterings, and lean soil. With the exception of rosemary (whose roots plunge down), most herbs are best grown in tight containers. Skip the fertilizer over the winter. (Many growers suggest forgetting the fertilizer all year because herbs tend to be more flavorful when they grow on lean rations. I find that to be true. The compost in my organic potting soil is sufficient to keep them

Herbs

ALSO CALLED: marjoram, oregano, thyme, winter savory, and others

FLOWERS	Usually to be dissuaded
FOLIAGE	The look varies, but the foliage is usually aromatic
OTHER ATTRIBUTES	Often good-looking and readily available
SIZE	6–12 inches (15–30cm) in height
EXPOSURE	South or bright west
WATER REQUIREMENTS	Thyme can tolerate drought; other herbs tend to wilt easily
OPTIMUM NIGHTTIME TEMPERATURE	50–65°F (10–15°C)
RATE OF GROWTH	Medium
SOIL TYPE	Good, heavy potting soil with compost added
FERTILIZING	Herb growers suggest not fertilizing because lean herbs are more flavorful
PROBLEMS	Aphids

Why not use a creeping herb as a groundcover below a taller plant? Try covering the soil below the bromeliad *Neoregelia marmorata* with *Origanum vulgare* 'Aureum Crispum'.

chugging along beautifully.) Furnishing the cool temperatures is easy for me; I just nestle the herbs close to the windowpanes. But if you live in a normal, comfortable, toasty house, your herbs will also probably be fine. However, they might make leggy growth. And the remedy is to snip them often and add them liberally to dinner. Even those of us who cannot cook become instant chefs with marjoram and some thyme at our beck and call.

HOLIDAY PLANTS

When you receive the inevitable gift of *Cyclamen persicum*, switch it into a clay pot immediately and it will survive rather than sulk.

IF YOU WERE hoping for an ode to poinsettias here, I've got bad news. Enter my home for the holidays, and I can guarantee you won't see a single one. I'm just as fascinated as the majority of the world with all the new introductions out there. My jaw drops with the rest of humanity when I encounter the speckled, spangled, jingled, edged, crinkled, shrunk, and otherwise "improved" novelty poinsettias that have popped up recently. But I admire them from afar at garden centers and go home empty-handed. I live in a Poinsettia-Free Zone conspicuously lacking in those finicky, flouncy, whitefly-beckoning, extremely ephemeral winter performers.

Before you accuse me of general bah-humbuggery, let me explain. My house is full of holiday plants. I go shopping for friends and family, and end up keeping most of the plants I had planned to wrap and proudly present to nephews and nieces. Unlike those who pause before saddling folks with living things that require water, care, and quality time, I don't think twice about it. Any friend of mine is bound to have a botanical bent. And, like it or not, plenty of the relatives are horticulturally gifted. In fact, I invariably overbuy. And that's how my windowsills get into a pickle by January.

The beauty of holiday plants is that they are generally easy to grow (with the exception of poinsettias). Not only that, but membership in this elite group is so selective that only tried-and-true, definite, you-can-set-your-watch-by-it midwinter performers are affiliated. If you were afraid to test the houseplant waters before, this would be the perfect juncture to jump in. Or if someone gave you a gift and you are wondering what to do with it now that the party is over, read on. Not all holiday plants are keepers, but there's a good ratio. Here is a rundown of holiday plants that get two thumbs up.

CYCLAMEN

Undoubtedly, you have seen cyclamen lurking in garden centers with their unique, shooting star–like blossoms above heart-shaped leaves. They blossom intermittently throughout autumn, winter, and early spring, and come in colors ranging from snow white to pink, magenta, and cherry red, with creative combinations of those shades. Although they are among the most majestic holiday plants, cyclamen tend to be misunderstood. And killed. Most often, too much water plays a role in the murder. But even I tend to overreact when faced with a cyclamen in its death-like swoon when I am only a few hours late serving drinks. Too little water, and a cyclamen faints. Too much water, and it dies. It's a balancing act.

But there are ways of keeping the watering issue within bounds. First, transplant a cyclamen out of its plastic nursery container immediately. Cyclamen roots prefer clay. They need repotting, but it's better to be Scrooge when it comes to pot sizes—slightly cramped quarters work best for the roots. Water lightly when the soil is slightly dry. Underwatering is better than drowning the poor thing. Grow your cyclamen in indirect light. The gentle light will also ease the watering conundrum.

Do right by your cyclamen, and it will blossom wildly throughout the winter. I prefer the more demure types to the flashy giant hybrids, but that's just me. Feel free to go over the top.

Cyclamen persicum cultivars

CYCLAMEN

ALSO CALLED: **florist cyclamen, Persian violet**

FLOWERS	White, pink, red, magenta, and combinations of shades on the same shooting star–shaped flower
FOLIAGE	Beautiful heart-shaped leaves with patterned markings
OTHER ATTRIBUTES	Initiates from a handsome, above-the-ground bulb
SIZE	6–12 inches (15–30cm) in height
EXPOSURE	East or west
WATER REQUIREMENTS	Even watering—don't allow it to wilt and don't overwater
OPTIMUM NIGHTTIME TEMPERATURE	50–60°F (10–15°C)
RATE OF GROWTH	Medium
SOIL TYPE	Well-drained potting mix is important
FERTILIZING	I don't bother in winter when they're in growth
PROBLEMS	Can perish from overwater (mine never get insects, though). Cyclamens are toxic.

The beauty of *Echeveria* species is midwinter blossoms that coincide with the holidays. Each individual flower is intriguing. All together, the presentation is remarkable.

ECHEVERIA

Okay, so echeverias are not official holiday plants. I confess, this is just an idea I'm hoping might catch on. The fact is, most echeverias are sending up flower spires right about when the holidays are looming around the bend. And they're mighty snappy when in blossom. Actually, with their neat rosettes of swollen, succulent leaves, echeverias are always finely dressed. Some have velveteen-textured foliage; others are smooth. Some have a silver hue; others have a blue cast. And because of that fetching foliage, echeverias are the sort of plants you can give with the confidence that your gift will never have a downtime. Not only that, but they come pretty close to being no maintenance. A sunny window is a must. Beyond that, these succulents don't want to be overwatered. Watering once every week or so is perfect in winter. Plus, you can purchase small plants for a song. Snatch them up and plunk them into a funky, snug container (too much room for the roots will lead to overwatering), and you have saved somebody's winter from blahsville.

Echeveria species
ECHEVERIA

FLOWERS	Arching spires of waxy pink or coral blossoms
FOLIAGE	Cunning rosettes of thick blue-green or coral leaves, or sometimes furry and silver
OTHER ATTRIBUTES	A cinch to grow, and they add rosettes with age
SIZE	6 inches (15cm) in height and under
EXPOSURE	South
WATER REQUIREMENTS	Only once a week or so
OPTIMUM NIGHTTIME TEMPERATURE	55–65°F (12–18°C)
RATE OF GROWTH	Slow
SOIL TYPE	Sandy, heavy potting soil mix
FERTILIZING	Early spring to late autumn only, and then very lightly
PROBLEMS	Prone to root mealy bugs

The crown of thorns, *Euphorbia milii*, has a certain barbed beauty, and it blossoms during the holiday season.

Euphorbia milii

EUPHORBIA

ALSO CALLED: **crown of thorns**

FLOWERS	Red, but new cultivars are available in peach, yellow, pink, and combos
FOLIAGE	Small green leaves, variegated versions available
OTHER ATTRIBUTES	Serious thorns line the stems
SIZE	Usually 12 inches (30cm) in height, but can vine larger
EXPOSURE	South
WATER REQUIREMENTS	Sparse, but does not like to dry out completely
OPTIMUM NIGHTTIME TEMPERATURE	50–60°F (10–15°C)
RATE OF GROWTH	Slow
SOIL TYPE	Sandy, well-drained, heavy potting soil mix
FERTILIZING	Early spring to late autumn, but lightly
PROBLEMS	Prone to root mealy bugs. Euphorbias are toxic and can cause a dermatological reaction.

EUPHORBIA MILII

Any plant with a name like "crown of thorns" is bound to be prominent around Christmas. And, true to its name, a heavy artillery of barbs lines the stems of this euphorbia. These are big thorns, by the way; the type that makes a statement but could also do some harm to pets or people. Thorns are not the only game for this particular holiday mainstay; in winter, *Euphorbia milii* produces flowers, too. The foliage is generally dark green and tidily tucked between the thorns, but variegated versions are also available. The plant tends to drop leaves, especially on older growth, but that just makes the thorns more prominent. And the vining habit makes it possible to train mature plants into a circular crown shape.

Just like its relative, the poinsettia I so snidely maligned earlier, *Euphorbia milii* is triggered into blossom by the shortening days. Like the poinsettia, the floral bracts make the show. The species (native to Madagascar) has scarlet-red bracts, but hybridizers have increased the spectrum into the realms of cream, yellow, peach, and various speckled combinations.

The beauty of crown of thorns is that it is trouble free. Give it sun and do not overwater (keep in mind that this is a succulent, and you will remain on the right track). It rarely needs repotting (thank goodness, because that could be a painful endeavor). It's the perfect gift for beginning gardeners.

HIPPEASTRUM

I almost skipped the amaryllis (hippeastrum) this year. With a new kitten—indeed, with a new kitten who had a penchant for gnawing on just about everything at first (including broom handles and wrists)—I figured that amaryllis inside my house were a thing of the past. After all, they are on the ASPCA list of toxic plants for pets. Fortunately, Einstein outgrew that phase. As soon as he swore off plant ingestion (with the help of considerable training), I put in my order for umpteen hippeastrum and placed them out of his realm. Now, in the dead of winter, they provide plenty of entertainment. This is a plant with a will to rivet. Some of my amaryllis have sent up multiple tall spires, each composed of several trumpet-shaped flowers, some opening to a diameter that competes with your aver-age Frisbee. 'Exotic Star' and 'Lemon Lime' win the "most spikes" competition. The doubles have been improved from the raggedy originals to beautiful forms that bring double water lilies to mind. For that reason, I am a big fan of 'Zombie' this year.

By all means, give everyone on your list an amaryllis. It is one of the best values available. If possible, hold off planting until right before giving the gift. That way, the recipient gets to witness the entire show, from the flower buds' first appearance until they pop. In most cases, multiple spikes initiate over the course of the winter. This is truly a gift that keeps on giving.

If possible, provide amaryllis with bright light to diminish the flower stems and coax brighter colors from the petals, but they also blossom in an east or west window. Too much heat can lead to tall, stretching stems, I sug-gest keeping the thermostat below 70°F (21°C). Amaryllis don't like overwatering, and for that reason I pot mine in a container that is an inch or two wider than the bulb all the way around. A heavy terra-cotta or metal container and a stake counterbalances the tall, heavy, blossom-laden flowering spikes. Then sit back and watch the show.

As far as keeping amaryllis year after year, they want the good life in summer, with plenty of water and food—I put mine outside and treat them grandly. In late summer, start to dry them off and push them into dormancy. By early winter, get them rolling again by applying water and furnishing light.

One of the longest-blooming amaryllis, *Hippeastrum* 'Papilio Improved' sends up multiple flower spikes, and blooms reliably year after year.

Hippeastrum cultivars

AMARYLLIS

FLOWERS	Outrageously beautiful star-shaped and double blossoms in white, pink, peach, green, red, and burgundy, with stripes possible
FOLIAGE	Long, strap-like leaves, often after the flowers
OTHER ATTRIBUTES	Smaller flowering versions are also available
SIZE	12–18 inches (30–50cm) in height when flowering
EXPOSURE	East or west
WATER REQUIREMENTS	Allow to dry out between watering; don't overwater
OPTIMUM NIGHTTIME TEMPERATURE	55–65°F (12–18°C)
RATE OF GROWTH	Fast
SOIL TYPE	Well-drained is important; otherwise, any potting soil
FERTILIZING	Early spring to midsummer
PROBLEMS	It can be difficult to achieve blossoms on the second and subsequent years. Keep all members of the *Liliaceae* family away from pets who are prone to ingest, especially cats. Also toxic to humans.

Why not take one of the traditional holiday chestnuts, such as *Kalanchoe blossfeldiana*, and jazz it up with a smart presentation?

KALANCHOE

I didn't always love *Kalanchoe blossfeldiana*, but flaming Katy grew on me. Especially when breeders came up with such a vast array of flashy flower colors, it was hard to maintain an attitude against a plant that forms large heads of blossoms that linger week after week in absolute prime condition. Who can choose? Right now I'm doting on the orange version with yellow toward the center. But I could just as easily fall for the terracotta edition, or the brick red, ruby, magenta, yellow, or white variations on the theme. All are composed of constellations of little stars set in clusters above the not-particularly-exciting flat, succulent, green leaves. But variegated versions are entering the scene, and crinkled leaves are also newly on the horizon.

In most parts of the country, you are unlikely to witness very bright sun in winter, so a south window is fine for a flaming Katy. But when the sun shines in, you might want to switch the kalanchoe to an east- or west-facing exposure. In fact, I have occasionally stored *Kalanchoe blossfeldiana* in extremely poorly lit conditions and the plant didn't complain. I have also forgotten to water it for a spate of time. The leaves crinkled slightly, but beyond that the plant was unscathed. And it fully recovered.

The only problem with flaming Katy is that it only blossoms in autumn and winter. But that is still a good long

Kalanchoe blossfeldiana

KALANCHOE

ALSO CALLED: flaming Katy

FLOWERS	Little stars in clusters in a staggering color range, including yellow, brick, orange, red, and magenta
FOLIAGE	Succulent oval leaves, sometimes variegated
OTHER ATTRIBUTES	Pretty much unkillable
SIZE	12 inches (30cm) in height
EXPOSURE	East or west
WATER REQUIREMENTS	Allow to dry out slightly between waterings
OPTIMUM NIGHTTIME TEMPERATURE	50–65°F (10–18°C)
RATE OF GROWTH	Slow to medium
SOIL TYPE	Heavy, rich potting soil mix
FERTILIZING	Not necessary, but early spring to late autumn if you want
PROBLEMS	None really

For the holidays, who wouldn't love to receive *Kalanchoe thyrsiflora*, which resembles a massive rosebud? It's dramatic and different.

run. When the flower show is over, there is not much to recommend keeping the plant. Toss it. You can bet that garden centers will be well stocked next year. But if you yearn for a kalanchoe that you can keep (or someone on your list can sustain), go with *Kalanchoe thyrsiflora*. They're not much for blossoms, but the wavy pewter-colored leaves burnished with bronze accents make stupendous gifts. They look like gigantic roses with wavy leaves. In summer, shuffle them outside as a focal point in the garden.

SCHLUMBERGERA

Back in my retail nursery days, I was besieged by customers panicking because their Christmas cactus was not performing on schedule. The calls came in; the end of the world was predicted. I remained cool in the face of Armageddon. I will pass along the counsel I offered: Keep in mind that succulents don't check out our daily planners. Vendors might be able to prompt plants to perform in tandem with holidays that ramp up their sales, but in subsequent years you might not be able to jive your calendar with the plant's internal clock. And, after all, it is only a name. Christmas cactus, Thanksgiving cactus, Easter cactus—the plant has nothing to do with ratifying its label.

However, sometime in winter, the Christmas cactus, *Schlumbergera ×buckleyi*, will probably be doing its thing. Often, it comes in late for Christmas activities. A cross between *S. russelliana* and *S. truncata* originally bred in 1840, the Christmas cactus has segmented leaves (that easily break off) and profuse, gaping, jaw-like flowers that are often likened to lobsters. It comes in purplish red, and

a mature plant can produce hundreds of blooms. But then, to confuse the issue, there is the Thanksgiving cactus, *S. truncata*, with pointed jointed segments and similar flowers to its Christmas cactus kin. It often starts blooming in October, and the show is generally over by the end of December. Breeders went to work and wed these two, so the color range has increased to include yellow, mauve, white, and magenta. Plus, the holiday cactus clan tends to reblossom in early spring, so the timetable has been totally blurred. If you think jazzy blossoms-within-blossoms will light up the eyes of a certain someone, go for them. Promise them anything, but don't commit to a blooming date.

If you want to make a schlumbergera happy, give it bright light, water it sparingly, and, most important, don't rush to repot the plant when it fills its container. Schlumbergeras like cramped roots, and repotting might curtail blossoming.

Schlumbergera species
and cultivars

SCHLUMBERGERA

ALSO CALLED: **Christmas cactus, lobster cactus, Thanksgiving cactus**

FLOWERS	Dragon-like or lobster claw–ish blossoms in an array of glistening colors
FOLIAGE	Segmented green, succulent leaves
OTHER ATTRIBUTES	Can make a huge specimen; blossoms in winter theoretically in time for the holidays
SIZE	6–12 inches (15–30cm) in height
EXPOSURE	South, east, or west
WATER REQUIREMENTS	Meager
OPTIMUM NIGHTTIME TEMPERATURE	50–60°F (10–15°C)
RATE OF GROWTH	Medium
SOIL TYPE	Well-drained potting mix is important
FERTILIZING	Early spring to late autumn
PROBLEMS	Mealy bugs

The name is a handful, but everything else about *Oncidium cheirophorum* × *O. ornithorhynchum* 'Twinkle' is manageable. And the scent is heaven.

ORCHIDS

PART OF MY morning ritual entails leaning over the plant stand to turn the shower knob on the claw-leg tub, and then ducking before the initially cold spray hits me. The tub is massive, so it's a long reach in. As I stretch, my nose makes contact with *Oncidium cheirophorum* × *O. ornithorhynchum* 'Twinkle', and no matter where I need to go or what I have to accomplish, I'm stuck. I linger in sensual bliss. The hot shower will be divine and my sister's handmade soap will be therapeutic, but the orchid is almost sinful.

To take a stab at dissecting the scent, I'm going to weigh in with warm milk chocolate with a trace of vanilla. I challenge you to imagine a more stirring configuration. And in the dominion of floral fragrances, orchids emit some of the more lustful aromas. With the possible exception of *Cosmos atrosanguineus* (which doesn't bloom as a houseplant, by the way), the only botanical candy store where you will find a strong emanation of chocolate is in the orchid realm. And the beauty of 'Twinkle' is that it throws its aromatic voice out into the room. Once I have jostled it, the air is impregnated. A million times better than any manufactured air freshener, this is the real thing. And, not to gloat, but only a houseplant grower can sample the special brew. Cologne doesn't come close.

I cannot claim to be an orchid expert. I just aim at a few tried-and-true performers to make winter a brighter season. Several are fragrant, because winter needs all the help it can get. I grow winter-blooming *Dendrobium kingianum* for its profusion of little white, beaked blossoms with a honeyed scent when you touch nose to flower. I have a few cattleya hybrids that unfold with light, fruity scents. Beyond 'Twinkle', I host other oncidiums. In the nonfragrant realm, who can live without the pert, elf-like, long-lasting blossoms of tropical lady's slippers (paphiopedilums)? Although I thought I had my fill of phalaenopsis, the moth orchids, I can't resist the newest trend in moths. The novel miniature phalaenopsis are just too adorable (and easy to grow). And after assuming that masdevallias were beyond my scope in the house, I took the leap. They have been blooming happily, mostly in summer, ever after. They need nothing more than good light and ample water.

In an orchid you need willing flowers year after year, and that's exactly what *Dendrobium kingianum* delivers.

I think the difficulty of growing orchids is overhyped. I do not treat orchids drastically differently from anything else in my windowsills. I detest orchid containers with the holes in the sides. Have you ever tried to water them indoors? The water spouts out of the sides like a sieve. I would never grow an orchid in plastic, but clay is plenty porous without introducing the wild card of side-seepage. Then there is orchid mix. The last thing I want to anchor a plant in is Styrofoam. It looks gross, it sheds all over the place, and with the least provocation the plant jumps out in a suicide plunge. I mention this only because many orchid mixes are nothing more than wood chips mixed with packing noodles. After trying several, I tossed together my own mix by adding a very coarse organic potting soil to wood bark. Coconut husk chips also work. My oncidium couldn't be happier. It is blooming its head off for the third winter running. Fool's luck, maybe, but I intend to keep bumbling through my winning streak.

Watering an orchid can be a challenge. Although I preach monitoring for dryness rather than watering on a schedule, orchids are the exception. Because the water runs right through the porous growing medium into the saucer below, there is no way to monitor for moisture. I water twice a week when the weather has its normal distribution of sunny days and cloudier intervals.

Orchids are worth the investment (to a degree— I wait for ultra-expensive novelties to go on sale). They also warrant a little extra consideration. Once you get a rhythm going and are accustomed to their ways, orchids are no hassle whatsoever. I go for beginner's fare. I find that oncidiums, paphiopedilums, phalaenopsis, some of the species dendrobiums, and masdevallias are easily accommodated in the average home. And they give me all the glitz I need.

You can find tropical lady's slipper orchids in flashier colors, but I go for the simple plain green-and-white-flowered *Paphiopedilum* cultivars. Reblooming them is a cinch.

Moth orchids may have reached cliché status. But no one can tire of the new minis, such as this dwarf magenta phalaenopsis beside foolproof *Drimiopsis kirkii* (not an orchid, but a fine companion).

Orchidaceae
ORCHIDS

FLOWERS	The main attraction; they imitate moths, butterflies, and all things beautiful
FOLIAGE	Many of the paphiopedilums have handsome mottled foliage
OTHER ATTRIBUTES	Fragrances beyond any other flower group
SIZE	Usually 6–12 inches (15–30cm) in height
EXPOSURE	East
WATER REQUIREMENTS	Twice a week
OPTIMUM NIGHTTIME TEMPERATURE	60–70°F (15–21°C)
RATE OF GROWTH	Slow
SOIL TYPE	A special orchid medium, or configure your own bark mixture or coconut husk chip combo.
FERTILIZING	I use fish emulsion every three weeks
PROBLEMS	Orchids require high humidity; they're not prone to insects

PELARGONIUMS

The heirloom zonal geranium *Pelargonium* 'Crystal Palace Gem' is mildly amusing in summer, but those cheerful red blossoms make your life in winter.

I TRY NOT to look visibly shaken when huge clots of snow go thundering down the greenhouse glass and land with a reverberating thud down below. I try to take in stride the three-foot drift out the back door. After all, I've got to keep up appearances for Einstein. So I focus on the geranium that persists in blooming its little heart out on the warm side of the panes. Judging from the howl of the wind, the power might go off at any moment. We lost it for nine hours last week. Fearing for the orchids and begonias, I shuffled them into the warmest canyons of my office. But there was one plant that was not on my worry list: the pelargonium. Even if the thermometer tottered precariously near the freezing mark, the pelargonium would be just fine.

Not only will it survive, but the steady roll of blossoms will not miss a beat. The beauty of pelargoniums is that they are impervious. If you're hitting a blank when I use the term "pelargonium," it's understandable. You undoubtedly will be more comfortable with the more commonly used name of geranium. Most popular are the zonal geraniums, those much-adored, almost clichéd houseplants with a history that stretches back to the first rustlings of indoor gardening in this country. Zonal geraniums are indomitable. Although they perform their stunts most impressively in a bright window, these plants will soldier on with less light. True, the growth will become lanky. And yes, the flower colors will not be as vibrant. But if all you have is an east or west window (even an obstructed east or west

window), go for it. And when I said that pelargoniums would withstand nippy temperatures, I should also mention that they will withstand dry heat just as stoically. Few plants are as cheerful as a geranium.

Everyone knows that zonal geraniums blossom in summer (think Memorial Day plant sales). But their winter escapades are not so well publicized. Since they root like weeds with no fancy propagation systems necessary, it is no challenge to tuck a slip into a pot and bring it indoors. For your foresight, you have a plant that will probably continue blooming throughout the entire winter without missing a beat.

Distinctively different *Pelargonium* 'Appleblossom' blossoms throughout the winter, but the blooms are never as deeply hued as they are when light levels are brighter in spring and summer.

What I love about geraniums, Gertrude Jekyll, that nineteenth- and early twentieth-century legendary gardener, designer, artist, writer, and trendsetter, reputedly hated. She disliked the unmitigated magenta blossoms that I hold dear. But magenta is just the tip of the iceberg. Zonal geraniums also come in white, pink, and scarlet. There are singles with open-face, five-petaled flowers and doubles that mimic rosebuds. They are borne in clusters, like round lollipops. And an umbel can continue its dance over an extended period of time while the blossoms slowly open, linger, and then fade to form the signature cranesbill-shaped seeds that prevail throughout the family. Also readily available are fancy leaf varieties, such as 'Crystal Palace Gem', an heirloom with two-tone apple-green and forest-green leaves.

In a home environment, you will find plenty of opportunity to wield pruners when it comes to pelargoniums. Like cane begonias, they form woody, unsightly, almost arthritic-looking stems that are best minimized in favor of new, spritely, green growth. They are rarely self-branching, and need the stimulus of pinching to send the message to make side shoots down the stem. Never fear that you will be curtailing blossoms. The beat goes on, no matter how much pinching and clipping you've applied. You do not want to fertilize pelargoniums during the dark days of winter. With fertilizer, they will form stems fatter than your index finger. And who needs that? Lean is wiser.

In summer, *Pelargonium* 'Crystal Palace Gem' is mildly amusing. In winter, this heirloom zonal geranium makes your life. Especially when you throw in a variegated philodendron accenting the mottled golden leaves.

Pelargoniums can endure without water for a while, but their survival tactic is to lose foliage. Dry soil will lead to yellowing leaves almost immediately. And from yellow it goes downhill to brown. Because pelargoniums do not shed their browned leaves hastily, the ugly evidence of your neglect remains as an eyesore for all the world to witness.

The stellar pelargoniums are an amusing spin on the familiar theme. Generally much more compact in growth habit than a standard-size zonal geranium, they have intriguing fingered foliage crowned with an endless supply of small flower umbels. The blossoms have the same color range, but they tend to be smaller than the zonals while sporting pointed and notched petals. They prefer more light, and pout when deprived of a south-facing window.

I am a confessed sucker for the scented-leaf geraniums. My favorite is 'Nutmeg' or its progeny, 'Old Spice' or 'Logeei'. The scent is a homey combination of spice, apple, and rum, which acts like an olfactory version of comfort food for me. But the growth habit is the clincher. 'Nutmeg' and its kin form whorls of leaves and can be coaxed to take a prostrate stance. Full-grown, lush, and lovely, with bluish-gray leaves and little white flowers that almost go unnoticed, this group only stands a couple of feet in diameter. Plus, they are easy as pie in a south window. Compare that to 'Peppermint', which can grow up to your shoulders and gropes toward the glass even

Pelargonium species

and cultivars

GERANIUM

ALSO CALLED: cranesbill, zonal geranium

FLOWERS	Very showy in umbels, range of colors includes magenta, white, and pink
FOLIAGE	Rounded and soft felted for the zonal geraniums; varied for other species
OTHER ATTRIBUTES	Scented geraniums have aromatic leaves
SIZE	6–12 inches (15–30cm) in height
EXPOSURE	East, west, or south
WATER REQUIREMENTS	Do not overwater, best to water in the morning
OPTIMUM NIGHTTIME TEMPERATURE	50–60°F (10–15°C)
RATE OF GROWTH	Medium
SOIL TYPE	Rich, humusy potting medium with compost included
FERTILIZING	Early spring to late autumn only
PROBLEMS	Aphids, whiteflies

Because they're compact and cheerful, stellar geraniums such as *Pelargonium* 'Happy Violet' are custom made for crammed windowsills.

in a sunny window in winter. Also, the lemon-scented group, *Pelargonium crispum*, is notoriously prone to fungal infections and generally melts when not grown in a bright greenhouse. However, the rose-scented group is more accommodating, especially 'Little Gem', a compact rose hybrid with pert, frequent red flowers. Great flowers, tidy form, easily grown, and head-ily scented. Sounds like the best of all worlds, no?

PEPEROMIAS

Peperomia rubella (in the foreground) isn't the swankest houseplant on the block, but it's cute and compact. The more finicky *Pilea involucrata* (prone to melting away) sits behind.

WITH ALL THIS talk of orchids, pelargoniums, and South African bulbs, perhaps you've jumped to the conclusion that my home is filled with flashy plants. Not so. Some plants are part of my collection simply because they are indomitable. How can you fail to love a survivor? And peperomias definitely fall into that category. Saturation coverage is my goal, and my mantra is that every nook needs nature, so peperomias fill a niche that few other plants could endure.

Peperomias are not wildly thrilling, but they do have a certain flair. With limited space and unlimited plant lust, there is no way I'm going to bother with "foliage plants," such as spider plants (chlorophytums), peace lilies (spathiphyllums), and similar ilk. But occasionally, you need a plant with a stiff upper lip. That's where peperomias prove invaluable.

To give you a mental image of peperomias and their breadth, the foliage in this genus is impressively diverse. However, the flowers are never going to send shock waves. In fact, I have heard them likened to rattails with a thin, seemingly naked spike that runs through the clan. There are exceptions. *Peperomia fraseri* is topped by small, white, feathery plumes, almost like someone drastically downsized the astilbe. But by and large, the foliage is the draw.

On the foliage front, peperomias have plenty going on. Take *Peperomia incana*, for example. With thick stems, thick leaves the size of your average oatmeal cookie, and silver felt covering all surfaces, it rates as semi-riveting. And, despite its succulent look, the plant can tolerate shady conditions. More mainstream is the wa-

If you have less-than-perfect growing conditions (low light, low humidity), *Peperomia caperata* 'Ripple' is bulletproof. Mine sits on the low-light corner by my bedside without flinching.

termelon pepper (also known as the watermelon begonia, but that's confusing—it is not a begonia or a watermelon), *P. argyreia*. The name refers to the silver striping that follows the contours of the leaf. The foliage emerges around a central stem, and it is a total no-brainer to cultivate. Also ultra-easy and readily available (stop by your local supermarket) is *P. caperata* and its many cultivars, including 'Emerald Ripple', 'Tricolor', and a never-ending batch of spins. Its leaves are smaller than the watermelon pepper, and they're thinner and rippled, with a less waxy substance. Search a little deeper into specialty nurseries, and you can find several peperomias with swollen, succulent leaves lining their stems, such as *P. asperula*, *P. ferreyrae*, and *P. dolabriformis*. Some are upright, others trail, and some, such as *P. rotundifolia* var. *pilosior* (with tiny, pill-like leaves on limp, threadish

You could treat *Peperomia ferreyrae* just like a succulent, water it forgetfully, and it would be fine.

Peperomia species

PEPEROMIA

ALSO CALLED: **radiator plants**

FLOWERS	Most have something in the rattail line; some are a little more feathered
FOLIAGE	With markings, ripple effects, and intriguing colors, the leaves are the main attraction
OTHER ATTRIBUTES	Durable. You don't get a nickname like "radiator plant" for nothing.
SIZE	Some are trailing, others grow from 6 to 20 inches (15–50cm) in height
EXPOSURE	East, west, or south
WATER REQUIREMENTS	Tolerates occasional drying out
OPTIMUM NIGHTTIME TEMPERATURE	50–65°F (10–18°C)
RATE OF GROWTH	Slow
SOIL TYPE	Friable, rich potting soil would be nice, but they're not finicky
FERTILIZING	Early spring to late autumn
PROBLEMS	Mealybugs can be an issue

stems), are groundcovers. This is just the tip of the iceberg for peperomias. With more than a thousand species, many are in cultivation.

Do not expect your peperomia to break speed records. Do not even expect your peperomia to do more than move just one step ahead of suspended animation. But the flip side is that peperomias do not require much upkeep. Of course, they would love to be watered when dry, but they do not complain if you forget. They even take repeated offenses in stride. They tolerate heavy shade, but sun is dandy too (as long as you make the transition gradually).

If you dislike bare
soil as much as I do,
Selaginella kraussiana
'Aurea' is the solution.
Here it's covering
ground below
Clematis 'Rooguchi'.

SELAGINELLAS

I'VE NEVER BEEN a big fan of bare soil. I decided long ago that a little green around the ankles wouldn't be a bad thing for potted plants. An uplifting frill at the base might liven things up in a cheerful sort of way. Fortunately, I found just the plant to do the job.

The way windowsills work, at least in my house, is that sunbeams don't always hit the container rim, especially in winter. The foliage basks in the beams, but the lumens never penetrate down to soil level. Instead, they are obstructed by window ledges or bogarted by other plants standing in the way. I needed a plant that wouldn't pout despite low light levels. Fortunately, selaginellas dote on indirect light. Meanwhile, my collection overflows with plenty of individuals who could

use a little action around the base. Take plants with woody stems, for example. Why leave that real estate naked? Blanket it, I say. So I put a team together between selaginellas and just about everything from hippeastrum to fuchsias.

If ever there was a plant qualified for a career as a groundcover, it is the *Selaginella* species. Spongy, fluffy, almost sea foamy, and with strong survival instincts (against all odds), the beauty of *Selaginella kraussiana* is its indomitable spirit. Depending on the garden center you frequent, you will find this plant under a vast array of confusing common names, but almost all mention moss. Whether it is spike moss, club moss, mat moss, or Irish moss is governed by the day of the week and the mood of your merchant. Deservingly popular, *S. kraussiana* does more than merely survive under adverse conditions—

it expands. If you treat it halfway decently, it grows by leaps and bounds until it requires dividing or cutting back (I usually just give my mosses a haircut with a pair of barber's shears). I prefer *S. kraussiana* 'Aurea' for its golden hue. Certainly not blaring yellow, it is sufficiently flaxen to provide a striking contrast with whatever plant is growing above. You can work some nice dialogues back and forth, color-wise.

Direct sun doesn't penetrate into the midst of my converted barn, but *Selaginella kraussiana* 'Aurea' (right) and 'Frosty Fern' (*S. kraussiana* 'Variegata') thrive beside *Asplenium nidus* in its gigantic terrarium.

Other spins on *Selaginella kraussiana* are all more or less easy to grow. During the holiday season, you will find *S. kraussiana* 'Variegata' tempting you at every turn. Go for it. With more upright growth than the typical spike moss and silver accents on the edges, it has been dubbed "Frosty Fern" for commercial purposes. I find that it does not divide quite as successfully as the old staple *S. kraussiana*, but it is a close second and nearly as ironclad. You can occasionally find *S. kraussiana* 'Brownii', a slight variation on the theme with more compact, tuft-like growth that makes little foamy whorls, like a Romanesco cauliflower. It is slower growing, but worth the patience required.

Another option is peacock moss, *Selaginella uncinata*. We're talking wandering, bluish purple strings of foliage that trail along haphazardly and cover ground rapidly. Just as shade tolerant as plain old *S. kraussiana*, it shimmers with an iridescent sheen when a sunbeam happens to graze the foliage. I just snip the brownish older wisps to encourage fresh, colorful growth.

Not all selaginellas are equally simpatico with the average home. Unless you happen to dwell in a sauna, many require too much humidity for most of us to easily host. Alas, *Selaginella umbrosa* is just a wish and hope for most gardeners. With snappy reddish burgundy branchlets, it is petite, compact, and striking. It is common on the market, but mission impossible for me. Heaven knows, I've tried.

You can stash 'Frosty Fern' (*Selaginella kraussiana* 'Variegata') just about anywhere, and as long as you remember to water, it thrives.

Selaginella species

SELAGINELLA

ALSO CALLED: club moss, Irish moss, mat moss, peacock moss, spike moss

FLOWERS	Not in the cards
FOLIAGE	Mossy, fluffy, and sometimes colorful
OTHER ATTRIBUTES	Makes a great groundcover for the container of taller plants
SIZE	2–4 inches (5–10cm) in height
EXPOSURE	East or west
WATER REQUIREMENTS	Generous, prefers not to dry out
OPTIMUM NIGHTTIME TEMPERATURE	55–65°F (12–18°C)
RATE OF GROWTH	Fast
SOIL TYPE	Rich, humusy potting soil
FERTILIZING	Early spring to late autumn
PROBLEMS	Will scorch in bright light

Lachenalias are the best-kept secrets in the South African bulb realm, and *Lachenalia purpureocaerula* is just one shade in the wide color range.

SOUTH AFRICAN BULBS

STARVED FOR SOMETHING new (even with some 300 houseplants), I pulled on a scarf, parka, insulated gloves, an extra pair of wool socks, and galoshes; grabbed a snow shovel; dug the car out; and went to the local garden center. Empty. Went to another garden center. Nada. Long story short, no one had any houseplants for sale— not boring houseplants, not mall-type foliage plants— nothing. This strikes me as such a brilliant (?) business strategy—cut off the supply of indoor plants in winter just when demand crests. I went home fairly glum until the light bulb went off. I picked up the phone and dialed Peter Wooster's gardener, Rob Girard. "Your South African bulbs need dividing," I announced. "I'll be there in five minutes." He never knew what hit him.

Fortunately, my hunch was right on target. They were pot-bound. And while unloading several souvenirs from the car into my house a few hours later, I congratulated myself for having gone to the mother lode. I had scored several lachenalias, a chasmanthe, and a babiana. The next few months were looking mighty bright indeed.

Except for my own collection of lachenalias, I don't usually delve too deeply into South African bulbs. Of course, there are a dozen or so amaryllis (hippeastrum) on my premises during any given winter, but they lack the snob appeal of other South African bulbs. Why? Well, they are entirely too easy, I suppose. Real South African bulbs take skill.

Or that's what I've always assumed. People clucked their tongues and revered my expertise simply for venturing into lachenalias. And I handled them like the aristocrats I assumed they were. Gave them a special sandy soil, lavished them with all the light I could muster, offered them a few miserly dribbles of water only once a week. Well, they despised me for it. In the end, when I managed them like all the other plants in the crowd, with regular potting soil and a normal watering regimen, they performed much better. End of preferential treatment.

You could go absolutely nuts with South African bulbs, and there are specialist nurseries that encourage you to wade in deep. But here are a few of my favorites to date. I expect more romance to unfold in the future.

BABIANA ANGUSTIFOLIA

Part of the booty from my potting binge at Peter Wooster's greenhouse, these bulbs were given to me as *Babiana pulchra*, but apparently they've been reclassified. They sprouted their long, grass-like leaves immediately, but sat in suspended animation for a while. Finally, those royal blue blossoms on their long wands emerged and thus started an extended stint of several weeks in sheer ecstasy (the kind you savor only in winter).

Babiana angustifolia's flowers are about the size and shape of a forsythia bloom. But the color is a royal purple like few other flowers can claim. As with most South African bulbs, several should be clustered together in a pot. The combined statement of many bulbs brandishing their wands of blossoms is impressive. I'm thinking at least half a dozen per pot for starters. I sit them in the best sunbeams in the house and give them the chilly reception they prefer. After flowering, babiana goes completely dormant in summer, starting in spring when the foliage turns the color of wheat. Dry it out and let it sleep until late autumn, when it's time to divide it up and begin watering again.

BOWEIA VOLUBILIS

Although you will not find *Boweia volubilis* listed in most books on South African bulbs, it is a bulb from South Africa and winter growing, so I am profiling it here. Although the climbing onion, as I have always called it, is not available at every corner garden center, I cannot seem to live without it. Something about its lacy, succulent stems curling their way up the curtains has always intrigued me. Plus the round, ever-expanding, onion-like bulb also has just the sort of weirdo comportment that is my kind of draw. The sheer energy of this plant, plus its stubborn will to live, is not only endearing, it is also reason to recommend it for the windowsill. Right now, mine is in a south-facing window and upwardly mobile around the curtain. The swollen bulb (which remains in evidence even when the vine isn't actively growing) should be planted so it is slightly above the soil. The potting medium should be well drained. You would be wise to give the plant a wide container at the start, because repotting as it expands is not so easy. In winter, the strange, frothy, seaweed-like stems begin to jut out and grow an inch (or more) daily. Tiny, star-like green flowers emerge (you might not even notice them at first). And that's the full performance. In spring, the growth dies back and you can water only occasionally until early autumn, when growth resumes. Pest-free, prone to taking summer vacations (when we're all preoccupied elsewhere anyway), and with minimal water demands, nothing could be easier.

CHASMANTHE BICOLOR

South African bulbs have a total advantage over the local talent (meaning forced hardy spring bulbs) because they are capable of delivering outrageous color in a few simple steps. *Chasmanthe bicolor* has long, tubular blossoms that could be likened to a dragon. To complete the analogy, they are fiery red-orange with a yellow lip at the tip. They come in loose spires crowning bolt upright, one-foot-tall (30cm) stems that tend toward pale pea green in color. The only effective way to display *C. bicolor* is to do it in mass. Rob Girard fills window boxes and puts them on the floor of his greenhouse. When you've got a dozen flower spikes or more all united, the combined effort makes a statement. Otherwise, a single bulb or two on display is a little awkward.

I treat *Chasmanthe bicolor* like the other South African bulbs that go entirely dormant after their performance. I just let it slip away, keeping it dry, and then I store it out of sight and mind in a dark, dry closet until late autumn, when I trot out the whole South African bulb menagerie and treat it to drinks and the cold conditions they dote on to begin growth again.

Like a herd of gaping dragons, the fiery blossoms of *Chasmanthe bicolor* last long, and the bulbs form abundant babies to increase the show rapidly.

Although most of the cyrtanthus I've encountered have lackluster, flesh-colored flowers, *Cyrtanthus mackenii* 'Hobgoblin' is pumpkin orange.

CYRTANTHUS MACKENII HYBRID

Not many plants have followed me throughout my adult life, but *Cyrtanthus mackenii* 'Hobgoblin' came along wherever I have roamed. Actually, it lives in Peter Wooster's greenhouse down the street right now, but that's certainly close enough to qualify. And how could you leave behind a bulb that has persistent foliage and blossoms from autumn through winter, especially if the blossoms are abundant, tubular, very showy, and Halloween orange in hue. Full disclosure: I was responsible for naming this orange version 'Hobgoblin'. It blossoms to beat the band.

Cyrtanthus mackenii is probably the easiest South African bulb to grow indoors. It has robust green, grass-like leaves that stand about 6 inches (15cm) tall with the flower spikes jutting just slightly above. Give it full sun and do not overwater (overwatering can cause the foliage to rot, but the bulbs generally remain intact), and you are home free. Reputedly, the plant flowers best when pot-bound. That's rarely a problem, because side bulbs appear with such gusto that keeping abreast of repotting is close to impossible. In this rare case, repotting delinquency is rewarded by an enthusiastic round of applause of the floral kind.

LACHENALIAS

I couldn't make it through winter without a lachenalia or two somewhere in close proximity. They are the easiest, most beguiling little bulbs you can possibly imagine. Envision a plant about the dimensions of a grape hyacinth with flowers about the size of a genuine hyacinth. Like tulips, the blossoms come in a broad array of colors, including purple, yellow, and lipstick red, with hues often combined on each tubular flower. Fragrance—lovely sugary sweet, anise-light fragrance—can also be a facet of the configuration, depending on the species. As the foliage emerges, it's also part of the show. Some have speckled leaves, some have warty leaves. However, as the flowers begin to mature, the foliage often becomes floppy. That downside probably isn't a factor in a bright greenhouse, but in my less-than-fully-luminous abode, the leaves always seem to sulk. As for water, be generous. My lachenalias dry out and wilt frequently. I originally potted them in a very sandy soil medium, but couldn't keep up with the watering. In a regular, well-drained potting soil, they are fine.

My lachenalias tell me when they want to come out of dormancy in early autumn. They begin growth, and I have to whisk them out of the closet where they summered and begin watering immediately. I usually summer them in their containers. Somehow, an inner bell always seems to go off reminding me to check them out just as growth is emerging. If you forget to get them into the light, they begin to elongate and the whole package isn't as natty.

When the show is over, lachenalias begin to go downhill with appalling speed. One day they're your pride and joy, and the next week they are a bit of an embarrassment. I just cut them back and stash them in the closet until next year.

Although lachenalias are thrilling when several bulbs fill a pot, even a couple of bulbs of yellow-flowering *Lachenalia* 'Romaud' effectively relieve winter doldrums.

You wouldn't choose
*Ornithogalum
longibracteatum*
on the basis of its
flowers. But if you're
into sharing the
bounty, you might
grow it because of
its proliferation
of baby bulbs.

ORNITHOGALUM
LONGIBRACTEATUM

Unlike the other South African bulbs here, this performer is not really about flowers. Granted, in winter, *Ornithogalum longibracteatum* sends up tall, arching wands of uneventful, small, cream-colored flowers with a green stripe, but they are generally overlooked. Instead, the bulbs themselves are the intriguing factor. The pregnant onion, as I've always known it, makes babies. The rounded, onion-like bulbs (ornithogalum is in the *Liliaceae*, along with onions) swell above ground to become the size of plump, green baseballs with a sheath of paper-thin coating drawn around each. From the sides of the main bulb, little bulbs continually pop. The mama bulb sends up a regal sheaf of long, thin leaves that swoop

and arch. The piggybacked progeny start making thin grass-like blades sticking out of their little swollen pouches and then future generations develop from there.

Best of all, this plant is a living social network. When people admire your pregnant onion, you can turn around, nonchalantly break off one of the developing bulbs with roots (and they send down their own roots as soon as they hit soil), and become instantly popular for your generosity. Pass it along. This serves a dual purpose. If you hoard the whole display, the extended family will soon require larger accommodations.

When you share this ornithogalum, you can do it with a clear conscience because it's absolutely trouble free. Given an east, west, or south window, it is one of the easiest houseplants around. Dry it out

Ornithogalum thyrsoides 'Alaska' has just recently made the scene as a winter potted plant, but it's bound to gather a following based on its lingering, lovely performance.

or give it water—it's all groovy. I've never even tried to over-water mine. Neglect seems to be its preferred treatment.

And if flowers are your heart's desire, go for chincher-inchee (*Ornithogalum thyrsoides* 'Alaska'), with its dense, foxtail-plump wands of creamy white, star-shaped blossoms that last for many weeks. This maintenance-free performer used to be summer fare, but now it's marketed for Thanksgiving entertainment.

Various South African bulbs

FLOWERS	Often very colorful and the main perk, except *Ornithogalum longibracteatum* and *Boweia volubilis*
FOLIAGE	Usually part of the display, especially the lachenalias
OTHER ATTRIBUTES	The bulbs themselves can be part of the display
SIZE	Mostly 6–12 inches (15–30cm) in height
EXPOSURE	East, west, or south
WATER REQUIREMENTS	It's important not to overwater bulbs
OPTIMUM NIGHTTIME TEMPERATURE	50–60°F (10–15°C)
RATE OF GROWTH	Rapid for most
SOIL TYPE	Heavy but humusy potting soil mixture with compost included
FERTILIZING	I fertilize lightly at the beginning of the bulb's growing season in autumn, then taper off
PROBLEMS	Foliage can be pestered by spider mites as it begins to slip into dormancy. I prefer to cut it off to preclude the problem. Keep all members of the *Liliaceae* family away from pets who are prone to ingest, especially cats.

Let's talk about sunbeams and
bask in their bright splendor
as they beat their path through
the windowpanes. Let's find
excuses to loiter around the
houseplants and coat our
bodies in the warm glimmerglow of the brightening light.
If spring strikes you as
sensual, join the crowd. The
fever certainly quickens my
pulse in a heady sort of way.
And long before there's desire
or hope of going outside,
the indoor garden is pulsating.

On a visual level, spring
might be about primroses pop-
ping and tiarellas blooming on
the windowsill when they're
no more than a promise in the

garden. But spring also introduces the smell of unthawing soil floating through newly opened windows. It pushes the curtains into billowing where they once lay limp and stood sentinel against the cold air. Spring in a windowsill might be a prelude for impatient gardeners longing to rush headlong into the scene about to happen outside. But that's only part of the picture. Spring has stunts all its own.

Little wonder that spring inducts everyone from casual supermarket shoppers to innocent Easter revelers into the houseplant halls of fame. Try—just try—to get past the salad bar without veering over to select a primrose or two just begging to jump into your shopping cart. Knowing that summer is right around the corner, adopting a houseplant seems less of a responsibility-fraught commitment. We all jam an expanded assortment of plants onto the windowsill in spring with the full expectation that the doors will soon be thrown open and they will spill outside onto porches and patios.

Friends come because they're no longer snowbound and because I've got the only live show in town. They open the door and exclaim about the fragrances filling their noses from plants that just a few weeks before were nothing more than impediments to taking off their galoshes. When they pick me up for dinner, they can see those plants clearly in daylight because the days are longer (and we switched the clocks).

Spring is the season for boasting. It's when indoor gardeners parade their proudest moments before the world at flower shows. And even if we don't exhibit, we go to the shows, peruse the plants, and tell tall tales about how impressively our succulents are growing and claim beefed-up bud counts on our rhizomatous begonias. But most of the time, there's no need to exaggerate. Spring is looking pretty darn impressive in my home. And I return from those spring flower shows feeling fairly smug. I open the door, I walk into the entryway, and I applaud all those botanical warriors who made it through the long winter by my side. No wonder they're all bursting to blossom. They're survivors, and spring is their moment of glory.

Primroses are spring's happiest moment. And that's why everyone absolutely needs a container of *Primula denticulata* 'Confetti Blue' and *Primula denticulata* 'Rubins' close by.

Pity the poor shirkers in spring, because their picture will not be pretty. All the plants that were not repotted in a timely fashion last spring and summer will haunt them. All the pots fitted with insufficiently wide saucers will overflow. All the plants that are not watered will wilt, wilt again, and come down with aphids. Spring is an unforgiving season.

The key to spring, as I see it, is twofold. First, you must deliver water on a timely basis, or else. A stressed plant is a sitting duck for all sorts of problems (and spring seems to be a hotbed for issues to flourish). Second, you have to throw open your windows generously and without dallying or undue deliberation. Toasty is not the way to go in spring. Hesitate too long in the ventilation department, and the repercussions might reverberate far beyond just some uncomfortably stuffy situations. In spring, prudence will get you insects.

But why am I harping on this? Nothing is more fun than sprinkling water around in spring, ministering to the needs of house- plants making fresh, new growth. And when it comes to throwing open the windows, it's usu- ally a hold-me-back state of affairs. I rush to push open the storm windows and pull down the screens so I can crack the windows without watching Einstein go flying out. Then I turn down the thermostat so the furnace won't labor when I get home late while the tempera- ture has plummeted. The houseplants love the fresh air, and the bugs are held at bay.

Meanwhile, I push the food. A week or two before the calendar actually chronicles the official beginning of March, I'm looking at the fish emulsion with longing and anticipation. I can hardly wait for that smell to permeate the house (and I don't care how adamantly the label proclaims a product to be scentless; fish emulsion always emits its own unique odor). Initially, I dispense fertilizer prudently and in partial portions. Being a gal who believes in moderation in all things (at first, anyway), I dilute the fertilizer beyond the usual label rec- ommendations for the first couple of feedings and gradually edge into full strength. And the plants respond. Given the additional sun and the ramped-up feeding schedule, houseplants begin thinking about pollination. They start producing the flowers that might make it hap- pen. Even indoors, spring raises the bar in the performance arena.

If ever there was a season that changes drastically from start to finish, it's spring. At first, it's just a nebulous sense that light levels are increasing. But this state of affairs improves daily as plants that had no blossoms begin to initiate buds galore. It's incredibly thrilling. They are shaking off their holding pattern and coming to life. Spring is a celebration. It's payback time. Everything kicks up its heels and starts performing. Other folks palpitate when treated to bonbons; my cartwheels are sparked by bud counts and energetic new growth.

Just like any card-bearing gardener, I'm outdoors as soon as I can beat a path out the door and into the yard. Likewise, the forced potted bulbs are also sent outside as soon as I can safely throw them there. I do it gradually, by exposing them daily to the cold, cruel world that isn't tempered by a thermostat and then trundling them inside by late afternoon. Whenever temperatures remain safely (very safely, especially before they've been hardened off) above freezing overnight, I leave them outside. Finally, they stay out permanently and are part of the patio display for passersby to enjoy. There's a reason for this. I find that forced bulbs are the first plants in the house to come down with aphids. If possible, I don't leave any bulbs that have finished flowering inside. As the foliage dies back, it calls insects from nowhere. In other words, it becomes a liability.

If it weren't for diversions indoors, I'd be getting into deep trouble. I'd be out there with the hair dryer, trying to unthaw a cavity to insert something that is probably only marginally hardy. Instead, I repot. Some plants let you know in no uncertain terms that this should be in the cards. As light levels increase, houseplants dry out every half day, becoming a time guzzler. But it's not a bad idea to check the entire assemblage for repotting requirements. When the roots have filled the container, it's time to move on. And the beauty of doing a "repotathon" is that you can just engineer a switcheroo. Start by repotting something large and work down to the smaller containers, and you can enlist plenty of hand-me-downs without digging around in your basement or investing in more terra-cotta.

Of course, spring typically has a lot of false starts. It's a fickle season. That's why you need to do horticultural therapy by beginning seeds indoors. Seeds are a predictable, direct tangent from sowing to germination to transplanting—all in the comfort of your home while the weather waffles outdoors. During those inevitable spring showers, while the chilly drizzle is putting a damper on your best-laid plans to fiddle around in the backyard, you can do something constructive and creative. Besides the promise that garden seedlings imply, I keep the focus steadily inside. Only hardy plants (like forced bulbs and perennials I've brought indoors for early spring feats) are sent outside this early. Why take chances? Spring is a yo-yo. Look outdoors all you want, but do your tasks inside.

BEGONIAS

I'M ON MY 160th sit-up and begging for an excuse to pause, so it's fortunate that 'River Nile' happens to be thirsty. Yep, it needs a drink immediately. Preferably before I tackle the leg lifts or sun salutations. In fact, now that I notice it, 'Texastar' could use a drink too. In fact, all the begonias in the bathroom window would benefit from some watering-pot attention.

The bathroom windows are monopolized by rhizomatous begonias, with a few ferns, orchids, and bromeliads thrown in. It's not because they need the humidity from my daily shower or the heat from an abundance of vents. The begonias live in the bathroom by default because it gets filtered eastern light, and they are fine with that. In fact, they dote on it. Witness the fact that 'Texastar' is waving promising flower spikes that somehow emerged from nowhere when I was otherwise preoccupied during the past week or so. Life should hit an elevated level of excitement in the bathroom sometime soon.

Surprises are not unusual with the begonias. Because they don't require frequent watering, they're apt to catch you unaware with new leaves and flower stalks. And that's half the fun. Chancing upon that unforeseen flower spike is like finding a forgotten twenty-dollar bill tucked into your knapsack when the bank is closed. And it's even better because you earned it. Because of your benign neglect, because you didn't overwater or overpot, and because you sat that begonia close to the window that wasn't too bright, you've achieved blossoms. It's the begonia's method of training you to keep up the good work.

On the plant stands in my bathroom, *Begonia* 'Bunchii', *Nephrolepis exaltata* 'Emina', *Paphiopedilum Maudiae* cultivar, and *Begonia* 'Dryad' watch me huff and puff through my morning exercises.

Begonias have been training me for a while now. In fact, most of my adulthood has been spent working intimately with begonias (I use the word "intimately" without reserve—I used to hybridize them professionally). For 25 years, I curated the begonia collection at Logee's Greenhouses. Even though I arrived at that job with only a rudimentary awareness of wax begonias, daily proximity fanned the fires of admiration for the rest of the family. But that was in a greenhouse setting. When I moved, the begonias came along (not all 1000 of them). The pleasant surprise? They thrive in a house. If you disregard the challenging rex types, there's really no difference between a greenhouse and home as a setting for cultivating primo begonias.

Hands down, I find that rhizomatous begonias make the best houseplants. Granted, a few species are too persnickety for the average home because of their elevated humidity requirements. But most stunners turn cartwheels inside. If you like tiny, dime-size leaves, you'll find the rhizomatous begonia of your dreams. If you prefer big, flouncy foliage, they've got you covered. And there's everything in between, ranging in size from plants that remain under 2 inches (5cm) indefinitely to massive 3-foot (90cm) behemoths. Size is one variable; shapes are another. Perfectly rounded leaves, serrated foliage, maple-shaped leaves, curly foliage, star-shaped leaves—they run the full gamut. Felted, furry, eyelash-edged, hairy, smooth, and shiny leaf surfaces are available. In the color spectrum, the foliage doesn't move far out of the green, bronze, red, and brown range, with markings that are varied and artistic, but not overdone.

The miniature eyelash begonias, *Begonia bowerae* var. *nigramarga* and its close cousins, are readily available and foolproof to grow.

The rhizomatous begonia, *Begonia* 'Palomar Prince', has both handsome striped foliage and abundant spires of flowers.

In the rhizomatous begonia realm, leaf shapes vary from rounded to ruffled to star-shaped, such as *Begonia* 'Texastar'.

Lack space? For years, miniature *Begonia* 'Zip' has happily existed in suspended animation tucked into this tiny container.

Add late winter and early spring flowers to the package. Held in wands, each blossom is small, but perceived as a unit, they make a subtly significant statement. The colors range from white to pink blushing into the soft reds and peach. A few species move into the yellow realm. As with all begonias, the females, with their potential seed pouches, are larger than the males. But the shape doesn't vary much, and they're never going to wow the gardener who needs something the size of a Frisbee to be fulfilled.

I palpitate for rhizomatous begonias, but angel wing begonias are equally easy to host in a home. Actually, any fibrous begonia—the type with a woody stem—will grow beautifully without fuss. The angel wings have feathery leaves of different shapes and sizes initiating from cane-like stems. Some have showy blossoms that can swell to the size of a shooting marble, while others are more about foliage. The only stumbling block that most gardeners face is having the discipline to cut them back brutally to encourage branching. Beyond that, you're home free. Ditto for the prostrate hanging types. Same story for the hiemalis types, with their abundant winter-spring blossom load.

Rhizomatous begonias don't have immense flowers, but the blossoms (this happens to be a spire of *Begonia* 'Bunchii' flowers) are just what you need in early spring before you can escape outdoors.

Although some of the fibrous begonias can be a handful size-wise, this Brazilian species begonia is sufficiently compact to sit beside any windowsill without bogarting the beams.

I can't grow rex begonias in my home. They totally elude me. Although I grew them for 25 years in a greenhouse setting, they always seem to succumb to powdery mildew in my house. I have the same issue with semi-tuberous begonias, although heaven knows, I try. I've never attempted a tuberous begonia in my home because they grow from bulbs only in summer (and they're prone to powdery mildew). Wax begonias (*Begonia semperflorens* hybrids), with their lettuce-like leaves and little crowns of cute blossoms, are all well and good for the bedding scheme in the local park, but they totally bore me in my house.

The trick to growing any sort of begonias is to water sparingly. They detest soggy roots. I've found that neglect will get you nowhere with a begonia, and they're not fond of a yo-yo wet/dry cycle. They prefer an even supply of water when they're slightly dry. And along the same line, it's a killer to overpot a begonia. Start small, and graduate one inch (2.5cm) all around the root ball at a time. A light, humusy growing medium is the way to go.

Originally, I imagined that any begonias on my premises would have to remain confined to the bathroom; I figured they'd complain about my chilly home. Wrong. Begonias have infiltrated just about everywhere.

Begonia species
and cultivars

BEGONIAS

FLOWERS	Late winter and spring for most rhizomatous, variable on the other types, usually handsome
FOLIAGE	Wide diversity in leaf shapes and markings
OTHER ATTRIBUTES	Begonias run the gamut. There's a size for every situation.
EXPOSURE	East or west
WATER REQUIREMENTS	Lightly moist
OPTIMUM NIGHTTIME TEMPERATURE	55–65°F (12–18°C)
SIZE	2 inches (5cm) to 3 feet (90cm) in height or larger behemoths
RATE OF GROWTH	Medium
SOIL TYPE	Any rich, humusy soil
FERTILIZING	Early spring to late autumn
PROBLEMS	Powdery mildew is an issue with some begonias. Mealy bugs can also be a problem.

CARNIVOROUS PLANTS

I keep up with the excessive drinking habits of *Sarracenia purpurea, S. flava,* and *S. 'Love Bug'* by sitting them in a pan of water.

*T*HERE IS A fairly broad chasm between me and anything having to do with greasy grimy gopher guts. I never embraced sci-fi, horror movies, or anything remotely leaning in the gory direction. Indeed, I'm a lifelong vegetarian, and that should tell you a lot. However, some of my best friends are meat-eaters. Take the pitcher plant, for example.

I like to think I'm attracted to sarracenias because they are gorgeous. Solely on the basis of their physical appearance, I made a beeline in the pitcher plant's general direction. And why keep an oddball of this caliber at arm's length outdoors? Fortunately, sarracenias turned out to be possible and pleasurable houseplants. We're talking funnel-shaped, tube-like leaves that poke up from the ground (or lay back, in the case of *Sarracenia purpurea*). They're leathery, their veins are accented, and they have a little bonnet at their tip, sometimes shaped like a lid that is ajar. In other words, pitcher plants look vaguely supernatural. Add their eating habits to this outlandish garb and you've got the makings of an Alfred Hitchcock movie. The foliage has nectaries that attract insects. While the insects are in exploratory mode, they crawl around the tube, which gets waxier further from the opening. It's so slippery that hapless bugs (and the misadventures of bugs seemingly make the world go round) tumble into the depths of the leaf. In this case, a second chance isn't in the poor little pollinator's cards as it drowns in the accumulated water. The pitcher plant ingests the lip-smacking goodness of its yummy prey, leaving the outer body parts to form a slurry in its depths. Look within a tube on a pitcher plant, and

Admit it. You're just as drawn to the macabre gaping mouth of a sarracenia as its prey.

there's going to be considerable grossness going on. It's the smoothie from hell. Be prepared for yuck even indoors—sarracenias manage to wine and dine on any stray fruit flies that happen to be carousing. If that image bothers you, feel free to empty out the pitcher periodically. Or you can turn the other cheek and let nature take its course.

When one of my nursery friends divulged the knowledge that sarracenias need a sub-freezing sequence, it was news to me. I'd always grown them successfully indoors throughout the winter. Granted, they're not in their finest form at that juncture (although they never went completely dormant), but they survived to rally and blossom in spring. The blossoms are deep burgundy and shiny, and look like a combination spaceship-parachute-umbrella. They shoot up twice as tall as the leaves and are definitely an event in spring.

The sarracenias aren't the only carnivorous plants in my inventory. I also do a few sundews (*Drosera* species). They aren't equally thrilling from a distance, but I love the sparkling, jewel-like quality of the tentacles that enwrap and strangle their prey. Mine don't seem to have an appetite equal to the pitcher plants, but they are easy to grow, mildly entertaining, and definitely different, so I invite them to the party.

Occasionally, I try (and fail with) a Venus flytrap (*Dionaea muscipula*). It lives for a month or two under my stewardship, and then goes dormant (also known as dead). I've tried them in the open and in terrariums. Nothing seems to work. Dormancy is the kiss of death in my house. Although they are undeniably thrilling for a while, it isn't a lasting relationship.

Just for the record, I have never grown a nepenthes in my home. Their preference for warm temperatures, high humidity, and warm water is just too daunting. It's fine to host a modest carnivorous plant that demands high humidity in a terrarium, but nepenthes are huge plants with dangling lidded pitchers that catch bugs. In other words, they are not easily clapped into a humid chamber. They are undeniably fascinating, but I leave them to reside in toasty greenhouses and visit them there.

All carnivorous plants enjoy similar growing conditions. They love bright light and soggy roots. My entire collection sits in a watertight metal tray with sides that can be filled and refilled with water as the level dwindles. The even moisture factor is key, and I find that it's more important than light. Because I don't really have any super bright venues in my home, most of the carnivorous crowd

Look closely at *Drosera capensis*— its leaves seem to be lined with glittering (but deadly, if you're a fruit fly) jewels.

is relegated to part shade. The whole menagerie takes lower sunbeams in their stride (except the Venus flytrap).

The potting medium can be dicey. I've seen a combination of peat moss and sand used (50-50 is usually recommended). Sphagnum moss has been associated with carnivorous plants as a potting medium, but it has also been linked with a very serious skin condition, so I avoid it entirely and urge you to do likewise. I have never needed to repot my collection—they seem to grow fine in their original pots indefinitely. Keep in mind that carnivorous plants are custom-made to survive in protein- and nutrient-poor ecosystems. They are indigenous to bogs and supplement their diet with their kinky meals. They detest fertilizer. Carnivorous plants don't actually need to eat insects to survive; the bugs are supplemental. Of course, there's no way to dissuade kids from trying to cram flies into their carnivorous pets. But an arm of a Venus flytrap with prey inside will remain shut, and then turn black and rot. Pitcher plants, on the other hand, can gorge on thousands of insects and still be their handsome, smiling selves.

Sarracenia species, *Drosera* species, *Dionaea muscipula*

PITCHER PLANTS, SUNDEWS, AND VENUS FLYTRAP

FLOWERS	Sarracenias have burgundy parachutes on tall stems; Venus flytraps have small white flowers jutting above the foliage
FOLIAGE	Ornamental in all cases
OTHER ATTRIBUTES	Pitcher plants make great cut flowers
EXPOSURE	South
SIZE	Sarracenias are 1–2 feet (30–61cm) in height; Droseras and Venus flytraps are ground hugging
WATER REQUIREMENTS	Heavy drinkers; use purified water
OPTIMUM NIGHTTIME TEMPERATURE	50–55°F (10–12°C)
RATE OF GROWTH	Slow
SOIL TYPE	Mossy, boggy
FERTILIZING	None
PROBLEMS	They can go dormant and fail to return. But they aren't pestered by insect attacks—instead, they are their own eliminators.

FICUS

A study in contrasts within the same genus, upright *Ficus benjamina* 'Too Little' juts from its bed of creeping *F. pumila* 'Snowflake'.

THROUGH THE YEARS, I've found all kinds of reasons to covet figs. The first rustlings of the affair were sparked by the creeping fig, which might not seem particularly dramatic, romantic, or exotic at first glance. But *Ficus pumila* gave me the veiled mystery and sense of nature encroaching on human domain that I strive to attain. The rambunctious creeping fig swings into action in three winks of an eye (or less) and clambers into the dark recesses of your life. It requires almost no light for encouragement. It needs almost no nurturing. You plant it and stand back while it conquers ground, via its ivy-like stem roots, swiftly, efficiently, thoroughly, and with a ruthless take-no-prisoners policy. I actually had to put a crimp on *F. pumila*. It was ruining the walls. I now grow the miniature versions.

Recent years have seen the introduction of adorable little creeping figs that travel around with less frightening agility. There are several spins on *Ficus pumila* 'Minima', the smallest of which is 'Quercifolia', with notched oak-shaped leaves. 'Snowflake' is also downscaled and polite, and it has variegated white edges and wavy leaves. I harness these as groundcovers below taller plants.

On a whole different note and with an entirely different habit, *Ficus benjamina* has become something of a cliché for interior landscapers. You might have noticed it in malls and corporate headquarters.

Or you might not have noticed it. With thick, tree-like stems (often braided) and long, slender, deep-green leaves, it's so boring that you might have walked by *F. benjamina* a million times and failed to register it. It's a bear to grow in the average home. In fact, it comes down with scale so often that I avoid it entirely. But I do have the miniature version, *F. benjamina* 'Too Little' (often used for bonsai), which has slightly sickle-shaped leaves and reaches only 8 inches (20cm) or so in height. It can also fall victim to scale, but if you treat it right (and it's a lot easier to royally host a small plant compared to an indoor tree), it will do just fine.

I'm also fond of *Ficus deltoidea*, the mistletoe fig. Absolutely trouble-free, it tolerates very low light, forms a dense little tree with deep-green, triangular leaves, and produces pea-size, yellow-orange fruit. The fruit isn't edible, but it's a handsome package and as easy as they come. Compare that to *F. aspera* 'Parcellii', the clown fig with long, deep-green leaves and continual supply of shooter marble-size, variegated figs (also not edible). It requires much warmer temperatures and more light than I can provide. Its need for bright light throughout the winter is a rare exception in the fig group.

Now for the juicy part: edible figs. Although I bring in several cultivars of *Ficus carica* that produce a few figs over the winter, they are

Sandwiched between *Begonia* 'Bethlehem Star' and *Saxifraga stolonifera* on my windowsill, *Ficus deltoidea* is a singularly handsome fig.

Not all edible figs are houseplant-size, but *Ficus carica* 'Petite Negra' stays small and begins producing fruit in winter.

Ficus species

FICUS

ALSO CALLED: clown fig, creeping fig, edible fig, mistletoe fig

FLOWERS	Not in the cards
FOLIAGE	Varies greatly, but usually handsome
OTHER ATTRIBUTES	Fruit on some ficus is edible
SIZE ATTRIBUTES	A groundcover for *Ficus pumila*, varies for other figs
EXPOSURE	East or west
WATER REQUIREMENTS	Low except *Ficus carica*, which is a heavy drinker
OPTIMUM NIGHTTIME TEMPERATURE	50–60°F (10–15°C)
RATE OF GROWTH	Fast on *Ficus pumila*, medium on other species. Painfully slow for *F. benjamina* 'Too Little'.
SOIL TYPE	Good organic potting soil with compost included
FERTILIZING	Early spring to late autumn
PROBLEMS	Scale can attack any of the members of this genus. Ficus can be toxic and can cause a severe dermatological reaction.

typically too large to suggest as houseplants. I recommend putting your edible figs in the basement and letting them slumber in their dormant, naked cigar state. The exception to this rule is 'Petite Negra', a dwarf fig that remains delightfully compact, retains its foliage over the winter, and forms fruit. It's divine decadence indoors. Can you imagine taking a scrumptious bite from your own figs grown in your kitchen window? It's fully possible with 'Petite Negra'. Except for a voracious drinking habit, I've discovered no problems with this fig. I feel like Cleopatra.

GARDEN PREVIEW

Right alongside succulents in the tough-as-nails category, *Armeria maritima* 'Rubrifolia' grows its tufts of foliage all year, but sends up little spaceship-like orbs of flowers when light levels increase.

THERE'S SOMETHING about spring that melts your heart. Maybe it's the courage of those brave little blossoms that forge ahead against all odds, or maybe it's the daintiness of the first blooms to emerge. But no need to wait for the thrill. You can sneak a glimpse of spring long before it pops outdoors. And a little riot inside is truly welcome right about now. Not only can you bask in the debut, but you can watch it unfold in the comfort of your own home. If you've never had the opportunity to snuggle up to a columbine and examine its intricacies face to face, this is your chance.

Spring never arrives soon enough for me. In a perfect world, I would segue from January straight into the growing season. A little winter is okay, but it doesn't need to linger as long or as fiercely as it does in New England. So why not pull some stunts? All you need for a little seasonal foolery is a windowsill and a good nursery that starts its own stock.

In a few cases, I dig plants in autumn to remind me of the garden throughout the long, boring, brutal winter. I plunder tiarellas and heucheras from the garden in autumn, before the ground seizes up, to become part of spring's prelude in the windowsill, and I just put them back in place after the show. But mostly I wait for late winter and haunt garden centers so I can be the proud and precocious purchaser of perennials as the trucks arrive hot from the wholesalers in early March. If your garden center is open and willing (and why not?), taking a few plants off their hands can save them a lot of work. That labor now falls on your shoulders, but aren't you ready to lavish all your latent nurturing instincts on some perennial acquisitions raring to go?

The beauty of the season's first bloomers is they're poised to perform ultra early. You're just pushing them to speedier levels of precociousness. No special lights or heating units are called into service. Simply acquire the plants, pot them up, put them in position, and sit back. Because this is a temporary performance, you don't need to think long term for containers, but a certain amount of short-term practicality makes the whole process more fun and less laborious. To do this right and to keep the plants from becoming holy nuisances because of watering demands, give them ample containers. Spring-blooming plants generally have roots that plunge down, so deeper pots are usually better than shallow ones. Don't try to cram the plant's roots into something painfully pinched.

As far as temperatures and care are concerned, keep in mind that these plants prefer spring showers and cool temperatures to make their alarm clocks ring. Turning the thermostat down would create the best of all worlds for most spring bloomers trying to keep you entertained inside ahead of schedule. A constantly moist soil extends the show.

The result is great entertainment. Do it for your psyche. Do it for all the friends you'll invite over to savor the premiere. With a bleeding heart or two close by, spring can be as poky as it wants in the garden, and your patience will know greater limits.

AQUILEGIA VULGARIS

Columbine is an incredibly complex flower. But who wants to crawl around on hands and knees outdoors in chilly spring weather to check it out? It's a different story at your elbow inside. Sometimes I just can't keep my eyes off the resident columbine's intricate artistry, and I sneak over to catch another glimpse.

Single columbines come faster to the punch than the double types. The singles also tend to have shorter stems, making them a more succinct unit in a container. They are adorable and they linger long.

There is no trick to coaxing columbines early. You can hardly hold them back. The moment after they start to grow, they begin shooting up blossom spires. An east or west window is all you need. Starting them from seeds is a cinch, so that might be a way to go if you don't mind dealing with a little nurturing and transplanting. I often take that inexpensive route to fulfillment.

Not only is *Aquilegia* 'Origami Rose & White' precocious inside, but it blithely blossoms for weeks.

ARMERIA MARITIMA

Spring starts small, and isn't that the ideal dimension for a windowsill? For example, the individual blossoms on sea thrift (*Armeria maritima*) are tiny, but they're packed together into walnut-size orbs. A whole crowd of those little balls massed together creates a show. Without blossoms, sea thrift would bear an uncanny resemblance to your average tuft of grass and wouldn't warrant any second looks. Fortunately, the flowers happen pretty much constantly as soon as light levels begin to increase, making the plant a perfect harbinger for a much-anticipated upcoming season. And seen on a windowsill, sea thrift is capable of stealing the show, unlike the same tiny little nugget crouching at your feet outside with infinite competition in your line of vision.

In a perfect world, sea thrift would prefer a bright, south-facing window. But it certainly doesn't pout with less light—it just doesn't produce the amassed pincushion-topped-by-balls-of-blossoms package that makes it overwhelmingly adorable. Fond of sandy-type drainage in the garden (rock gardens are its usual venue), you can give sea thrift the same sort of crammed root system, lean soil, and sparse water and it will be blissfully happy, producing plenty of blossoms and keeping your spirits buoyed until you have access to outdoors.

What you need in early spring is magic, and *Armeria maritima* 'Rubrifolia' might not wow you outdoors, but it's a different story inside.

Grow *Bellis perennis*
'Rominette Pink'
indoors, and the
button-like double
blossoms will linger
longer than they
would outside.

BELLIS PERENNIS

I don't bother with English daisies in the garden. They just don't perform sufficiently long to justify the space. (Not that they take up much space, but still.) The moment after they begin blossoming outdoors, it's curtains as soon as the sun glimmers and the temperatures rise. So I get my English daisy fix indoors, where I can enjoy front row seats, see them day and night, and do so in preview mode.

If you're thinking the usual daisy package of big, open-face disks of flowers standing on tall stems, you've got it all wrong for *Bellis perennis*. It creeps along the ground with small oval leaves to send up mini pom-poms of blossoms just above the foliage. The flowers are shaggy little balls about the size of a button in shades of white, pink, and red. They're infinitely cheerful and the epitome of spring.

Bellis daisies need cool temperatures, which makes them a perfect match for my home. Outdoors they wouldn't mind bright light. But since our affair doesn't linger indoors, I give them an east or west window and keep them away from the heat to extend the show. They love it.

Treat *Dicentra spectabilis* 'Gold Heart' like a temp in your home. Buy a budded plant, tuck it into a great container, and enjoy the show, then send it out into the garden. Not all houseplants are meant to be long-lasting relationships.

DICENTRA SPECTABILIS

Bleeding heart is literally spring-loaded. It practically sprouts from the soil with its dangling arch of blossoms all breathless to pop. Convincing bleeding heart to make blossoms is not an issue. In fact, the only challenge with this plant is trying to wedge the immense network of rhizome-like roots into a container. You'll need something large to balance out the top growth because bleeding hearts just don't read unless you get a fairly hefty mass. And cramming the plant into small "shoes" is not going to work, even over the short term.

Obtain your bleeding hearts as early as possible, preferably before they've begun to sprout or when they are just emerging from dormancy. The roots fall apart easily and do not like to be jostled. Pot them immediately and let them recover before the flowers peek out. Then find an east or west window to display the plant and leave it alone to do its thing. Savoring the gracefully arching stems of dangling pink broken hearts with their melodramatic white teardrops hanging is glorious indulgence indoors. The white version also works and isn't quite so hefty. And the gold-leaved edition adds great foliage to the presentation. Generous moisture to mimic spring showers will push things along. And after the show is over, you might as well incorporate them into the garden.

HELLEBORUS HYBRIDS

While the rest of Easter is rife with bunnies delivering eggs, it's refreshing to find supermarkets sporting hellebores to celebrate the holiday. Hellebores fully deserve the holiday connection. They bear clusters of individual bell-shaped flowers in profusion above a frill of pointed leaves. I'm fond of 'Candy Love' for its apple blossom–colored blooms and nice frill of leaves around the base, but any hellebore will provide months and months of intrigue indoors and then make the move outside absolutely seamlessly.

Hellebores are not finicky about light conditions inside, although they will blossom longest in an east or west exposure rather than a brighter south window. They never wilt. Body language isn't their forte. Keep an eye on the soil to make sure it doesn't dry out. Despite the fact that they're not complainers, they tend to be heavy drinkers and will last for months and months in blossom when treated right. A fluffy organic soil does the trick.

When the snow is still blanketing the garden outdoors, a *Helleborus* hybrid takes the edge off the wait.

HEUCHERA

Winter is long and bittersweet for a gardener, so even though I have umpteen houseplants, I always invite a heuchera or two inside in autumn to go through the winter as a memento of a season gone by. Low-maintenance souvenirs of summer, heucheras are perfect. They don't monopolize much space, they require almost no care aside from occasional watering and tidying, and they're much more thrilling indoors than outside.

When growing heucheras inside, the foliage is the focus. You're unlikely to see flowers, and you're not missing much, as the flowers on most are merely wispy, easily overlooked spires of tiny blooms. The leaves, on the other hand, are broad and often smartly lobed, like a thoughtfully designed collar on a vintage blouse, and they come in a carnival of colors. We've been barraged by heucheras in the full color spectrum, and you can take your pick according to preferences. I find the darker types do better during the winter in the average home, whereas the orange hybrids ('Caramel', 'Marmalade') sort of limp along until spring.

Heucheras are one of the rare cases when I actually dig from the garden and hustle a plant indoors just hours before the soil goes solid with frost or snow blankets the whole shebang—whichever happens first. The roots of a huge, full-grown heuchera can be massive and will require a generous container, so go for a dwarf version. In an east or west window, they give me the garden throughout the year.

PAPAVER NUDICAULE

I tried Icelandic poppies on a lark a few years ago, when I needed a lift (in March, don't we all?) and walked into a nursery to find some cheerful ones in full bud. Not only did they perform in a west window, but they continued to stay agape much longer than they would when exposed to wind, thunderstorms, and direct sun outside. And, amazingly, they kept right on producing buds. Like other poppies, they have tissue-thin petals. But the colors of Icelandic poppies are luminous shell shades, the likes of which you won't find elsewhere in nature (except perhaps peonies, but you can't bring them inside). They're fluttery, they're delicate, and they begin as modest, nodding buds that straighten out to pop open above a nest of green, slightly disheveled leaves. They have a saucy little "wild child" type of persona.

I grow Icelandic poppies in a deepish window box to give the roots a chance to plunge down (as poppies will do) and to combine several Icelandic poppies, displaying masses of flowers in stages of coming and going. They never pout if I forget to water (it happens), and they never pause in their bud production until spring is nudging summer.

Icelandic poppies prefer as much light as you can muster indoors in early spring. I find that a west-facing exposure works fine. I water the poppies sparingly, and that is the full extent of my role. Even the spent flowers have a romantic quality.

Long before spring actually arrives, *Papaver nudicaule* makes it happen inside the panes.

PULMONARIA

Spring has its perks. When else can you find that clear, striking, sailor blue that lungworts feature? And wouldn't you like to have that little piece of the sky (or the sea) by your side, where you can drink it in on a regular basis? Not only are pulmonarias easy to push into bloom indoors, but they are delightfully easy all around. For one thing, the long speckled (or pale green or splattered milk-white) leaves that shoot from the base don't wilt as miserably as they do when the sun hits their leaves outdoors. There's nothing as sad as a pouting pulmonaria, but it isn't apt to happen inside, if you keep your plant well watered.

Pulmonarias tend to be deeply rooted plants, so a long tom container will make this more fun and less of a chore. Even after the flowering show is over, you could continue to host a lungwort for its handsome speckled (or otherwise dapper) leaves and still glean the intrigue. Because powdery mildew can be an issue if you plan to hold your lungwort over into summer, you might want to give the plant good air circulation (an open window should do it) and steer away from the solid silver-leaved versions that seem to fall victim to mildew more readily. But for a spring fling, pulmonaria is fairly trouble free.

Among the first plants to pop in the spring garden, *Pulmonaria* 'Raspberry Splash' and *P.* 'Blue Ensign' appear even sooner inside.

TIARELLA CORDIFOLIA

Ever walk into a nursery, see the containers of foamflowers (*Tiarella cordifolia*) in spring, and want to nab a couple for what they do in a pot? Why not? Thanks to totally hyperactive hybridizing programs, we have a plethora of foamflowers (and intergeneric crosses with foamflowers) on the market with foliage bearing all sorts of markings. The leaves are okay and rival your average rex begonia (with a whole lot less fuss about humidity, I might add). They display various dark markings and leaf shapes ranging from maple to bird's foot. But the spring wands of fluffy little whitish-pink flowers (like foam, especially when massed together, which is how they hang out) are an added dimension. Whereas you might walk right by them in a garden, foamflowers are much more of an event in a windowsill.

Foamflowers are disarmingly easy to grow indoors. They often blossom a month or more before their leaves begin to emerge outside, and they stay in bloom for a long duration of fulfillment. In the garden, mine tend to slip away in midsummer heat and lose leaves. But they don't do the same disappearing act inside. I'm beginning to think that they are more suited to life indoors. All they need is shade and moisture (not too much; just don't let them dry out) to furnish loads of pleasure.

Long before the snow has melted, low-light-loving *Tiarella* 'Sky Rocket' bursts into blossom. The foamflowers are cool outside, but they're downright bedazzling indoors.

VIOLA LABRADORICA

You could pretty much host any violet indoors and the result would be heavenly. You would have blossoms long before a single bud unfurled outside, and those flowers would set your spirits on wing. But most violets are prone to spider mites, and their foliage will begin to turn yellow and fail in a typical indoor situation. As soon as the temperatures climb into the 70s, the flowers will stop blooming. And what's a violet without blossoms? On the other hand, *Viola labradorica* keeps performing reliably until the weather becomes quite warm. And it never seems to be bothered by spider mite.

The Labrador violet is adorable. In addition to quantities of perky baby blue blossoms on longish stems, it has deep-green leaves with burgundy undersides. Most violets hug the ground (think shrinking violets). But *Viola labradorica* has leaves that stand slightly above the ground, especially if you grow it in a shady window. And, yet, it has infinite blossoms in the shade. It thrives in an east or west window and will tolerate a south sill, but could probably endure north, too. If you're the type who overwaters, that's groovy (to a degree). If you forget the drinks occasionally, no problem. I include it in my list of favorite plants, especially as a harbinger for a season long before it pops outdoors.

Various spring bloomers

FLOWERS	The main show for all, except heuchera
FOLIAGE	The main show for heuchera, but most have fetching foliage (armeria is a little like tufts of grass, but that's cute too)
OTHER ATTRIBUTES	A preview to an upcoming season up close and personal
EXPOSURE	East or west for most; armeria and papaver produce more flowers in south
WATER REQUIREMENTS	Most spring bloomers prefer evenly moist soil
OPTIMUM NIGHTTIME TEMPERATURE	50–60°F (10–15°C)
RATE OF GROWTH	For the brief time you've got them indoors, this isn't a factor
SOIL TYPE	Well-drained but humusy soil
FERTILIZING	No harm in feeding, but usually not necessary to get the blossoms out of the gate
PROBLEMS	The plants are indoors briefly but several are prone to spider mites. Pulmonaria is susceptible to powdery mildew.

JASMINES

In addition to the lure of scent, *Jasminum polyanthum* is also about its wending vining arms and legs.

JASMINUM LAURIFOLIUM
VAR. LAURIFOLIUM

I WOULD BE lying if I said romance has nothing to do with indoor gardening. In fact, it's all about intimacy all hunkered down, sensual, and exotic. It's heady stuff. It's the smoldering synthesis of the *Rubaiyat* (although jasmines were never actually mentioned in those pages), *Arabian Nights*, and other steamy imagery. That's why we grow jasmines. Their flowers aren't frequent or even particularly noticeable. They aren't wildly handsome plants. But we grow them for their associations, so we can sample a heavy dose of aroma from the depths of some perfumed past. Jasmines deliver an evocative element into our humble homes. That alone is worth plenty.

"Ah, jasmine," the uninitiated might say, as if there's only one jasmine scent and one jasmine aroma. Jasmine takes on many guises. If I had to choose just one jasmine to live with and inhale on a daily basis, it would be *Jasminum laurifolium* var. *laurifolium*, hands down. Saddled with a new, hellishly clumsy name and formerly known as *J. nitidum*, let's just call it the star jasmine (although it's also known as the angel-wing and pinwheel jasmine, but so are several other commonly cultivated plants). Not only does the star jasmine blossom throughout the year, but it emits a fragrance that's more livable than most of its brethren. Of course, the perception of fragrance is highly subjective, but who doesn't like the scent of freshly washed laundry hung on the line? *Jasminum laurifolium* var. *laurifolium* has an outdoorsy-soapy aroma that's universally admired.

Beyond having good scents, *Jasminum laurifolium* var. *laurifolium* flowers are pretty in an open-face, star-shaped, white-tinged-with-pink sort of way. The growth habit is bushy (making them easier to manage than a vine for many indoor gardeners), the plant remains compact, and it has tidy, shiny, deep-green leaves. Grow it in an east or west window and it will thrive. In other words, this is a beginner's jasmine.

If the clean, fresh scent of soap is your perfume of choice, then veer straight for the prolific blooming *Jasminum laurifolium* var. *laurifolium*.

JASMINUM OFFICINALE

Without their scent, jasmine flowers would be nothing to write home about. They're generally dime-size, white or cream, and so unremarkable that you would easily pass them by if they weren't sending their scent-signals floating. *Jasminum officinale*, the poet's jasmine, is particularly modest as a visual package, but it also bears the banner scent we associate with jasmine. Walk by *J. officinale*, and the essence of fine perfume will tickle your nose. It's sweet, seductive, echoingly mysterious, and altogether delightful. If only the vine was easier to grow.

Jasminum officinale isn't on the mainstream plant market, probably because it doesn't lend itself to windowsill cultivation. The vine is loose and gangly. It's prone to browning and dying back. And those divinely fragrant flowers are not sufficiently profuse to lure anyone into adoption. Instead, they are produced in open clusters of two or three flowers grouped together. Ever wonder why fine perfume is so expensive? It's because the top note is this jasmine, and it's stingy with blossoms (and the process of extracting the essence is also incredibly laborious). Granted, the vine can withstand quite cold temperatures. But who lives below 50°F (10°C)? Fortunately, *J. officinale* does equally fine in regular home temperatures. Unlike other jasmines, it prefers a bright south window and mopes with less light. My advice is to leave this jasmine for the perfumers, and go for something more productive and conducive instead.

Although *Jasminum polyanthum* isn't easy to coax into blossom in the average home during winter, if you throw the windows open in early spring, you might just trick it into performing.

JASMINUM POLYANTHUM

Even without blossoms, I'm keen on this vine. It just has a wonderful roving, graceful beauty. If treated well, it always seems to be tidy and well clothed, with segmented leaves running up and down the meandering stems. You can wind it easily around a support or just let it wend its way around the furniture or a curtain rod. But the potential for aroma is an additional perk.

Not everyone agrees that the winter-blooming jasmine's scent is pleasing. Say the word "jasmine," and we're trained to expect good things. But some people jump straight to musk when describing the scent of *Jasminum polyanthum*. Others invoke something more potent. No matter how you feel about the fragrance, the flowers of *J. polyanthum* are unarguably some of the handsomest in the genus. They're white with a throat tinged in rose, and they form constellation-like clusters of stars. Plus, they come in quantity, and that alone is a digression from the rest of the clan.

At any rate, coaxing forth flowers is a feat for dedicated gardeners. The easiest way to attain blossoms is to skip any hopes of a winter display and go straight for a spring performance. To get those midwinter flowers that have secured renown, you would have to leave it outdoors to be exposed to temperatures below 50°F (10°C) for a month or so in autumn while keeping it no warmer than 60°F (15°C) during the day. I find it easier to put this jasmine outside in spring and let it rev up. And if I leave it by the front door without giving it entry, its scent isn't so bottled up, so it's more of a "come hither" and less of an "ugh." Beyond that, *Jasminum polyanthum* tends to be more sensitive to bright light than most jasmines, and it dislikes heavy fertilizer. In other words, generosity in all forms is not appreciated.

JASMINUM SAMBAC

Erase all the common associations of jasmine vines—*Jasminum sambac* is something different entirely. The commonly available form, known as 'Maid of Orleans', has button-size, semi-double blossoms shaped loosely like an African violet with more petals. They are creamy white but burnish to rose-colored before dropping. And they easily drop. Don't transport this jasmine in blossom and expect to show off the flowers at your destination, because it's not going to happen.

Unlike most of the other jasmines, the leaves of *Jasminum sambac* are oval and deep green. But keeping them that shade requires a lot of feeding. Plus, *J. sambac* is a thirsty plant compared to its brethren. But the fragrance is lusty. It combines wine with deep-throated honey and a touch of musk. It is the veiled essence of passion.

JASMINUM TORTUOSUM

In the search for jasmines that perform readily and without hassle, combined with the quest for the sort of scent you can live with happily at close quarters, *Jasminum tortuosum* is a strong contender. It is a wispy, elongated vine with deep-green leaves (and they remain this color even when not being fed a breakfast of champions). The flowers come in small clusters, are pearly white, stay attached to the stem, and emit a fragrance I liken to Ivory soap.

The beauty of *Jasminum tortuosum* is that it doesn't have strong opinions about light, food, water, or temperatures. You can give it any window except north-facing, and it will be just fine. You can forget to water occasionally and it won't pout. And it will thrive whether you live at 50°F (10°C) or 70°F (21°C) (I haven't tried it warmer than that). I fertilize it with the rest of the clan and I've kept it fairly pot-bound, and still it persists in producing a ready supply of those soap-scented flowers. If you like that squeaky clean scent, go for *J. tortuosum*.

Most jasmines aren't thrillers for their physical charms, and *Jasminum tortuosum* will never be accused of being an exhibitionist. But its throaty scent compensates.

Jasminum species

JASMINE

FLOWERS	Mostly star-shaped and white; intensely fragrant
FOLIAGE	Usually long, slender, and deep forest green
OTHER ATTRIBUTES	The fragrance is the stuff of romance
SIZE	Mostly vining
EXPOSURE	East or west
WATER REQUIREMENTS	Moderate, except *Jasminum sambac*, which is thirsty
OPTIMUM NIGHTTIME TEMPERATURE	50–60°F (10–15°C)
RATE OF GROWTH	Very rapid
SOIL TYPE	Good organic potting soil with compost included
FERTILIZING	Early spring to late autumn, might require a winter snack
PROBLEMS	Too much light can cause *Jasminum polyanthum* to scorch. Mealy bugs can be an issue.

KANGAROO PAWS

I can't fathom why *Anigozanthos* 'Bush Tango' isn't more prevalent as a houseplant. The flowers are bright, perky, quirky, and abundant.

I ADMIT THAT I'm easily amused in early spring. Plants that wouldn't normally get past the bouncer come filing through my front door. Just like the rest of humanity, I'm a sucker at the flower shows. I draw the line at dragging home those frangipani cigar-like sticks that have smaller-than-scant chances of sending out a root, let alone blooming. And I walk right on by *Dendrobium* orchids that will clearly never live up to the glossy photo tacked up beside the dying epiphytes on display. But I've come home with my fair share of quirky succulents. I'm apt to leap for anything else that veers off the beaten track. So I've always wondered why no one sells kangaroos paws (anigozanthos) for spring revelry.

Perhaps the problem lies in the fact that anigozanthos doesn't confine its performance to spring. It blooms sporadically through late winter, spring, and summer, with a smattering of flowers dribbling into autumn as well. It's not like we haven't seen anigozanthos since last spring and we're starved.

When they are in blossom, anigozanthos flowers are head-turners that would have the potential to pull in the crowds to a flower-show booth. The common name says it all—the flowers are long, fuzzy, tubular affairs groping out in elongated clusters. Each flower is only the size of a tootsie roll, but the tip opens up into something that resembles groping animal claws (without the barbs). The interior is green; the exterior might be golden, orange, or pink (depending on the cultivar); and it has a felt-like, touchy-feely texture. The blossoms are brandished on strong foliar spikes, which do not need staking, held above clumps of leathery pointed leaves that resemble fuzzy grass. Not surprisingly, kangaroo paws are native to Western Australia, where some other fairly bizarre members of the botanical kingdom reside. Who doesn't love an oddball, especially in spring?

Not only are these crowd-pleasers, but they are astonishingly easy to grow, despite their Australian connection. Indoors or outside on the porch (in summer), they require very little prodding to burst into yet another flush of blossoms. You can forget to water them occasionally (don't push it, or the foliage will whither and mope), you can overwater them occasionally (again, there are limits), and you can bake them in bright light or give them shade. But they blossom best with good light. And a kangaroo paw without blossoms is along the same lines as an iris without flowers.

The show goes on with scarcely a pause from season to season, except perhaps early winter. As soon as the days begin to lengthen, flower spikes develop. When I first encountered kangaroo paws, they were tall, rangy things, and not really conducive to your typical window. Breeders have now come forth with a generation of compact kangaroo paws that stand about 2 to 3 feet (60–90cm)

tall when in blossom and last for months before fading. I've hosted the glowing orange 'Bush Tango' and pink 'Bush Blaze' in my home.

Forcing yourself to cut back flower stalks that still hold a slight hint of color after the party is over is pretty much the full extent of the chores that accompany growing anigozanthos. Mine sometimes get brown leaf tips that should be snipped off. Every once in a while, one leaf in a fan (they form fans off a clumping rhizome) turns ugly and needs removal. That's the sum total of your interaction. Beyond that, it's gravy.

Anigozanthos flavidus cultivars

KANGAROO PAWS

FLOWERS	Golden, pink, or orange kangaroo paw–like flowers
FOLIAGE	Iris-like fans of furry green leaves
OTHER ATTRIBUTES	New cultivars are scaled down in size, making this a great windowsill plant
SIZE	1–2 feet (30–61cm) in height
EXPOSURE	South, east, or west
WATER REQUIREMENTS	Tolerates sporadic watering, but best to keep lightly moist
OPTIMUM NIGHTTIME TEMPERATURE	50–60°F (10–15°C)
RATE OF GROWTH	Medium
SOIL TYPE	Any rich, humusy soil
FERTILIZING	Early spring to late autumn
PROBLEMS	Leaf edges can brown

PRIMULAS

Like its parent, *Primula auricula*, *Primula ×pubescens* has a wonderful farina in the center of each uniquely colored flower, plus a haunting fragrance. I pair mine with ferns, such as *Polypodium formosanum*.

THE 'FLAMING PURISSIMA' tulips have joined my magnolia out front to make the view from my office window absolutely breathtaking. Granted, it's tough to confine my concentration indoors. But that's where I work until 5 p.m., when they unlock the chains that hitch me to the computer. Fortunately, *Primula ×pubescens* is sitting by my side in full flower to sweeten the time at my desk.

Without the auricula hybrids (and *Primula ×pubescens* is *P. auricula × P. hirsuta*), life would be dull and lackluster through winter and early spring. Even with all my other houseplants, the auricula hybrids are paramount. And for good reason: small clusters of nickel-size flowers open in improbable shades of cranberry, deep purple, wine red, and mauve running in bands. But there's more. The center of each flower is dusted with a signature powder that gives it substance. Meanwhile, the leaves are thick, leathery, and also powdered with stardust. The fancy, named-variety, green- or gray-flowered exhibition auriculas are far too pricey and finicky for me to grow. Nevertheless, my versions are sufficiently enthralling to send me hopping up periodically to catch yet another glance at their flowers.

Dangle an auricula hybrid in my line of vision, and I'll be waving dollar bills in response. The collection grows. In autumn, I repotted the whole crew. I gave them a rich soil mix heavy with compost and sank the rosettes into the soil (with time, they tend to push their shoulders up and out). I didn't graduate each plant into a larger container; instead, I shook away their

Nothing could be more cheerful or scream spring like primroses. Plus, *Primula denticulata* 'Confetti Blue' and *Primula denticulata* 'Rubins' are no-brainers—they burst into blossom in a blink.

soil and gave them fresh underpinnings. Then I bestowed the gang with prime seating in a west window throughout autumn and early winter. They did fine until the days lengthened, and then the wilting began. So I sprinted into action and moved the whole flock into a spot in the greenhouse that gets no direct sun. They expressed gratitude. Although auricula hybrids certainly don't need a greenhouse, they like the ambient indirect light. They've been blooming for several months now and coloring my life. A bunch of Easter eggs couldn't do a better job.

This has been going on for a few years. The auricula hybrid primroses are part of the permanent cast in the house. But they're joined by a chorus of spring-blooming primroses that perform for my edification indoors and then add their voice permanently (I hope) to the primrose garden under the black walnut outside. Who can resist *Primula denticulata*, the precocious drumstick primrose? Not only does the duration of their glory start earlier and last longer inside, but their little round drumsticks aren't splattered by the constant mud that kicks up in spring showers. Equally fab is the parrot-green-flowered *P. vulgaris* 'Francesca'. When it first hit the scene, I couldn't resist adding it to the compendium inside. Like its kin, 'Francesca' was a raving success.

The open-door policy doesn't extend throughout the entire clan. I go only for spring bloomers, knowing the house will be too warm over the summer. I steer away from the whitefly-attracting (and dermatologically irritating) *Primula obconica*. Similar troublemakers are the ordinary British primroses, *P.* ×*polyantha* (the primroses you find in the supermarket with little nosegays of brightly colored blossoms nestled into a rosette of leaves), now classifying as Pruhonicensis hybrids. They cause no skin angst, but get spider mites, whiteflies, and aphids. Plus, they always seem to be wilted—even in a shady spot. Who needs that?

If you want to try primroses, here's the secret: use indirect light and never let them wilt. And by all means, whisk them outside when they finish blossoming. Outdoors, they give additional years of pleasure. It's the best of all worlds.

Primula species
PRIMROSE

FLOWERS	Colorful flowers held above the foliage
FOLIAGE	Rosettes of leaves, silverish gray for the auricula hybrids, green and deeply veined for the drumsticks
OTHER ATTRIBUTES	Hardy outdoors; plant them in the garden when they finish flowering
SIZE	Under 6 inches (15cm) in height
EXPOSURE	Diffuse east or west
WATER REQUIREMENTS	Keep evenly moist but not drenching wet
OPTIMUM NIGHTTIME TEMPERATURE	50–55°F (10–12°C)
RATE OF GROWTH	Slow
SOIL TYPE	Good organic potting soil mix with compost included
FERTILIZING	I give the auriculas fish emulsion in late winter and spring; I don't fertilize the other primulas
PROBLEMS	Mealy bugs can be a pressing issue, but only occur when growing conditions aren't ideal. Aphids, whiteflies, and spider mites occur on the other primulas. Some primulas can cause a dermatological reaction.

SEEDS

The vegetables I start in small seed flats are eventually transplanted to individual pots before weather permits shifting the whole crop outside.

STARTING SEEDS IS hope. Starting seeds is promise. Starting seeds is the lure dangled to prod me out of bed early in the morning, when spring is not really keeping abreast of the calendar. Curiosity over whether something has sprouted gets me up, dressed, and wielding the mister. At the flip end of the day, it coaxes me to check the seed flats one more time before going to bed. Although this book isn't about vegetable and outdoor flower gardens, starting seeds for those venues is one of my windowsill's major roles.

Every spring, I save money by starting my own seedlings for the garden. Actually, budget-consciousness is only one motivation for planting seed. By ordering seed from mail-order providers, I can find interesting varieties that give me the edge over the neighbors. Plus, with the numbers available using a seed packet, I can plant novelties and heirlooms in quantities that would break the bank. It gives the garden cohesion. And, as we all know, you need at least 25 of anything before the neighbors notice.

I have a fluorescent light stand in a side room. It's a veritable tower of lights and trays with heating mats. I never use it anymore. Instead, I start my seedlings in a warm, sunny, south-facing window that I visit frequently with a spritzer (and this is one valid application for a mister). This method might not work so well in March. But by April, the sunbeams have increased sufficiently to make those babies sprout without artificial lights; plus, my method builds stronger seedlings. And by starting late, I can shuffle the transplanted seedlings in their individual pots outdoors during (warm) days rather

Maybe not as glam as the more exotic houseplants, trays of vegetable seedlings are equally essential.

than overcrowding my already jammed windows. Every evening, I rescue them inside, where they perch on temporary tables just footsteps from the door so I can trundle them out again before I become ensconced in my office for the day.

I know what you're thinking. Sowing seed is labor intensive, no question about it. But it's worth the effort. I use little seed flats recycled year after year. I fill them with organic potting soil mix (I don't bother with special seed-starting soil mixtures), tamp it down, sprinkle the seed on top, and cover them if the packet directions suggest doing so. The sowing isn't the time drain; it's the constant sprinkling that steals me away from my computer. I've found that any type of watering-can nozzle washes them out, so I minister to their watering needs by wielding a mister until they've successfully sprouted and are well on their way to sending down anchoring roots.

Various seedlings

EXPOSURE	**South**
WATER REQUIREMENTS	**Use a mister to apply a gentle spray of water. Never allow seedlings to dry out.**
OPTIMUM NIGHTTIME TEMPERATURE	**60–65°F (15–18°C) (that's all I can muster, but the sun warms the seedlings)**
RATE OF GROWTH	**Fast**
SOIL TYPE	**Well-drained potting soil**
FERTILIZING	**None**
PROBLEMS	**Fungus gnats can become an issue if the seed flats are kept too moist**

Because the seedlings are all destined for life outdoors, I get them accustomed to the change in climate as soon as possible by bringing them outdoors. The trick lies in remembering to whisk them inside before the temperatures fall in late afternoon.

When the time comes, I transplant them into individual pots (I hate cell packs—just a personal prejudice). This is the only instance when I use plastic pots, and I recycle them year after year. I wish that I had enough quaint little clay thumb pots to service all my seedlings, but alas, I grow hundreds and hundreds. Sometimes you've got to skip the aesthetics and go for efficiency.

What do I gain from all this fussing? Everything from celery to delphiniums. I start my own heirloom cabbages, regional broccoli, annual rudbeckia, cut flower basil, and zinnias like you'll never find at the corner garden center. By the time frost is no longer a danger, my garden is well on its way.

Not many plants stay inside during the summer sojourn, but succulents are so low maintenance (and I would be so lost without them) that they remain inside. So does Einstein's fescue.

Just like gardeners everywhere, I welcome summer with open arms. In fact, like most of humanity, I warm to sunshine, the great outdoors, the hum of industrious insects, and the distant war whoops of children playing on athletic fields. With the same outrush of pent-up kinetic energy, I heave a sigh of relief when the forecasters stop harping on the F-word (frost, of course). I passionately embrace the growing season when it finally stabilizes. But I have mixed emotions.

Around here, summer means I won't be quite so close with the houseplants. For the rest of the year, we're intimate. We share space. I maneuver around them, and they brush against my thigh as I make my way from desk to telephone and from dinner table to front door. But with gardens galore on my property's seven acres and plants outdoors vying for attention, my affinities and time are just as split as everyone else's. That's why most of my houseplants are outward bound in summer.

I miss them. I miss the constant physical contact despite the fact that, in their outdoor summer quarters, they're just footsteps away. I suffer a sense of spatial emptiness indoors even though several favorites are kept in for sentimental reasons. But for a few months I wave a fond farewell to manipulating the sloshing watering can back and forth from the kitchen sink to the distant points in the house. With the increased sun of summer, houseplants dry out much more frequently.

And the plants are proverbial happy campers outdoors. They feel the gentle breeze rustling their leaves, which are freshened by dews and washed by sprinkles. They have ringside seats for watching the skateboarders glide by and hearing the car stereos. Or, from a less anthropomorphic view, they are street performers in the town's comings and goings. So far, not one representative from the steady stream of joggers, dog walkers, and postal workers has swung into the driveway to pay my houseplants their compliments. But I know they're watching. I know they've got their noses poised and their eyes peeled for that first promisingly plump bud on the passion flower to open.

As much as I dote on the houseplants indoors, they make a proud showing outside as well. Plus, they impress the neighbors.

The beauty of sending plants to summer camp comes with the perk of reduced watering. When drinks are dispensed with a hose, it takes a fraction of the time.

SUMMER AGENDA

Summer is a double-edged sword. Who doesn't love the opportunity to throw open the windows and feel the warmth of the sun falling on your forehead through the panes? But summer also cranks up the chore load when ministering to container plants. That's why most of my plants are sent outside, where the duties are divided between Mother Nature and me.

From a houseplant's perspective, it's like someone turned up the high beams. For plants indoors, the sun comes streaming through the windows to serve up a full dose of seething-hot wattage. Here in New England, that's a welcome thing for light-loving plants. They bask in the bright light and add new growth galore. In the South, Southwest, and Midwest, the ramped-up solar exposure can be brutal unless it's filtered through a curtain. Wherever you live, take a moment to assess what's going on light-wise.

Even in New England, the story changes drastically for plants that aren't rigged up genetically for sunbathing. Sometimes low-light lovers of the botanical kind gravitate onto south-facing windowsills. During all seasons but summer, a south-facing window usually won't harm them. But in summer, I've seriously scorched orchids and African violets (even *Sinningia* species that come from a caudex) by forgetting to move them when the sun shifts. The moral of the story is to monitor the way sun moves into your home. No need to bring in the light meters; just eyeball the situation and move plants immediately based on the beat of the rays. But don't hope that the plants will send out warnings before suffering from oversaturation. Scorching and foliar damage from too much sun generally happens without forewarning (although for some plants, the new growth might be disfigured or reduced in size). Fortunately, damage is generally not lethal. New, unscathed leaves will resume when you hasten the plant to a more appropriate position. But the ordeal is painful for everyone involved.

Some plants remain inside, but the bulk of my botanical collection goes outdoors. The egress isn't haphazard. According to their light requirements, the houseplants have assigned seats. The sun-lovers are marched onto the sun-baked back patio. However, before taking up their permanent stations, they're given a critical adjustment period. This part is important. No matter how seemingly bright their window seat was, the sun isn't as intense as it is outside. Blasting noon sun can be a killer. In the best of all worlds, time your exodus for a rainy, cloudy spate of weather. If you can't, protect all sun-loving plants in partial shade (or covered by cheesecloth) for the first few days when making the transition from inside to outdoors. After a few days of shade, my houseplants-on-vacation receive a parceled-out dose of sun. After a week or so of coddling, they're finally exposed to the full brunt of noonday sunbeams.

Meanwhile, shade-tolerant plants, which constitute the bulk of my collection, go out front to lounge under the protective skirts of a massive sugar maple. By that time, the maple is fully clothed and capable of casting an expansive shadow, so no transitional intervention is needed. The same bleachers the houseplants sat on inside are moved into position outdoors to receive the crowd. Plus, dozens of indoor plants spill out the front door to form a bounteous tableau outside. I spread mine out. But you don't need acreage to do the summer-camp thing—it can happen on your city terrace or fire escape.

All that additional light has other ramifications, as well. Watering is more of an issue in summer. Generally speaking, container plants need more frequent watering as light levels increase. When the temperatures are soaring and the sun is beating, plants with abundant foliage might need water more than once a day. In general, I minimize watering chores by selecting plants that are not drama queens. Plants that swoon after only a few hours of dry roots aren't for me. I want to have a life.

I have no experience with soil-wetting agents because I veer toward a more natural approach to gardening. But my gut reaction is that water-retaining soil additives are not the ticket for plants that prefer to dry out between waterings, such as begonias. Similarly, I have not used drip systems because I'm based at home, and I like the intimacy and familiarity of caring for plants. But not everyone is homebound. Irrigation tubes are certainly an option, especially if you do not have a lifestyle that allows constant contact with your plants at home. Needless to say, a container must be wide enough to balance the accoutrements of drip irrigation, which brings me to container sizes and repotting.

It's a good idea to check all your plants coming into summer to make sure they are not pot-bound. You will save yourself time and potential heartbreak. While in the process of ferrying most of my houseplants outdoors, I knock them out of their pots and check the root systems; a quick appraisal is the fastest way to diagnose a plant's overall health, and it does absolutely no harm. When a plant's roots have filled a container and there is little or no soil showing along the outside edges of the root ball, that plant becomes a water-monger. Every time you turn around, it is dry or wilted. Some plants can tolerate

pinched toes and the resulting thirst better than others. But if the root ball is all roots and no soil, you are stressing the plant on many levels, including nutrition and moisture. And that is not a good thing.

Then again, do not overpot plants just because the growing season has arrived and the houseplants are going out to play. When you water a plant that has large expanses of excess soil without root penetration to drink up the water, the rootless soil will remain damp, and that can lead to trouble. Plus, when repotting, remember that autumn will come someday. Because I'm hosting multitudes of plants (and trying to convince you to do likewise), each one can't be an instamatic incredible hulk (except the staghorn fern...and the agave). To maximize my space and keep every plant happy but not piggy, I give graduations of an inch or two at a time. This system has served me well.

Summer is when plants crave fertilizer. Since I go organic with fish emulsion, I fertilize every three weeks or so. That's not sufficient for some super hungry plants, such as gardenias. But they let me know when they need food. When their leaves begin to pale from deep green to a lighter shade, dinner is served. A little sensitivity goes a long way with plants. Sometimes you have to fill custom orders in nature.

When mercury soars in summer, we wilt, but plants love it—if they receive sufficient water. I'm a fan person myself, as opposed to air-conditioning, and find that plants do not mind a light wind—in fact, they love a little breeze. Indeed, for some plants (rex begonias come to mind), stagnant air can lead to powdery mildew. Air conditioners are okay if they do not blow cold air on the plants.

High humidity is also fine for most plants. Even succulents take it into their stride on a temporary basis. Over the long haul, it might get under their skin, but almost all houseplants can handle the occasional stifling heat-and-humidity wave.

During the summer, your plants both indoors and outside might be so delighted with the warm weather and increased sun of an open window or an outdoor location that they make new growth. When the light quality increases, plants tend to make tighter growth compared to the spindly appendages that happen in autumn and winter. If you want to keep the plant within bounds, prune back that new growth. (If you are aiming for more mass, let it grow.) Pruning also encourages a denser specimen. Prune to shape in early summer to give

the plant time to make side branches and react to your input. But do not fear pruning. I am a major advocate for brandishing prune shears on a regular basis. We benefit from periodic haircuts, and so do plants.

While my houseplants are outside having fun, I do likewise. I hit the perennial borders and concentrate on the great outdoors. I know plenty of people who incorporate their plants into the garden during the growing season, and that's brilliant. I lack the energy to run around digging up all 250 of them at summer's end, so I leave them in their containers. And I've got to say, they look glorious out there.

The bleachers in front of the house are shaded by a huge sugar maple, which further reduces the need to water.

BROMELIADS

So you've invited the town socialite over for dinner. *Tillandsia fasciculata* var. *hondurensis, Tillandsia stricta* (hard-leaved form), and *Tillandsia caput-medusae* make edgy centerpieces— no florist needed.

IN THE MASS exodus that happens every summer as soon as I can send the indoor contingent out to revel on the front and back porches, some plants are held back. I need them close, but it helps if they're low maintenance. The bromeliads have all the qualifications to remain indoors year-round. The tillandsia nests in a bowl and doesn't jump hoops. It doesn't grow by leaps and bounds. It's pretty much the same today as it was three months ago. But that's why I love it. It's solidly, constantly, dependably, exceptionally, superlatively gorgeous.

I don't mind if a plant grows slowly, just as long as it looks great along the way. That would describe most bromeliads, the members of the pineapple family. At any stage in their maturity, they are sensational. Many have intriguing foliage, most eventually have blossoms as well, and almost all of the bromeliads in popular cultivation are ridiculously easy to host in anyone's home.

There's a lot of diversity in physical traits within the *Bromeliaceae* family. I imagine some are slackers, but members of the pineapple family tend to come up with some of the snappiest foliage in the plant world. We're talking leaves that stem from a central rosette and are noticeably striped or spotted, bright red or silver. Some are broad, smooth, and strap-like, while others have serrated edges. Some stick straight up, while others curl around like ram's horns. And the flowers are equally diverse. They jut from wands stacked up like rattlesnake rattlers, or they settle within a ray of surrounding leaves. The pineapple, ananas, is topped by edible fruit. So far, I've never met a bromeliad I didn't like. This takes a toll on my wallet.

Orthophytum gurkenii
grows slowly, but it
makes a statement
every inch of the way.

Depending on the time of day and the moon cycle, I am in the throes of an ardent crush on one bromeliad or another. If I fail to get this manuscript to my publisher in time, it will be because the tillandsia and I were making love. Every once in a while, I jump up to get yet one more glimpse of my *Orthophytum gurkenii*. (I actually carried it home from Michigan so it wouldn't get mauled or nicked by airport security.) Or a vriesea might be my current heartthrob. Or it may be a cryptanthus. I'm fickle.

A few air plants, tilland-sias, invariably remain inside over summer. If you haven't encountered one of these sea urchin–like little wonders, you need to wrangle an intro-duction. They are enthralling. As the nickname implies, they need no soil. Amazingly, they can survive without being planted into any sort of growing medium. Some

look like spiny little silver balls. Others have leathery, felted leaves in a Shirley Temple hairdo. They range in size from golf ball to soccer ball. Not only do I find them infinitely entertaining, but they're so easy to host. I keep most of mine in glass jars, cups, beakers, and tureens, so I just soak them weekly for a few hours and then toss out the water. Outdoors, I tend to forget to drain off the water, with disastrous results.

The rest of the bromeliads need some sort of anchor-ing medium. They have long, strap-like leaves that form a vase in the center. Some are smooth, like the vrieseas. Others bare razor-sharp teeth on their edges, like the orthophytum that I (painfully) carried home by hand. Many have foliage that has abso-lutely outlandish markings. *Vriesea hieroglyphica* has wavy, irregular stripes across its brittle leaves. *Vriesea gigantea* has a cross-thatched web of pencil-thin lines. The aechmeas have striped leaves but add brightly colored blossoms to the brew. Neoregelias have spots or stripes going the long way up leaves that often blush cherry-red toward the center. When the leaves form a cup, such as in the aechmeas and billbergias, they love having their vase filled with water; in fact, that's their preferred mode of drinking. But keep their moss-based medium (the preferred potting mixture) lightly moist as well. Don't over- or under-water them, although they will endure a lot of torment before voicing displeasure.

Bright, indirect light is best for bromeliads, especially in summer. During the rest of the year, pretty much any exposure will work except north. But baking sun in summer can be stressing. By the end of the season, you might have achieved blossoms. If so, the flowering rosette will die back. Don't take offense, don't panic, and definitely don't toss the plant. Although a new rosette might not be visible, it is probably poised in the wings if you've been giving the plant the proper care. Keep treating your bromeliad right and the replacement will become manifest. And then it's another year of seduction and split affinities. If you thought that you were free to post blogs and check out Facebook pages without distractions, you were dead wrong.

Container gardening is all about pairing pots with plants. The baby blue pigmentation in the leaves of the earth star, *Cryptanthus* 'Black Mystic', is more pronounced if the container underlines the color.

Who needs flowers when you've got something as weird as *Tillandsia stricta* to contemplate?

Various members of the

Bromeliaceae, including *Aechmea*, *Billbergia*, *Cryptanthus*, *Neoregelia*, *Tillandsia*, and *Vriesea*

AIR PLANTS, PINEAPPLE

FLOWERS	Various presentations of blooms coming from bracts or snuggled in the vase of the leaves
FOLIAGE	Extremely colorful and riveting in form
OTHER ATTRIBUTES	Do you know of any other plants that grow on air and air alone?
SIZE	2–24 inches (5–61cm) in height
EXPOSURE	East or west
WATER REQUIREMENTS	Water when dry for most bromeliads; soak air plants once a week for a few hours
OPTIMUM NIGHTTIME TEMPERATURE	55–70°F (12–21°C)
RATE OF GROWTH	Slow
SOIL TYPE	A combination of moss and wood chips works—most like an acidic soil, and air plants need no underpinning
FERTILIZING	Early spring to late autumn, but not critical
PROBLEMS	Pest-free for me, prefer not to dry out completely

CROTONS

Put *Codiaeum variegatum* var. *pictum* 'Gloriosum Superbum' in the wrong setting, and even this flashy plant seems hackneyed. Give it the right container and it rises to the occasion.

AS A RULE, I am not sucked into the flashy vortex when it comes to tropical plants. I like a spark as much as the next guy, but a little zing of bright color pretty much does it for me. For the most part, my houseplant collection takes its cue from the same design tenets that rule outdoors: A little showing off is encouraged, but upstaging everything else is not cool.

I couldn't resist a couple of perfectly matched, fiesta-colored crotons when they went on sale halfway through summer. Despite the fact that they tend to be associated with malls (and who wants to bring them to mind?), the garden was in a serious lull. I saw *Codiaeum variegatum* var. *pictum* 'Gloriosum Superbum' and felt uplifted.

I gave a pair some snappy containers in keeping with the mood of my place. I had a couple of metal Industrial Era canisters with drainage that bridged the gap between the ultra-tropical look and my equally uncompromisingly New England cottage front porch. That's the trick. Given the right trappings, you can marry the tropics with just about any vernacular.

If ever there was a plant that tickled a smile onto the lips of everyone who walked their dog for the rest of the summer, it was the croton. In the post office and at the dump, they all gave me a high-five. Inside, I did a victory lap.

The beauty of the crotons is they require almost no care. And that's a good trait on a front porch. I stationed them where the hose doesn't quite reach, so they did not receive the usual regular dousing. Did they quibble? No. Did they pout? Never. I guess that's why they earned mall status.

Now that I've admitted the torture sequence that I inflicted on my crotons, I'll tell you how to treat them right. Give crotons indirect light, water them regularly (when grown indoors over the winter, they tend to be thirsty), and there's not much else to your duties. Granted, they will sit in suspended animation, but they do thrill the crowd. Which might be another reason why they are so often invited to dwell where the masses gather.

Codiaeum variegatum var. *pictum* 'Gloriosum Superbum'

CROTON

FLOWER	None
FOLIAGE	Extremely colorful
OTHER ATTRIBUTES	Pretty much maintenance free
SIZE	1–2 feet (30–61cm) in height
EXPOSURE	East or west
WATER REQUIREMENTS	Thirsty but forgiving outdoors
OPTIMUM NIGHTTIME TEMPERATURE	55–70°F (12–21°C)
RATE OF GROWTH	Painfully slow
SOIL TYPE	Any rich, humusy soil
FERTILIZING	Early spring to late autumn, but not critical—they seem to be in suspended animation regardless of whether you feed them
PROBLEMS	Can drop leaves if totally dried out. Crotons are particularly toxic.

EUCOMIS

You need not look far for a pineapple lily. Recently, it's been possible to find *Eucomis comosa* 'Leia' in supermarkets for late-summer thrills.

EVERY YEAR, THE back patio hosts a totally different configuration of plants, depending on my inclinations and how successfully I've fended off the merchants at the local plant sale. Some years, half the dahlias remain clustered around the back door because they're too riveting to send farther afield. Other years, I load as many herbs as possible into containers and sit them by the door knowing that I will be making mad sprints between the boiling soup and the seasonings. But there are some constants. On an annual basis, a few pineapple lilies (eucomis) are part of the display. If gaudy colors alone groove you, you might not notice them initially. But if a eucomis is in blossom, sooner or later it will turn your head.

I grow eucomis because they require almost no upkeep. Initially, the bulbs are potted in a shallow container (they don't like to be overwatered) with their neck and the flare to their shoulders showing, sort of like a turnip. After the ugly weather has shut down the summer performance, I store the bulbs throughout the winter, out of sight and mind. I store them in their containers (I use a closet, but just about any dark, dry space will do), so there is no need to repot the eucomis when they are fetched from the dark recesses of the house. I just tidy up their pots, add a little fresh soil if needed, and commence with watering. Often, they have begun to show signs of sprouting even before they see the light of day and the rejuvenating sprinkle of a hose. But when they are cracked out of their dormant digs, they begin to grow in earnest, sending up furls of leaves from the bulb, like a rosebud about to pop. Then I bring them out again when danger of frost is just a distant memory.

It's a long stint of glory from the time *Eucomis comosa* 'Leia' first opens until it fades.

Eucomis are among the few bulbs to start their entertainment segment even before flowering begins. The leaves are thick (almost succulent), long, thin, pointed, and comely in their own right. They sometimes have speckling (I am thinking in particular of 'Van der Merwei') or they might be dark maroon ('Sparkling Burgundy' comes to mind). And then along comes the flower presentation that has won the plant its pineapple connection. The flowers themselves surround long stems (with the exception of *Eucomis* 'Van der Merwei', with 4-inch [10cm] spires) in a series of open-face stars colored white, cream (with a maroon rim in the case of *E. autumnalis*), or pink-raspberry. At the tip of the spike sits the pineapple-like topknot of leaves. They last for weeks in prime condition, and pollinators pay court. Then they form fat, swollen seedpods that look almost like plastic.

I suppose you could plant eucomis in the ground. That's how they grow in their native South Africa. But they seem more suited to display in containers rather than being planted directly in the soil. This trait alone puts them in the houseplant category. That's one reason my eucomis have survived year after year. Once a nonhardy bulb gets into the soil, what are the chances it will be dug up and brought into safety before the weather smites it into mush? In a pot, a bulb can be whisked in and out at whim. If the eucomis are still performing in autumn, which is generally the case, I move the act inside for the duration. Then it's an easy shift over to the closet after the final curtain call. Die-hard that it is, sometimes my eucomis does not want to quit for the year. The flowers begin to look weary, summer is long gone, and I've moved on to other dalliances. So I just pull the plug and stop watering. The shock treatment always sends the message that it's time for bed.

Eucomis make nearly no demands on your time. Of course, the plant would like to be watered when the soil goes dry, but it does not hand out demerits if you forget. Overwatering might be more of an issue, so I do not recommend hooking this plant into a constant drip system outdoors. Other than that, pineapple lilies are absolutely apropos for mixed containers, where they are worthy of centerfold status.

Eucomis species
and cultivars

EUCOMIS

ALSO CALLED: pineapple lily

FLOWERS	A pineapple-like topknot crowning the foliage
FOLIAGE	Long and fanning from the base, sometimes speckled, sometimes burgundy, always tidy
OTHER ATTRIBUTES	The whole package is handsome
SIZE	4–20 inches (10–50cm) in height
EXPOSURE	South
WATER REQUIREMENTS	Moderate, but don't overwater
OPTIMUM NIGHTTIME TEMPERATURE	50–65°F (10–18°C)
RATE OF GROWTH	Shoot up quickly from bulbs in spring
SOIL TYPE	Any rich, humusy, but well-drained soil mix
FERTILIZING	Summer only when in growth
PROBLEMS	Dislike overwatering; no pests that I've experienced. Keep all members of the *Liliaceae* family away from pets who are prone to ingest, especially cats.

FUCHSIA

WHEN I BOUGHT my eighteenth-century cottage adjacent to its converted barn on the main street in town, I figured my role was to give passersby a "grandmother's house" experience. So I marched a quaint little perennial garden up to the front door, set out rocking chairs, and tried my best to coax roses up the pillars that supported the porch. I knew that I succeeded in my mission when I came home from work one day to find the town historian, a rumpled old fellow fond of wandering the street, rocking away. He took a liking to the porch, filled me in on the town's past, and counted the cars going by. I tried to give him suitable surroundings year after year, but drew the line at fuchsia baskets.

Don't misunderstand. I have nothing against fuchsias. In fact, I'm a sucker for the single-flowered versions.

I keep them in the summer and I can't bear to part with them in the winter. Upright fuchsias are some of my favorite plants. But I detest hanging basket plants. Maybe it's the macramé association, or perhaps it's all those retail years of conking my head on low-hanging pots or mounting ladders to water those beyond my reach. I find hanging baskets to be a bear. Indoors, their saucers are forever overflowing onto the floor. They're awkward, they block incoming light, and they swing. Outside is no better. They have to be "grounded" in a stiff wind, they're difficult to water (and monitor for their watering needs), and they dry out twice as quickly as containers sitting on terra firma. I could go on, but you get the gist.

My dislike for baskets extends to my distaste for fuchsias bred specifically for hanging around. No doubt about it, they're flashy. But they tend to succumb to fungal diseases. They wilt easily (generally because of an overdose of light or heat), but the solution does not necessarily lie in watering; fuchsias detest overwatering. In other words, it's difficult to read their body language. Sun is death to them. You've got a plant with baggage.

All that grumbling aside, there are plenty of fuchsias in my life, especially in summer. I prefer the much more amiable, upright, small-flowering group stemming from *Fuchsia magellanica*. Their leaves are relatively small, and they tend to have modest double or semi-double flowers. Some personal favorites include 'Tom Thumb', 'Little Jewel', and 'Hawkshead'. True, their flowers in no way match the size of the beefiest basket brethren, but they are still remarkable in their signature earring configuration of tube leading into winged, flaring sepals above the dangling, skirt-like corolla. Not only are they smaller-size nuggets, but they can be equally colorful, providing a hit of purple and red, as well as more hushed shades. The miniatures have a tight habit with stems that don't break off (unlike the basket types). Like other fuchsias, they prefer indirect light. Most important, they flower profusely without bother. Comparatively, they're a cakewalk.

A close second for compatibility in the average home is the 'Gartenmeister Bonstedt' types stemming from *Fuchsia triphylla*. Their performance is legendary. They produce long, tubular, oboe-shaped flowers throughout the summer and combine those abundant blossoms with long leaves. Not all the offshoots from *F. triphylla* have intriguing foliage, but there is potential. Deep-burgundy leaves enhance 'Gartenmeister Bonstedt' and other cultivars in the group blush sunset shades. Plus, members of the *F. triphylla* group seem to tolerate more light than other fuchsias (don't push it, though).

I always hesitate to bring fuchsias inside in autumn. After all, what's the incentive? Only the *Fuchsia triphylla*, types such as 'Gartenmeister Bonstedt', blossom over the winter. And indoors, they tend to be whitefly magnets (and they attract spider mites and aphids, and are prone to botrytis). But this year, I tried 'Traudchen Bonstedt' because I couldn't cut its profuse performance of peach-colored blossoms short and look myself in the mirror. Not only did it continue to blossom without hesitation throughout the winter, it was impervious to problems.

Here's my advice: Don't listen to me. Grow whichever fuchsias strike your fancy over the summer. Give them liberally to whomever you want to honor on Mother's Day. Follow your heart. Keep them in a shady location, meaning a spot that gets no full sun at any time of day. Protect them from downfalls. Water them evenly. Don't take it personally when they unceremoniously go to the big hanging basket heaven in the sky. If they don't take their leave of you voluntarily in autumn, coax them toward the compost pile when frost is threatened. Only bring in fuchsias in *Fuchsia triphylla* or dwarf groups. Indoors, give them good light, but not full sun, and water sparingly (never let water sit on the leaves—aim your stream at the soil). Keep them in cool temperatures, around 55–60°F (12–15°C) indoors. But don't get invested. The moment they cause trouble or trouble comes to them, send them to the compost. It's not worth the risk to the other, less problematic plants in your family.

The miniatures have it all over the standard-size fuchsias. With a modest footprint, *Fuchsia* Shadow Dancers 'Marcia' packs in fashion statement–worthy color.

The long, oboe-shaped blossoms of *Fuchsia* 'Traudchen Bonstedt' might not be as flashy as more colorful fuchsias. But you can't beat their copacetic disposition.

Fuchsia cultivars

FUCHSIA

ALSO CALLED: **lady's eardrops**

FLOWERS	Colorful purple, magenta, and other shades. Earring-like in shape.
FOLIAGE	Blush for the 'Gartenmeister Bonstedt' hybrids, otherwise green. Micro-mini-leaf types are available, as well as well as the standard issue.
OTHER ATTRIBUTES	Unique blossoms your mother will love
SIZE	Varies greatly from 2–3 feet (61–90cm) in height to danglers; can be pruned smaller
EXPOSURE	East or west indoors; outside it wouldn't mind north
WATER REQUIREMENTS	Thirsty
OPTIMUM NIGHTTIME TEMPERATURE	55–60°F (12–15°C)
RATE OF GROWTH	Fast
SOIL TYPE	Rich, humusy soil
FERTILIZING	Early spring to late autumn only
PROBLEMS	Prone to aphids, spider mites, mealy bugs, and whiteflies, as well as leaf bacterial infections

GARDENIAS

Unlike any gardenia I've ever seen, *Gardenia carinata* adds flaxen color to its long, tubular flowers.

SUMMER IS YOUR only shot at gardenias. I know, I know—you're yearning for that aroma close in the warm cossets of your home throughout the year. But it isn't going to happen inside. At least, not easily.

Even I admit gardenias are a dilemma. Who doesn't want to grow a plant with a legendary fragrance? Say the word "gardenia," and everyone—gardeners and laypeople alike—brings up a mental image of a cream-colored, powdery, rose-like flower spewing the sort of scent capable of making a strong man's knees go weak. Part of the mystique has to do with the flower's dimensions. Most fragrant flowers don't have the physical presence that a gardenia blossom boasts. In size, it compares to a David Austin rose with all the poetry it implies. Pull it all together, and you have a package worth seeking

out. You yearn to have the splendor nearby. You bring it in. You swell with hope. And then the bubble bursts. As houseplants, gardenias are fraught with failure. I link with lots of kindred spirits who harbor houseplants. Across the board, gardenias have us all flummoxed.

I had pretty much given up on gardenias indoors. They came within a heartbeat of being filed into the Love Thwarted section of this book. I occasionally succumbed to a *Gardenia augusta* (formerly *G. jasminoides*) in summer on the strength of its hauntingly deep, throaty (verging on musky) aroma. But I've successfully grown gardenias only in open air. Even with Mother Nature as my ally in care and upkeep, gardenias require more maintenance than your average patio plant. Mine have never been large plants, because they don't have the benefit of several years' head start to get their growth in gear. Modest in size, they still need more feeding and fussing (mostly repotting) on their summer sojourn than most potted plants.

This year, I decided to give gardenias another chance indoors and tried *Gardenia carinata* (often said as *G. coronata*). I would not describe its performance as prolific in the bloom department, but a couple of flowers go a long way on a small gardenia. Not only was the scent spicier (in a good way) than the typical gardenia redolence, but the flower also has a unique shape and color. The flared mouth of the long, tubular, orange-darkening-to-cinnamon blossoms is about as wide as a pansy. In other words, if you have your heart set on a buxom, rose-shaped bloom, you might be disappointed with *G. carinata*. But if you keep an open mind and dote on diversity, you are going to love it.

When autumn arrived, the gardenia needed shelter. Gardenias prefer pretty much the polar opposite of the environment in your average home. They are fairly outspoken in their demands for bright light, high humidity, and toasty temperatures. The bright light might not be hard to secure, but warm temperatures and high humidity rarely go hand in hand indoors. Gardenias like a mildly acid soil, which you can achieve by adding a little fertilizer for hollies and rhododendrons. I fed *Gardenia carinata* with fish emulsion throughout the winter and gave it pot promotions to keep up with its growth and thirst. (Note that I usually don't fertilize or repot during the winter, but I made an exception because of the poor wee thing's body language. I know a cry for food when I see it.) The gardenia drank copiously and dried out twice as fast as any other plant in my collection. It dislikes soggy roots as much as any other houseplant, but this heavy drinker never got soggy. By the end of winter, my gardenia had good growth and only slightly pale leaves compared to the usual yellowing and browning that the plant suffers. I figured I was doing well. After all, it was still alive. Now it's back on the porch again and loving the outdoors, but still drinking up a storm.

With that small victory under my belt, I tried a *Gardenia* species sold as "hardy" and I took the claim (they

I've tried to host
the buxom standard
gardenias, but
couldn't convince
them to tolerate
the conditions in
my home. *Gardenia*
species doesn't have
those wonderful
rosebud-like
blossoms, but it's
more obliging.

said Zone 7; I am skeptical) as an invitation to host this particular cultivar in the colder part of my chilly home through the winter. With a lot of extra work (following the same regimen as *Gardenia carinata*), the plant also fared far better than the typical *G. augusta* cultivars, which generally come out of winter looking like someone torched the foliage. It didn't appear salubrious, but it wasn't a basket case, either. In a warm, humid greenhouse, the tale would be different and might have a much happier ending. But not many of us can claim that luxury.

The moral of the story? If you can keep your gardenia alive through winter, summer will provide the reward. Gardenias produce flowers in summer, often extending their bloom cycle into early autumn. If you live for that fragrance, I suggest getting a full-grown plant for summer delights and then waving good-bye in autumn. It's so much simpler.

Gardenia species
GARDENIA

FLOWERS	White or cream, and often rose-like
FOLIAGE	Optimally deep green
OTHER ATTRIBUTES	Fragrance that's out of this world
SIZE	3–4 feet (90–122cm) in height at maturity
EXPOSURE	South
WATER REQUIREMENTS	Thirsty
OPTIMUM NIGHTTIME TEMPERATURE	65–75°F (18–23°C)
RATE OF GROWTH	Fast
SOIL TYPE	Rich, humusy, acidic soil
FERTILIZING	Throughout the year on this one
PROBLEMS	Lots. Leaves tend to yellow or brown over winter. Prone to aphids, spider mites, mealy bugs, and whiteflies. Prone to die.

PASSION FLOWERS

When it comes to bells and whistles, what flower can compare with tricked-out *Passiflora caerulea*? (What you can't see in this picture is that it adds fragrance to its dance card.)

YOU KNOW WHAT all this is about, don't you? It's living *The Secret Garden* indoors on a daily basis. Not so subliminally, I'm striving for that life of lost-and-found flora throughout the year. For me, this boils down to entering a house with greenery concealing what lies around the bend. The fantasy is about the lure of adventure and being submerged in nature. There's got to be volume, density, and a feeling of delicious abandon. Passion flowers are a big part of the illusion.

When passion flowers are part of the formula, there is no maybe—you have a bona fide jungle. At least, you feel transported. Passifloras do not blossom reliably in winter, but they still have those groping appendages, plus tendrils galore. Flower power might be lacking inside, but there is ample greenery to reinforce the sense of carefree abandon.

Did I say carefree? Keeping up with passifloras can be time consuming. I pulled passion flowers out from the other vines because they deserve a closer look as individuals. But like most other vines, passifloras are athletes. They race around grabbing onto other plants, requiring support, extending their reach beyond whatever support they have been allotted, and getting into mischief. If you don't love that freewheeling energy, steer away. But if a gung-ho plant with a pioneer spirit is your idea of a companion worth inviting into your home, you and passion flowers will make beautiful music together.

In winter, passion flowers are grown pretty much for foliage purposes only. But in summer, they blossom, which is why I've included them in this section. With a bright, south-facing window, you might enjoy a smattering of flowers indoors in winter if you grow a passiflora that readily blossoms (and not all passion flowers are created equal in this department). During summer, if you sojourn your passifloras outside or in an ultra-sunny window, you are bound to enjoy a steady supply of blossoms with all their outrageous perks.

As far as endowments go, passifloras have more intrigue per square foot than any other botanical I can think of. The foliage is comely, for sure, but each blossom is a circus. We're talking a truly bizarre combination of a trio of stigmas overlaying five stamens above the frill of corona filaments on top of colorful petals and sepals sometimes jutting from an elongated calyx tube. Then there's the fragrance that wafts from this tricked-out set of gizmos. Although all passifloras have their own signature scent, the aroma is generally sweet and lightly perfumed. Note the "generally" qualifier—I know of at least one passion flower readily in the trade that is a stinker. *Passiflora jorullensis* is compact with abundant, small, cream-petaled flowers overlaid by a ray of sunrise peach filaments. It's adorable and no one could fail to fall for it. The only problem is that *P. jorullensis* produces the most nauseating scent, akin to sweaty gym socks. You literally can't be in the same room as this little number.

Flowering is probably in your cards, but don't bank on passion fruit as one of the bonuses (and note that not all passion fruit is edible). Only a few passion flowers readily set fruit—*Passiflora edulis* (the purple granadilla) and *P. quadrangularis* (the giant granadilla) are best known for this trait. But it's unlikely to happen in a window, and probably not even in a greenhouse. In fact, you are not apt to succeed in setting fruit outside unless your growing season is prolonged. In other words, do not plan on going into the passion fruit smoothie business unless you live in a frost-free area.

That's the flowering-and-fruiting end of the performance, but passion flowers offer much more. The leaves are usually intriguing, too. They are often glove-shaped or deeply fingered, and they sometimes change shape, which scientists tell us is an adaptation to flummox all the creepy-crawly things that devour passion flower vines. In particular, passifloras are the staple of voracious Heliconius butterfly larvae, and that can mean murder on a population of vines. So these ingenious plants have developed other survival tactics. The leaf stems are studded with little nectar-secreting glands that emit tiny drops of sticky sweet stuff meant to attract the ants and wasps that threaten the passion flower–nibbling larvae. The secretion often glistens in the sun, so the leaves have a jewel-like quality. That's it for the survival tricks, but there are other delights. For example, the stems wind gracefully around into a head-strong tangle, grasping onto supports (including neighboring stems, curtain rods, and furniture, if you don't monitor their moves) with those curly tendrils that are cute unto themselves. Bundle all these attributes together and you get an over-the-top act. But that's nature for you.

There are so many passifloras out there, I confess I haven't tried them all in my home. Who can keep up? New hybrids are being introduced on a regular basis, and they are all gorgeous. It's difficult to keep from slipping into insatiable collector mode. The old standbys for surefire blossoms are *Passiflora caerulea* (the best) and *P.* ×*alato-caerulea* (a close second). I find *P. caerulea* to be easier to

You've got to be creative with vines. An upside-down egg basket provides a jungle gym for *Passiflora caerulea*.

Not all passion flowers behave well enough to sit on a windowsill. But *Passiflora citrina* minds its manners and stays on its own trellis.

host in a home environment because of its more compact habit and willingness to produce abundant large (3-inch [8cm]) blue-petaled blossoms. You could easily wind *P. caerulea* around a large orb and accommodate it indoors. Compare that to *P. ×alato-caerulea*'s looser growth habit, which requires a tuteur of some sort but also bears larger (nearly 4-inch [10cm]) pink-tinted blossoms. Many of the hybrids have proved equally entertaining. I've only worked with 'Jeanette', which performs beautifully. I suspect the other progeny and species are similarly satisfying. My favorite at the moment (don't you love the way favorite plants change with your mood and the weather?) is the little canary yellow–flowered *P. citrina*. The leaves are about one inch (2.5cm) wide, and the vine is relatively polite in size and easily woven onto a 3-foot

(91cm) trellis. It will wander a little, but be firm and send those appendages back to the target support. Then come the profuse flowers.

To host a passion flower, a south-facing window is non-negotiable. Without bright light, a passion flower is going to pout. Give your vine a 5- to 6-inch (12–15cm) container for starters. Although the tradition is to pot three cuttings in a container for most vines, don't bother with a passion flower—it will fill in. And rather than pinching it out to encourage branching, I just wind it around more densely to give it girth. When bringing a passiflora indoors (in my Zone 5 garden, only *Passiflora* 'Incense' is reliably hardy), cutting back the vine is the key to fitting it through the door. I find that passifloras drop foliage anyway when they are moved inside in autumn. They can also turn pale with the transition from bright light to window-filtered sunbeams. Then they adjust and move

on. To feed the appetite of hungry passion flowers, I fertilize every three weeks or so with fish emulsion, which seems to do the trick.

In your home, Heliconius larvae aren't likely to be an issue. But whiteflies can be a problem. Passion flowers aren't the whitefly magnet that fuchsias are, but they will be targeted if there's an infestation close by. Besides that little wrinkle, passifloras are fairly trouble free. I shear mine back enough to maintain that delicate balance between delightful entanglement and the sense of being choked by vines. If nothing else, I try to keep the passion flower confined to its own trellis. Sometimes I succeed.

Passiflora species
and cultivars
PASSION FLOWER

FLOWERS	Absolutely otherworldly, very complex and floriferous flowers
FOLIAGE	Usually lobed or glove-shaped, but other leaf shapes occur
OTHER ATTRIBUTES	Fruit is rare indoors, but the tendrils are adorable
SIZE	Energetic vine knows no limits
EXPOSURE	South for flowers
WATER REQUIREMENTS	Thirsty
OPTIMUM NIGHTTIME TEMPERATURE	50–60°F (10–15°C)
RATE OF GROWTH	Lightning fast— lock up your daughters
SOIL TYPE	Rich, humusy soil with compost included
FERTILIZING	Early spring to late autumn; in winter if the foliage pales
PROBLEMS	Prone to aphids, spider mites, and whiteflies. Foliage and fruit may be toxic.

SUCCULENTS AND CACTI

When you keep a succulent, such as *Gasteria* species, for several years, the reward is a display of its full potential.

WHEN MEMORIAL DAY is pending, I hasten most of my houseplants outdoors for a season of frolic and fresh air. But everything can't go; the house would be empty. So I leave many of the succulents inside.

Several factors inform this blaring example of favoritism. First and foremost, succulents make me smile (and this is all about me, right?). There's something inherently comical about plants with all the bells and whistles that succulents brandish; they are the world's most bizarre and creative creations. Kalanchoes with little baby plantlets dangling from their edges, pachyphytums with fat, swollen appendages, and sempervivums wrapped in web-like gossamer might give anyone else the jitters, but I love them. I don't drink coffee. I don't even do chocolate-covered donuts. But the day would sputter out of its morning jump-start without a quick glimpse at the echeverias as I round the bend into the kitchen. They are my dose of adrenaline.

But there's an ulterior motive behind selecting the succulents as year-round housemates. They require almost no care. I can (and do) forget to water them for days, even weeks, and they don't whine. Indeed, their physical appearance following a brush with deprivation is about the same as when I remember to serve drinks on a regular basis. After all, these plants are adapted to the extremely arid regions of the world, and their weird leaves and stems have evolved to store water for times of drought. Not that you want to stress them. It's sometimes a precarious balance between letting them dry out and parching them to death. But even during the sunniest weeks, succulents require only a light dowsing with water once a week or so. More, and you'll drown them with misguided kindness. This fits perfectly into a season when I tend to be madly rushing around the garden trying to weed, mulch, plant, transplant, and water simultaneously. You know the feeling. If you're looking for a plant that doesn't give you grief over neglect, choose a succulent.

It might sound reckless to jam a whole group of plants together in the same blanket category for care and requirements, but I treat all the succulents as equals. I give them as much light as I can muster all year long, which sometimes entails moving them closer to the windowpanes in winter. A south-facing window or a very bright east or west window works fine. I water them all lightly. I give them "tight shoes" by potting and transplanting only when they truly outgrow their containers. And I pot them in an organic soil that is fairly gritty and not heavy on the peat. I frequently amend their soil to add sand (I buy what is called "traction sand" at a builder-supply store; beware of sand from the town garage, which is often laced with salt).

Some succulents (aloes come to mind immediately) make "pups," or baby plants, that require either repotting or division. Give them the space they crave or divide off the pups. The entire brood (parents included) will suffer if they are crammed together. Beyond repotting when necessary, I rarely fertilize succulents. When parceling out the fish emulsion, I generally pass them over. And they look wonderful.

Of course, I don't hoard all of the succulents inside. Some go out in summer, and I give them the sunniest position possible. I put them up on a white marble table where they can soak up the beams, but not on their first day out. They get the same gradual adjustment period as all the other sun-loving plants.

Sometimes I worry about the succulents outdoors when it rains relentlessly day after day. Occasionally, I consider bringing them indoors in a deluge. But I never do. And they truck along just fine because they're sitting in a good, well-drained soil (that's key) and their containers have ample drainage (also critical). I pass them over during my daily rounds with the hose,

When I looked at its label, I thought *Cotyledon* 'Happy Young Lady' had the dumbest name ever, but it grew on me. After a while, it seemed to suit the plant.

It's little oddities like the profuse, star-shaped flowers of *Stapelia scitula* that give indoor gardeners incentive to try plants that aren't in the mainstream.

Counterpoise container textures with the plants they cradle, such as concrete against echeverias with a pot of *Pachyphytum oviferum*, *Echeveria* species, and *Echeveria pulv-oliver* on the side.

Like gems, succulents are all about their setting, which is why this gasteria cultivar shines in its retro pot.

except their weekly watering and perhaps for a splash every few days in extremely hot, sunny weather. During cloudy, balmy periods, I don't water them at all. They seem happy.

Let's describe a happy succulent. None of mine grow by leaps and bounds, which is pretty much the nature of the beast and fine by me. They slowly add rosettes or gradually send a new arm jutting out. They flower quite readily, though. And that's a major perk, because the flowers tend to be just as sci-fi as the foliage. However, keep in mind that some succulents bloom only sporadically by nature (aloes and agaves are in this category) and others blossom only at certain times of year (kalanchoes tend to be autumn-flowering). In

some cases, you will have to be patient. Oh, and speaking of blossoms, *Crassula muscosa* is charming with its chamaecyparis-like stems, and it has nearly imperceptible blossoms running along its stem. But it also emits, rather vigorously, a totally gross musk-like scent that's unsavory (to say the least) indoors. You might want to steer clear or use it as outdoor entertainment only. Even then, proceed with caution.

I'm not big on cacti. My mom is a fan, and I got my lifelong allotment of cactus barbs and jabs during my formative years. Every time a thunderstorm blew in and the window needed to be shut in a hurry, half a dozen prickly things had to be removed from the sill. That sort of soured me on them. I know they have a certain twisted appeal, but no

Crassula, Echeveria, Kalanchoe, Pachyphytum, Sedum, and others

FLOWERS	With sun, flowers are part of the show—they range from candelabras of dangling bells to open-face blooms
FOLIAGE	Very diverse and unique
OTHER ATTRIBUTES	These are the freaks of nature, and they're lovely
SIZE	Quite variable, some remain very small
EXPOSURE	South
WATER REQUIREMENTS	Water only when soil is very dry, especially in winter
OPTIMUM NIGHTTIME TEMPERATURE	50–65°F (10–18°C)
RATE OF GROWTH	Very slow
SOIL TYPE	Sandy, well-drained soil
FERTILIZING	Very sparsely early spring to late autumn
PROBLEMS	Root mealy bugs tend to pester cacti and succulents

Part of the fun of oddball succulents like *Kalanchoe thyrsiflora* 'Flapjack' is finding a container that really struts their wares.

thank you. For those who are fans, give them the exact same treatment as succulents, and be especially sparse with water. And be careful. Although I got a little clutch of cacti last spring at a succulent sale, I haven't summoned the courage (or interest, quite frankly) to brave the barbs and repot them from their ugly plastic containers. I'll take succulents over cacti any day.

VINES

SEVERAL VINES ERASE the boundaries between indoors and outside, wrapping up the scene and frisking me as well as everyone else who wanders my way. Some spill out the front door in summer. But not all. A few of those vines could not be extracted from their indoor supports without tearing and mauling. So, several firmly entrenched vines remain inside, nourishing my need for green throughout the year. A case in point is the stephanotis. The prospect of moving the stephanotis's little jungle gym outside is far too daunting to undertake. And without a stephanotis wending around, the house would feel relatively stripped. So it remains indoors.

However, the stephanotis is an exception. Most of the vines are sent out to play, and they take full advantage of the recess, swinging from outdoor trellises or rambling along the ground. Of all the houseplants that go outdoors, the vines make the most growth. They are cut back sternly in autumn when it's time to come back inside. But in summer, I give them plenty of headroom and let them rip. The result is profuse blossoms, if they happen to be bloomers. If intriguing leaves are their gig, that's good too.

Generally, I covet sunlovers in the vine venue. After a brief adjustment period, I situate them where they can bask in the sunbeams. I give their roots the benefit of large containers filled with organic potting-soil mix to nurture their summer growing spree. Even so, they generally need repotting or root-pruning (which I do very gingerly, reducing the vine's head growth by at least a third in proportion to the quantity of roots I've eliminated) when it's time to come back into the fold in autumn. I fertilize approximately every three weeks, but rarely keep records. The vines themselves turn pale and nudge me to break out the fish emulsion again.

Rising to the challenge of matching a vine with the right support is half the fun. But it can be a difficult if you're in a new relationship and you don't know the ropes. Vines always seem to rampantly outperform your greatest expectations. For the most part, you can forget the "first year it sleeps, next year it creeps, finally it leaps" adage when working with tropical vines. Unlike their hardy perennial counterparts, they tend to go straight for leap mode. I'm just as guilty as everyone else of underestimating a vine's potential and coupling it with a trellis insufficient to shoulder its heft. But finding a support that will fit into a container can be a formidable and fruitless quest. For the most part, container supports are about 3 feet (90cm) tall at the most. To prevent the horror of toppling, be sure to get one with legs that can be inserted several inches into the soil. I also find that a support with several prongs poking into the soil leads to better stability than a single stick. I detest the flimsy plastic supports that come from the nursery with vines such as clematis. They're ugly and not equal to the task, and your vine will outgrow them in a matter of weeks.

But there's no reason why a vine needs to grow up. Rather than ascending, another option is to let a trailing plant descend. More often than not, I host trailing plants in tall containers, such as long toms, that let them swoop majestically down. Urns are another solution. In both cases, you've got plenty of space for a vine to spill before it hits ground level.

And long, tall containers are my answer to hanging baskets. I've never met a hanging basket I could live with. Perhaps because I'm short (I did confess that I'm ridiculously short, didn't I?), hanging baskets are a pain in the neck. There's no way I'm going to pull up a stepladder every time a hanging basket needs watering. It's just not going to happen. So they tend to go thirsty, which takes a rapid toll for a plant with desiccating breezes flowing all around the root system. For all these reasons, and for gardeners of average and above height as well, a tall container is a great solution.

ARISTOLOCHIA GIGANTEA

Call it the pelican flower or Dutchman's pipe or another name, this is one of the most bizarre blossoms in creation. Like the native *Aristolochia macrophylla* that will gladly encase your porch, the tropical Dutchman's pipe rapidly climbs upward in a tangle of deep-green, heart-shaped leaves. But while you could easily overlook the blossoms on the native version, you cannot possibly miss the otherworldly blooms that *A. gigantea* produces. They flare at least 3 inches (8cm) wide, with complex magenta and cream patterned markings moving into bright yellow at the center. The center marks the entrance into a curvaceous tube with bristling hairs directed inward to a chamber where the sexual organs await. It's all geared toward attracting flies. And the smell is part of the fly's version of "come hither." It's not the sort of thing most of us can live with on a daily basis. As soon as the novelty wears off, you're left with the stench. But if your nose has a high tolerance, give this vine full sun, warm temperatures, and a very hefty support with lots of headroom.

Aristolochia gigantea

DUTCHMAN'S PIPE, PELICAN FLOWER

FLOWERS	Huge Dutchman's pipe–shaped monstrosities with an uncomfortable scent
FOLIAGE	Heart-shaped and handsome
OTHER ATTRIBUTES	Totally strange flowers and a great, fast cover-up for a season
SIZE	Vigorous climbing vine
EXPOSURE	South
WATER REQUIREMENTS	Generous
OPTIMUM NIGHTTIME TEMPERATURE	55–65°F (12–18°C)
RATE OF GROWTH	Lightning fast
SOIL TYPE	Rich, heavy soil
FERTILIZING	Early spring to late autumn
PROBLEMS	Whiteflies; take extra care to penetrate the tangle of leaves when spraying a vine for organic pest management

I let *Boweia volubilis* climb the curtain rod.

Boweia volubilis
CLIMBING ONION

FLOWERS	Minute
FOLIAGE	Seaweed-like climbing strings
OTHER ATTRIBUTES	Impressive bulb is part of the picture
SIZE	Vigorous climbing vine
EXPOSURE	South, east, or west
WATER REQUIREMENTS	Meager
OPTIMUM NIGHTTIME TEMPERATURE	50–65°F (10–18°C)
RATE OF GROWTH	Athletically energetic
SOIL TYPE	Rich, heavy soil
FERTILIZING	While in growth in late summer, autumn, and winter
PROBLEMS	Keep all members of the *Liliaceae* family away from pets who are prone to ingest, especially cats.

BOWIEA VOLUBILIS

You want a plant with character hanging around, and the climbing onion (*Bowiea volubilis*) certainly qualifies. Although it is related to lilies, the flowers aren't the major show here. The blossoms are actually just little, tiny (very tiny) sparkling jewels on the roaming vine that wends its way hither and yon. The celery-green vines are cool and seaweed-like, but what they initiate from is even cooler. As the name suggests, the climbing onion sends its lacy foliage from the center of a massive onion-like bulb. Mine is many years old and the bulb has gradually swollen to 5 inches (12cm) over the years. Every summer, it goes dormant to start growing anew late in the season. By the time autumn is in full force, its lacework has formed a network. Give it a serious support. The vines are not heavy, but an older plant will need something to climb on. In the absence of something sufficient and sanctioned, boweia will look elsewhere. To give you a hint, the Victorians used them as green curtains.

Climbing onions prefer full sun and tolerate considerable drying out between waterings, thanks to their water-storage bulbs. If totally forgotten water-wise, they will slip into dormancy off-season, but mine always revives after a brief snit.

For some reason (that might have to do with its pillow of soft leaves) Einstein chooses to perch on *Lotus maculatus's* urn for his bed. The lotus takes it in stride.

Lotus maculatus and *L. berthelotii*

PARROT'S BEAK, PELICAN'S BEAK

FLOWERS	Colorful, claw-like blossoms in clusters
FOLIAGE	Silver, needle-like leaves
OTHER ATTRIBUTES	Great for window boxes or as a "spiller" in a container
SIZE	Trailing showering vine
EXPOSURE	South, bright east, or west
WATER REQUIREMENTS	Heavy drinker
OPTIMUM NIGHTTIME TEMPERATURE	50–60°F (10–15°C)
RATE OF GROWTH	Medium
SOIL TYPE	Rich, humusy, well-drained soil
FERTILIZING	Early spring to late autumn
PROBLEMS	Can litter foliage

LOTUS MACULATUS

In a windowsill, I can produce only a nod to the claw-like, yellow and red "parrot beak" blossoms that *Lotus maculatus* is capable of producing. I don't know where I'm going wrong, because my home is definitely sufficiently chilly to provoke flowers on this Canary Island native. But even so, the needle-like, shimmering silver foliage is entertainment enough, I suppose. I find that *L. maculatus* and its red counterpart, *L. berthelotii*, wilt easily, then shrivel their leaves and scatter them all over the floor. In summer, when your lotus is outdoors, this doesn't tend to be such an issue, making it a splendid plant for a mixed window box. Even though it can cause frequent fussing with the broom, I haven't banished mine from indoors for the simple reason that the kitten has adopted its soft bed of leaves for slumbering purposes. Because he's spoiled rotten, and to keep as much foliage on the upper portion of the plant as possible for his green cushion, I clip mine back regularly.

STEPHANOTIS FLORIBUNDA

If I could choose favorites (and I can't), this might be a finalist. Quite possibly the best vine for growing indoors, stephanotis is almost always either forming buds or in full blossom with waxy umbels of plump, tubular, sparkling white blossoms that linger long and emit a powdery sweet aroma akin to gardenia but not as cloying. On that rare occasion when the Madagascar jasmine is not forming buds, it has oval, deep-green foliage that is impeccably tidy, handsome, and buttoned down—a description we don't generally associate with vines. Even the ropy vine itself looks good and is easy to keep in check.

Like most other vines, Madagascar jasmines tend to be hungry. I try to keep abreast of container graduations and give them a beefy organic soil mix with compost included when repotting. However, fertilizing is absolutely required and can continue through winter, if needed. How do you know when to serve food? Your stephanotis will tell you. Watch the foliage. If it begins to pale a shade or two from its ideal dark forest-green hue, fetch the fish emulsion. Great for beginners, this vine tends to be trouble free as far as pests are concerned. Although a sunny window will encourage blossoms, the vine can winter in lower light and still survive perfectly well.

Stephanotis floribunda

STEPHANOTIS

ALSO CALLED: bridal wreath, Madagascar jasmine, stephanotis, waxflower

FLOWERS	Clusters of long, white tubes
FOLIAGE	Oval, deep-green, thick leaves
OTHER ATTRIBUTES	Intensely fragrant, used by florists for June bridal bouquets, also blooms for winter holidays
SIZE	Rope-like vine is best wound around a loose support, or trained in a circle
EXPOSURE	South, bright east, or west
WATER REQUIREMENTS	Medium
OPTIMUM NIGHTTIME TEMPERATURE	55–65°F (12–18°C)
RATE OF GROWTH	Medium
SOIL TYPE	Rich, humusy, well-drained soil
FERTILIZING	Early spring to late autumn, may need additional fertilizer in winter
PROBLEMS	Mealy bugs and scale

At certain times of year, flowers are at a premium indoors, but *Thunbergia grandiflora* continues its ongoing electric-blue show.

Thunbergia grandiflora

BLUE TRUMPET VINE, CLOCKVINE, SKYFLOWER

FLOWERS	Large, sky blue blossoms throughout the year
FOLIAGE	Deep-green, pointed leaves
OTHER ATTRIBUTES	A very reliable winter bloomer as well as summer
SIZE	Energetic climbing vine or dangling vine
EXPOSURE	South
WATER REQUIREMENTS	Medium
OPTIMUM NIGHTTIME TEMPERATURE	55–65°F (12–18°C)
RATE OF GROWTH	Medium
SOIL TYPE	Rich, humusy, well-drained soil
FERTILIZING	Early spring to late autumn
PROBLEMS	I find it to be trouble free but it can be pestered by scale

THUNBERGIA GRANDIFLORA

The beauty of vines is that they have the potential to spread color over a broad area. Take *Thunbergia grandiflora*, for example. Arrow-shaped, leathery leaves with clusters of several buds grow from sturdy arms that wind around uncomprisingly clockwise. At the end of a long, drawn-out drama that is part of the seduction, those buds finally unfold into sky blue tubular blossoms that flare 2 to 3 inches (5–8cm) and are absolutely ravishing. Summer is the main show. But my vines have budded up enthusiastically during the dull weather of autumn and stoically through winter, as well. Spring is also clad with flower power. Plus, pests never bother the thick leaves of this thunbergia, but a crystal-like "sweat" that does no harm and is part of the plant's eccentricities can appear on the flower buds. Full sun is imperative; indoors, this means a south-facing window.

Love Thwarted

Not all plants reward your hospitality. My relationship with *Heliotropium arborescens,* for example, is constant unrequited love as a roommate. We get along better when I admire it from a distance outdoors.

I wish that I could claim that it's all domestic bliss. But no. Some plants categorically refuse my most ardent affection and concerted attention. I try. I fuss. I nurse. I don't kill them with kindness, but I give them extra quality time. Nonetheless, they spurn me again and again.

Maybe it's only me. Perhaps these plants have an attitude against my happy little home. But I don't think so. From gossiping with other gardeners, I suspect the plants in this section thwart most of us with equanimity. Rather than just skipping over these plants, I decided to expose them. In the spirit of full disclosure, I feel you need to know what won't work on your windowsill. You also need the tools to give these plants your best shot. In most cases, I have suggested other applications so you can get these goodies into your life (like growing them outdoors in summer) and out of your indoor system.

All the houseplants in this section are desirable. There are plenty of houseplants I haven't mentioned in this book, but that's because I'm not even tempted to invite them in. You'll be intrigued by the plants I've included here. I wouldn't blame you for adopting them, bringing them home, and struggling to create a relationship, just as I did. But when they drop dead (or worse—when they slowly, painfully perish) let me be the first to say it: I told you so.

ABUTILONS

A hybrid of *Abutilon megapotamicum* 'Variegatum', *Abutilon* 'Yellow Cascade' is certainly desirable—indoor gardeners hunger for it, and so do insects.

AT ONE TIME, I was obsessed with abutilons. They have the wide-eyed wonder of their kin, hollyhocks, with big, bell-shaped flowers. And everyone loves a hollyhock. Why not bring that childlike ambiance into a home? Of course, there are several differences between abutilons and hollyhocks. For example, abutilons don't stack up their blossoms on lighthouse-like tall spires, but instead hold their blooms in clusters that dole out their goods one flower at a time. Abutilons are generous, but not effusive. You want that in a flower.

And they have history. Abutilons were originally known as parlor maples, grown in nineteenth-century homes before central heating kept things sufficiently (and evenly) warm for the average tropical. But mostly what I found appealing about abutilons is that they were the heroes of the working class. Florists such as my mother-in-law, Joy Logee Martin, would weave abutilons (which she dubbed "wedding bells"; she was no fool in the marketing department) into wedding bouquets and anniversary corsages for customers who could not afford roses in a little Connecticut mill town. She tucked them into teenagers' suit jackets (nobody had a tuxedo) before they left for the prom. Abutilons had a past. And I felt fairly strongly that they needed a future as well.

Since then, I've cooled on abutilons as houseplants. As I see it, the problem has a lot to do with their other fans. Unfortunately, whiteflies are also avid aficionados of this plant, and so are aphids. Spider mites pay call. And beyond that, even if you vanquish the pests, abutilons are a wild card. If you grow them indoors, they need a sunny window to secure flowers. If you grow them outdoors, bright light will shrivel the foliage and lead to general

On the difficulty meter, *Abutilon megapotamicum* 'Variegatum' is not as hard to grow as *Abutilon ×hybridum*. It can be coaxed into blossom in lower light.

decline. On the other hand (and this is where the guess-work comes in), give them too little light and you forfeit flowers. Achieving the right balance isn't always easy, and light is just the beginning. It can be dicey to find an equilibrium between overpotting and enough root room to prevent constant thirst. Stabilizing fertilizer between yellowing leaves and so much food that the plant fails to flower is tricky. Even in the best of all worlds, the leaves tend to sulk and turn downward in a home. I no longer bother with abutilons as houseplants. But I can never resist getting a few abutilons in spring to grow in outdoor containers footsteps from the front door, where they do just fine.

True, abutilons have sentimental value for me. But that's not the only reason I'm a sucker. Abutilons offer an incredibly broad flower color range that spans from white through all the pinks to peach and red. Those colors aren't just straight-on shades. Reminiscent of single peonies, they include luminous shell and coral hues that you don't find in every bloom up and down the block. The color range has increased, and abutilons have gained poise with time. Way back, the original parlor maples were tall, gangly affairs with flowers on the very top. But by the time I came on the horticultural scene, *Abutilon ×hybridum* had progressed to the point that it was no longer tree-size. You can grow a nice, full abutilon that stands 2 to 3 feet (60–90cm) tall and is covered with flowers. Some bloom better than others as small plants. The butter-yellow 'Moonchimes' and garnet red 'Clementine' became the benchmarks.

Abutilon ×*hybridum* isn't the only game in town. Along came *A. pictum* 'Thompsonii', with gold-flecked leaves and heavily veined, peach-colored blossoms in abundance on a compact plant. Other variegated abutilons are available, but none bloom with equal zeal. The exception is *A. megapotamicum* 'Variegatum', with small, mottled gold leaves and matching yellow blossoms dangling from bright red calyces. The flowers really do resemble a Chinese lantern. Another bonus of *A. megapotamicum* 'Variegatum' is that the overall growth habit is horizontal rather than stark upright. Recently, there has been much intermarriage, bringing larger, nodding flowers on compact plants.

Outdoors, abutilons maintain a stiff upper lip in chilly weather. More than once, I've watched abutilons endure a light frost (my advice: don't push it). Every year there comes a moment when I decide an abutilon needs to be sacrificed in autumn, and it refuses to die. In New England, however, it's just forestalling the inevitable. At some point, it's doomsday.

If you've opted to bring your abutilons indoors in autumn rather than going the sacrificial route, keep in mind they need bright light to blossom indoors. They should be watered when dry, they require strict pruning to keep them in shape, they should be fertilized regularly from spring through autumn, and they are bug magnets. That's all you need to know. Besides that, they're easy.

Abutilon cultivars

ABUTILON

ALSO CALLED: **Chinese lantern, parlor maple**

FLOWERS	White, pink, orange, red, coral, yellow, and all points in between
FOLIAGE	Maple-shaped; variegated versions available
OTHER ATTRIBUTES	New varieties blossom throughout the year when light levels are ample
SIZE	2–3 feet (60–90cm) in height
EXPOSURE	South indoors, dappled sun outside
WATER REQUIREMENTS	Very thirsty
OPTIMUM NIGHTTIME TEMPERATURE	50–60°F (10–15°C)
RATE OF GROWTH	Fast
SOIL TYPE	Any rich, humusy soil mix
FERTILIZING	Early spring to late autumn
PROBLEMS	Prone to whiteflies (major issue), aphids, and spider mites

BOUGAINVILLEAS

I HAD A vision when I bought my cottage, and bougainvilleas played a starring role. Of course, I wasn't under any delusions about hosting bougainvilleas outside. I know New England and its limitations. My plan involved bougainvilleas arching over the doorway between the converted barn and the little greenhouse passageway. I sought a sense of entanglement. I was striving for intertwining woody branches clambering over the doorway. I could almost feel the festively colored, papery flower bracts floating down like confetti as I walked by. I wanted the romance. What I got were mealy bugs.

For years, I struggled with bougainvilleas. My original scheme was to leave the bougainvilleas indoors throughout the year. The other plants get a summer exodus, but the bougainvilleas would remain captive no matter what the season. I reasoned that the vines wouldn't be able to scramble up and gain enough headway to achieve the tangled garden of my dreams if they were torn down periodically to spend summer outside. I acquired sufficiently large plants in various hues to staple their rambling branches in place. Just as planned, they formed an arch of blossoms and bracts in blazing magenta, burnt orange, and prom-gown pink all threaded together. Just as hoped, they sprinkled colorful bracts at my feet. But from the very beginning, the big picture also included wads of mealy bug masses. If you have ever battled mealy bugs, you know there will be no happy ending to this story. Not only will the bougainvillea be permanently jeopardized, but the evil cotton-encased culprit will jump insidiously from plant to plant.

For a few summers, the bougainvilleas went outside onto the back porch, where I labored for the duration of the season to rid the vines of mealy bug using all the organic means at my disposal. I kept calendars with spray dates (I sprayed roughly once a week, because eggs can hatch every 5 to 10 days), attempting to zap each consecutive generation the moment it hatched and before it could fall in love and make babies. I aimed my sprayer at all the nooks and crannies of the vine. I tried my level best to conquer the foul fiends. By summer's end, it always seemed as if the battle was won. But when autumn came and the bougainvilleas were marched inside, the mealy bugs surfaced again. In a fit of desperation, I even cut the bougainvilleas back to nubs, hoping to physically toss away any vestige of my foes. No luck.

To give you a preview of my little harangue on cultural basics in the back of this book, my theory is that a healthy, well-grown, faithfully watered and repotted plant will not fall prey to insects. It makes sense, right? You build them strong and they can fight back. Well, bougainvilleas are the exception. I'm convinced you can give your bougainvillea the best of all worlds, and it is nonetheless destined to come down with mealy bugs. I've given up. But so as not to dissuade anyone else, let me run through their list of desires.

Bougainvilleas are not difficult to grow indoors. Give them bright light—a south-facing window is paramount. Water them evenly, but don't overwater. I was taught that the secret to prompting blossoms is a slight wilt, but that felt like hosting a mealy-bug convention. And mine always responded to the prompt of fertilizer in late winter to jump-start bud formation. Give bougainvilleas plenty of root room in a generous container. Ideally, temperatures should not go below 60°F (15°C) at night. Mine went down to 50°F (10°C) most winter nights and survived, but dropped most of their leaves. I would hit them with that late winter shot of fertilizer, and they would leaf out immediately and burst into blossom. In fact, they spent most of the year in bloom, except perhaps autumn and early winter. And then I found a huge orange-bracted one, *Bougainvillea* 'Camarillo Fiesta', to fill that gap as well. In other words, it was great while it lasted. Although the bougainvilleas never quite reached the splendor of the vines in California, they came close. And no one but me knew about the mealy bugs. Yet, that dirty little secret was our undoing. I've never found a substitute that gives the same impact in my home. I'm still searching for the right match.

Bougainvillea ×*buttiana* and *B. glabra*
BOUGAINVILLEA

FLOWERS	White, but the more showy papery flower bracts are magenta, yellow, white, or orange
FOLIAGE	Mid-green and rounded, densely covering the woody stems
OTHER ATTRIBUTES	Woody vining stems have thorns
SIZE	Vining 6 feet (183cm) in height or more
EXPOSURE	South
WATER REQUIREMENTS	Medium; prefers not to wilt between waterings
OPTIMUM NIGHTTIME TEMPERATURE	60–70°F (15–21°C)
RATE OF GROWTH	Fast
SOIL TYPE	Any rich soil; a heavier soil seems to work better than a light, fluffy one
FERTILIZING	Early spring to late autumn
PROBLEMS	Mealy bugs with a vengeance. Bougainvilleas have thorns that can cause skin irritations.

HELIOTROPE

Summertime is my only shot at the heliotrope I can't survive without. To get the full dosage of their inimitable aroma, I jam a huge window box full of *Heliotropium arborescens* and *H. arborescens* 'Alba'.

SUMMER IS A series of sensations. Summer is sticky skin and beating sun streaming through the panes. It's the breeze from open windows. Summer is serenaded by the soothing saw of insects outdoors and the annoying hum of flies inside. Somewhere in that brew, there's the scent of heliotrope. Summer wouldn't be summer without that intrinsic element.

Certain scents are particularly seductive. The fact that heliotrope combines the aromas of baby powder, apples, and vanilla has everything to do with why I grow the plant. We're talking about *Heliotropium arborescens*, not to be confused with *Valeriana officinalis* (sometimes known as garden heliotrope, but with a decidedly cheesy smell and never used as a potted plant or houseplant, as far as I know). *Heliotropium arborescens* has a comforting, feel-good, uplifting scent. Nobody could be depressed for long with a heliotrope by your side. Your dog might be your best friend, but take a deep whiff of his wet fur and tell me, which would you rather inhale, Fido or heliotrope flowers? On the strength of its scent, heliotrope is often invited inside. But I've given up trying to accommodate heliotrope indoors. Its dimensions definitely fit—that's not the problem. The difficulty lies in my growing conditions. I just can't summon the necessary sun to grow a plant that was named for its love of light. To be honest, I'm not sure that any home could cobble together conditions that would please a heliotrope. In summer, you might stand a chance.

So I grow heliotrope outdoors on my porch. Every year, I stuff a window box chockfull of heliotrope to spill over its ample edges and billow its scent into the thick summer air. In fact, as I type this, the full force of a heliotrope blossom chorus is pouring its aroma through the screen of my office window to seduce me away from my desk. The ploy isn't likely to succeed, considering that I'm enjoying the benefits of the plant's company while also getting my work accomplished. This experience is what growing heliotrope is all about.

The foliage isn't bad looking. *Heliotropium arborescens* has long, slender, flannel-like leaves etched with pronounced veins. Their color is dark green, making the blue flowers stand out like jewels. Most blue heliotropes are upright and branching. The 'Alba' form (which takes the fragrance to another level) has a more lax, loosely trailing habit. All benefit from pinching, but are somewhat self-branching.

Not many blossoms boast the clear violet hue of heliotrope blossoms. The individual flowers are tiny, about the size of forget-me-nots. But they socialize together in long, dense clusters of flowers to achieve the composition. On the strength of their physical virtues, breeders developed a seed strain named 'Marine' that is particularly floriferous

and royal purple, but it lacks the deep-throated redolence for which the plant is prized, and that's a major pity. The lack of fragrance is nothing short of betrayal. On the other hand, 'Iowa' highlights the vanilla ingredient in the aromatic brew, while lightening the flower color to baby blue.

Other than full sun, heliotropes are relatively undemanding. They tolerate drought to some extent, but be careful. After a few wilts, they will be goners. On that note, heliotrope tends to do best with ample root room, so a deep window box is your best plan of action. And a city balcony would work beautifully for heliotrope, especially if it basks in sunbeams. If you're adventurous and want to try heliotrope indoors, give it a south-facing window, water very sparingly, and keep the foliage dry. The moment you see gray mold, whisk the offending part away and keep your fingers crossed. Don't expect blossoms in winter or even early spring. Summer is a heliotrope's moment in the sun.

Heliotropium arborescens

HELIOTROPE

ALSO CALLED: **cherry pie, turnsole**

FLOWERS	**Tiny purple or white open-face blossoms in dense clusters crowning the plant**
FOLIAGE	**Long, felted leaves**
OTHER ATTRIBUTES	**Heavenly and unique fragrance**
SIZE	**1–2 feet (30–61cm) in height**
EXPOSURE	**Bright south**
WATER REQUIREMENTS	**Moderate—do not overwater. Keep the foliage dry if possible.**
OPTIMUM NIGHTTIME TEMPERATURE	**55–65°F (12–18°C)**
RATE OF GROWTH	**Medium**
SOIL TYPE	**Organic container mix**
FERTILIZING	**Early spring to late autumn**
PROBLEMS	**Mealy bugs and whiteflies. Requires bright sun to blossom. Prone to bacterial infections, especially when grown indoors. Heliotrope is toxic.**

HIBISCUS

By all means, grow *Hibiscus* 'Tonga Wind' outdoors all summer. But forgo the heartache and sever the relationship when the first frost threatens.

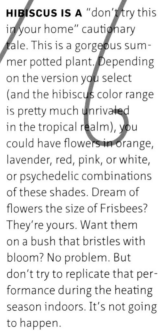

HIBISCUS IS A "don't try this in your home" cautionary tale. This is a gorgeous summer potted plant. Depending on the version you select (and the hibiscus color range is pretty much unrivaled in the tropical realm), you could have flowers in orange, lavender, red, pink, or white, or psychedelic combinations of these shades. Dream of flowers the size of Frisbees? They're yours. Want them on a bush that bristles with bloom? No problem. But don't try to replicate that performance during the heating season indoors. It's not going to happen.

Hibiscus are a delight outdoors. They aren't difficult to grow; just about anybody with some sun and a watering can (or, better still, a hose) can entertain hibiscus. You could even start with something fairly inexpensive and coax it into impressive size before summer's end. But when

frost arrives and it's time for reintroduction into the home, wave a fond farewell to your hibiscus. It won't translate into life indoors.

I've tried with hibiscus inside. A well-meaning friend once gave me her variegated *Hibiscus rosa-sinensis* 'Cooperi' to babysit when she went to Florida for winter. Of course, she figured she was doing me a favor. And I'm sure she meant well. But a winter of struggle ensued while I tried to keep the darn thing foliated. Its dimensions fit my home. 'Cooperi' is compact and can be kept 2 to 3 feet (61–90cm) in diameter. But as soon as the furnace started to roar, it began shedding leaves. That's a typical reaction—talk about a plant that tortures you for your hospitality.

Most of the hibiscus on the market are *Hibiscus rosa-sinensis* hybrids. And they all display their distaste for heating systems by unceremoniously dropping their leaves. Sometimes it's a dramatic protest that happens overnight. In other instances, they slowly shed leaves one at a time. By midwinter, they are virtually naked. Because my 'Cooperi' was someone else's babysitting favor, I kept it in that sorry condition until summer and then put it outside in the fresh air. Only then did it begrudgingly produce leaves again. A month later, it looked just fine. No one was the wiser.

Just a note to anyone who thinks they might have more luck than I did. When hibiscus come indoors, they tend to attract insects who feast on weakening plants in the process of decline. We're talking about the full spectrum of pests, including spider mites, aphids, whiteflies, scale, and mealy bugs (am I leaving anything out?). In other words, they are a liability for the entire horticultural home team. When they don't go naked, they are a worse problem than when they strip.

All warnings out of my system, there's nothing wrong with a summer romance with a hibiscus. They can tolerate baking sun, hot temperatures, and high humidity. They prefer to be watered regularly. And they need plenty of fertilizer and regular container promotions to maintain their deep-green foliar color. If given those conditions, they will reward you with blossoms like you've never experienced. Go ahead. Put a hibiscus around the pool, on your deck, or wherever they can bask in the beams. Their leathery leaves will even stand up against the winds outside your coastal cottage. But kiss that baby good-bye when cold weather comes.

Hibiscus rosa-sinensis

HIBISCUS

FLOWERS	Huge blossoms in a vast array of colors and color combinations
FOLIAGE	Notched, deep-green leaves; variegated version available
OTHER ATTRIBUTES	Great patio plant
SIZE	3–4 feet (90–122cm) in height
EXPOSURE	Bright south
WATER REQUIREMENTS	Water well, but will endure less-than-perfect watering regimen
OPTIMUM NIGHTTIME TEMPERATURE	50–65°F (10–18°C)
RATE OF GROWTH	Fast
SOIL TYPE	Rich, organic potting mix with compost included
FERTILIZING	Between early spring and late autumn
PROBLEMS	Mealy bugs, whiteflies, aphids, scale, spider mites, and leaf drop

Basics

There is no magic regarding houseplants. It's not necessary to be a garden guru, your digits need not include a green thumb of Master Gardener proportions, and a bank of special grow lights is not required equipment. All you really need is a bright window and sensitivity. Actually, the lumen quantity rushing through the window is negotiable. But sensitivity is key.

Frankly, I don't buy the "I don't have a green thumb indoors" excuse for a botanically bereft home. Green thumbs aren't in your genetic makeup. This myth is really just a rationale for attention deficit disorder in the botanical direction. After all, if you failed to give your pets food, water, and care, they would suffer. Same thing happens with your plants. If you pay attention to their needs and furnish their basic requirements, they will grow. If you go a few steps further to really get to know them—that is, if you establish a relationship and keep an eye on their condition—they will thrive. Neglect them, and they're history.

Of course, I'm generalizing. Some plants just don't do well in a home environment. Not all green things were meant to live with us indoors. That's really what this book is all about. I believe plants will empower you as an indoor gardener. I want to see you succeed. The last thing I want to propose is a plant that demands high humidity, very bright light, or all your time and resources. I avoid insect-magnet plants entirely, and so should you. I am recommending plants that work for me. I've actually gone one step further—I'm suggesting plants worth living with up close and intimate. I don't grow every houseplant. No one could, especially within the limited space of a home. I steer away from boring plants that do little or nothing for the decor or my morale. In other words, the plants in the previous sections are worth caring about. And with care, they have the potential to perform.

But I cannot spoon-feed the care formula. All home environments are unique, and weather patterns are always changing. After all, you are working with nature. Even though you are growing indoors, the available light, warmth, and humidity have everything to do with how a plant grows. So I cannot tell you exactly how often to water or when to fertilize. You cannot mark a date on your calendar to water the houseplants and have it bing! on your computer every Tuesday morning.

This is where the sensitivity comes in. Hopefully, you will glance at your houseplants often because they are gorgeous. You will admire their curves and check out their legs. But when you give them a second look, you should also see if the soil is dry. Notice if they are leaning toward the light, and think about whether the leaves are yellowing or browning at the tips. Indoor plants use plenty of body language to convey what they need. Take heed and act accordingly.

This section will help you understand what you are observing. Given my theory that no one is born with horticultural savvy, it follows that botanical smarts must be learned. Here's the crash course on what to watch out for, and how to make horticulture happen in your home. It works for me. Hopefully, it will do likewise for you.

Although it's undeniably athletic as a climber, *Thunbergia grandiflora* earns its keep with a continual supply of sky blue blossoms throughout the seasons.

MAKING THE MATCH

Chamaecyparis obtusa 'Blue Feathers' feels perfectly at home in the winter beside French doors that face east.

PERHAPS OPPOSITES attract with people. But when trying to work a marriage between your home and a plant, the winning approach seems to be matching similarities. Rather than struggling against the odds, I try to give my best shot at making a plant feel at home. Usually it's a bingo. Occasionally, my best intentions at matchmaking aren't good enough. But that's where it helps to be gardening with eyes wide open. When you've got your finger on the pulse, symptoms of discontent are visible early in the game, and you can take preemptive action before a life-or-death situation arises.

LIGHT

Most houses have several venues that can host a plant. The trick lies in bringing together the right plant with the ideal place. It's as simple as that. When you think about it, you probably intuitively know how the light moves around your home. You put the breakfast table in the morning (east) sunbeams and the cat sprawls on the overstuffed chair in the afternoon (west) sun to snooze after lunch. In summer, you might pull the shades on the sunny south side of the house. Apply this information to your plant selections, bearing in mind that your domain might not be able to give certain plants their optimal conditions. Avoid those plants. They won't make good housemates.

There is nowhere in my house that provides very bright sunlight in the middle of winter. Experience has taught me to steer away from plants that demand that sort of situation. Even though I have a lean-to greenhouse (it's actually a corridor with glass on one side connecting my office to a converted barn), the corridor faces east and throughout the winter my office obstructs the light (needless to say, I wasn't the one who designed the configuration). The greenhouse gives me lots of space to grow plants during winters, but the light levels are no better than your average bright window. Beyond that, I have some south-facing windows, some east- and west-facing windows, a set of French doors facing east, and only one window facing north. Every window except the northern exposure is jammed with plants. I'm not exaggerating.

When I hit a garden center and start trawling for likely horticultural housemates, light is the foremost issue on my mind. As Roger Swain pointed out to me long ago, you can change many things about your home to accommodate plants, but you can't (easily) move your windows.

A window doesn't need to be huge, but position a plant such as the Calamondin orange, ×*Citrofortunella microcarpa*, where the foliage will bask in the sunbeams.

So if I walk into a nursery and see an adorable miniature rose, I walk on by. I cannot furnish that plant with the sort of sun it demands. Ditto for the calceolarias parading their wares in the supermarkets for Easter (they also get demerits for being whitefly magnets). They demand the high beams. Without sufficient light, the plant might not blossom, so why bother? Even worse, it will probably take a nosedive. And a stressed plant is a bug beacon, because it will jeopardize the rest of its companions. Everything can go down with the ship.

Of course, it's not a totally cut-and-dried situation. Nothing in nature is absolute; many factors come into play. A white wall on the far side of a small room can reflect light (or a dark wall can have the opposite effect). You can stage plants so they sit close to the incoming light. And you can rotate a plant's container so exposure is balanced, which is important in creating a symmetrical specimen.

Generally, a south-facing window is brightest and works beautifully for sun-loving plants as long as they are not light-guzzlers, such as cacti. I find that west-facing windows are a close second, especially in winter. They work for shade-loving plants and might even suffice for some sun-lovers. East works for shade-loving plants. North might work for cast-iron plants, but I usually don't bother. Most plants stretch in north and look like a shadow of their potential selves. I have no experience with fluorescent lights or other auxiliary light units except for seed starting (and I don't enlist them anymore, opting for natural light instead). The fluorescent look just doesn't fit with the homey aesthetic I'm trying to create.

The beauty is, there is not a whole lot of guesswork. The plant will let you know when the situation is wrong. Too little light, and the plant will stretch toward the window or make long, leggy growth. It might develop yellow or brown leaves. Then the leaves might fall. Pay attention to the plant's body language and step in to fix the problem before things start to get ugly.

Maybe you've got too much light. That situation does not usually arise in a home in the Northeast over the winter, when most gardeners resort to houseplants. But if you're gardening on the upper floor of a tall building, or if you've got a reflective water source (a lake, the ocean) nearby, or if you live in the South, you might run into issues. The symptoms are leaf scorching. This might start as white burn marks on the leaves, but these eventually brown. Or a leaf might frizzle as if baked. If you bring houseplants outside for a summer sojourn after a winter in darker conditions, scorching can be a definite issue. All plants should be acclimatized, as discussed in the summer section. But the point is that light will probably be the primary issue to consider when selecting a botanical roommate.

TEMPERATURE

The general misconception exists that houseplants need a toasty environment. Over and over I hear that a home lacks houseplants because it is not warm enough. I'm here to tell you that heat is usually not an issue. For the vast majority of houseplants, if your home is warm enough for your family, it will be fine for plants.

Okay, my house is not typical, I'll be the first to admit. Because my living configuration includes a three-story-tall converted barn, heating is not streamlined. I just pile on sweaters and keep the thermostat at 60°F (15°C) during the day, with a five-degree drop overnight. I'm not suggesting for a nanosecond that you live in similarly Spartan conditions. But I would like to point out that all my plants thrive. That includes begonias, bougainvilleas, and chiritas—plants usually classified as heat-lovers. However, streptocarpus do not fare so well.

A good working thermostat range is between 65°F and 70°F (18–21°C) during the day, with a five-degree drop overnight. Of course, you can go up and down slightly. Too warm over an extended period of time, and you'll get stretchy growth over the winter and insect activity might increase. For each plant, I've recommended optimal conditions, focusing on nighttime temperatures with the assumption that the sun might warm the house during the day.

My advice is to set your thermostat where you are most comfortable, and hope for the best. Keep plants away from heat vents and cold drafts. I do not fret about proximity to windowpanes for temperature issues, however. Drafts or chilliness beside the window never seem to pose problems, even though my older noninsulated windows are admittedly breezy. But I do not grow plants that fuss over temperature fluctuations.

When in doubt, it's simple: use a thermometer. If you yearn to grow streptocarpus and your house is cool, there might be a space by the stove that is just a little bit warmer. Homes have ecosystems just like the varying habitats outdoors. My bathroom, for example, tends to be a few degrees warmer than the rest of the house. If a plant wants warmth, that's where it goes.

HUMIDITY

Lack of humidity can be an issue, especially during the winter. How can you tell if humidity is insufficient? If the cat starts sparking, your lips are chapped, and your skin feels like sandpaper, your humidity levels are probably low. Certain plants will not care—for example, cacti and succulents thrive in low humidity. But the majority of them might suffer.

How do you remedy the problem? Not with misting. I don't know how these ideas get started, but whoever began the association between misting and houseplants was all wet. You would have to apply mist night and day 24/7 to make any sort of impact whatsoever. And many plants become prone to disease when water sits constantly on their leaves, especially during clammy winter weather. Instead, a humidifier is the easiest solution. Or you might try a pebble tray, which is simply a tray with a lip, filled with an inch or so of pebbles and half an inch of water. The plants sit on the pebbles above the water, and the water evaporates around them.

My trick is to grow so many plants that their moist soil increases the humidity in my home. "The more, the merrier" theory definitely works for the plants. And my sinuses love it, too.

CHEMISTRY

I've been rattling on about practical issues to consider when selecting a plant to bring home. But really, whether you succeed or fail with a plant has a lot to do with attraction. If someone saddles you with a plant you really do not want but feel obligated to grow, the result will not be pretty. You will forget about it. You will fail to meet its needs, guaranteed. If you feel sort of lukewarm about a plant at point of purchase, the relationship might lack chemistry. If you feel the magnetic pull and it tugs at your heartstrings, that's a good beginning.

Of course, there are practical considerations, as well, like health. Do not try to be Mother Teresa to all the benighted plants in the supermarket. If they look like they are on their last legs, galloping to their rescue is probably not worth the investment. In fact, it might jeopardize the houseplants back at the ranch. A stressed plant is prone to insects and

disease, which can spread like an epidemic to your (formerly) healthy crew. No point in going there.

I avoid plants that look like they are headed downhill. If they are beginning to get leggy, if they are clearly pot-bound, if they are at the end of their blooming cycle, I go for something in a fresher state. Start with a sweet young thing and let the relationship blossom—that's my advice.

A note about toxicity: it's tricky. As you can tell from earlier chapters, I'm a cat lover. I couldn't survive without a cat or houseplants. And I wouldn't imperil my kitten for the world. I love kids, too. And some plants are toxic. Some do harm to certain animals and not to others. For example, deer ingest lilies like they are chocolate, but they are extremely poisonous to cats. Plus, plants might come into your home with leaves laden with pesticides from the nursery. I suggest keeping all plants out of the reach of children and pets. That's the safest approach. For more information on toxicity, search the web. An

excellent site to start with is aspca.org/pet-care/poison-control/plants.

Consider all these elements in your home environment and jive them with the preferences of the plants you select, and the match should work. Everything I'm addressing does not vary vastly from welcoming any new plant into your outdoor garden. You take into account available sun and your hardiness zone, as well as other conditions. But houseplants are even easier. You are in the driver's seat for soil and water when you garden indoors. And you can easily pick up and move around container-grown plants. If a plant pleads for brighter light, no need to dig it up and replant—just shuffle the pots around. Easy as that. You can succeed with houseplants. Gloriously.

CARE

TAKING CARE OF houseplants is not rocket science or anything remotely difficult. However, it does require a little insight. You might have to get into the rhythm of gardening indoors. But once you have mastered the art and science, the routine will become second nature. And the rewards will transform your home and life.

It is true that you shoulder more control (and responsibility) for houseplants than for their garden-grown counterparts. But that can work in your favor. When the weather fails to furnish rain for weeks at a time, it's pretty much business as usual for your houseplants. You just get out the watering can. As with outdoors, indoor gardening is affected by Mother Nature's antics. Paying attention to the environment is key when growing any plant. Proper watering, feeding, potting, and repotting can make the difference between success and failure. As for grooming, pruning, and all the other attendant aspects of gardening indoors, they might not be critical, but they will give you happier, healthier plants. Might as well go for the glitz, right?

POTTING AND CONTAINERS

Everything in this section is intertwined. That is the harmony of nature—you have to see the big picture. But the framework for successful indoor gardening starts when you fetch your new plant home and introduce it to the fleet. Without exception, I start by transplanting my new acquisition from its plastic container into a pot of my choosing. No chore about it; this is the fun part for me. I usually go with terra-cotta, but not always. I sometimes match the plant with a metal or faux container. But I always do something decorative. Beauty is what it's all about.

Well, not totally. Aesthetics are important, but practicality is even more crucial. I think about the root system. I consider the plant's future care. If it is a citrus, I am likely to give it a deep container because the roots tend to plunge down and I do not want to repot it again tomorrow. On the other hand, begonia roots are apt to grow outward, not down. So I give begonias wide, rather than tall, containers. When deciding on the size of the container, look at the roots. Have they filled the current container? If not, find a container of the same size. Sometimes I even demote the plant to a smaller footprint when the nursery has given it a huge pot to increase its perceived value.

In my houseplant-troubleshooting experience, I find that gardeners tend to overpot plants. Plants do get infinite root room in a garden bed, but that doesn't translate to container gardening. As a rule, graduate a plant only one or two pot sizes at a time. When a plant is swimming in too much soil without sufficient roots to soak up the moisture, the soil conditions tend to get soggy, especially over the winter. It's like giving a child shoes that are several sizes too big, hoping she'll grow into them quickly. Her feet might eventually fill the space, but they'll flop around while in the process. Same with plants. Whether you are potting a cutting or transplanting a plant, one step at a time is the way to go.

When you pot, be sure to firm the soil around the root system. Airholes will cause the roots to dry out. I am not suggesting that you cement the soil in, but make sure it fills all the gaps. I use my fingers to push it in (I have small hands). Another method is to use a pencil or stick to fill gaps. Then tap the container on the potting bench to settle it down, adding more soil if necessary.

It is critical to have space for watering between the soil surface and the container's rim. For a large container, leave at least an inch between the soil and rim for this purpose. For smaller containers, half an inch should suffice. Without that lip, water will flow over the side of the container. Not only will it be a mopping mess, but the water will never have the opportunity to percolate down.

When purchasing containers, I think about practicality first and foremost. But I also take a long, hard look at the shape of a container before plunking down my money. Bean pot shapes (tapering to a smaller opening at their rim from a stout middle) are

a bear when it's time to repot. I use them only if there is scant chance the plant will ever need promotions. I never enlist improbable salvaged things with insufficient root room as containers because they are rarely suited for this repurpose. But I do use industrial metal cylinders for plants, and they make the job switch seamlessly. I spend a lot of time drilling holes for drainage. Many containers lack holes, but it's simple enough to apply the cement drill. However, keep in mind that glazing might chip while you're drilling. Don't take the risk with anything expensive; that Ming vase would be better left empty.

A quick word about self-watering containers. I haven't experimented sufficiently with these systems, but my gut reaction is to be suspicious. It seems unlikely that the soil will ever dry out enough to give the roots the oxygen they need, but I haven't encountered a self-watering system that has lured me into giving it a try. And I enjoy watering my plants. It's part of the experience.

Select a container that is one size larger than the original when repotting. Always wear gloves and protective clothing when working with plants.

Drainage is critical. If a pot does not have drainage holes, create them. I no longer bother to insert "cracking" or pot shards in the bottom of a container. Drainage holes suffice.

SOIL MIXES

Finding the right potting soil also spells the difference between success and failure. It is paramount. When I first went to work in a commercial greenhouse, we concocted several custom potting soil mixes to suit the needs of specific plants. There was a fern mix, a begonia mix, a succulent mix, and so on. Nowadays, it's more of a one-size-fits-all industry. And that seems to be effective. My advice is to explore several potting mixes and find the one that works for the majority of your plants. Sometimes, it's not love at first sight.

I don't attempt to make my own potting mix from scratch. I don't have the time or facilities to sterilize loam or fiddle with a pile of ingredients. I rely on bagged, commercial potting soils. However, don't assume that a mix will work just because it features a label declaring it a "Container Mix." It's wise to look twice at the soil you use for potting houseplants. Don't assume all mixes are the same.

I use organic potting soils, but I don't think any old organic mix is sufficient for my plants. It's a mystery to me why soilless mixes have gathered such a following. Yes, they are lightweight, making your plants more portable and easier to ship. But do you carry your plants around continually? I move mine every once in a while, but it's more important to heft a healthy plant into a prime position than tote around a poor anemic specimen.

I seek out a potting soil with soil and/or compost included. I feel strongly about this. Plants raised on a purely peat-based mix look like they've been fed a fast-food diet. I can tell the difference. I give my plants a good, strong foundation, and they respond with vigorous growth.

Beyond being organic, I also select soils that have a friable consistency. Many potting soils on the market have poor drainage. Fortunately, you can do a simple "squeeze test" to discover if the soil has the proper makeup. Grab a handful of lightly moistened soil, ball it gently into your palm, and let go. If it falls apart, it's golden. If it remains in a glob, it will not drain well. Muddy soils can spell disaster for houseplants. The roots actually smother because of lack of oxygen, and it's often a slow, painful death. I avoid mixes with vermiculite because it tends to give the soil a sticky, globby consistency. Although pearly white perlite is not particularly good-looking, I prefer it to vermiculite. But I often work with soils with no perlite or vermiculite.

Before potting with any soil, moisten it lightly (keep in mind there is a vast difference between moistened and soggy). Ideally, you should do so a few hours (or at least a few minutes) before potting to let the water seep in. Then stir up the soil to distribute the moisture. After potting, give the new transplant another drink. During the potting process, you've probably teased out and disturbed the roots, and they need water to settle in. After that initial watering, check for cavities where the soil has migrated down. If it has, top off with soil.

The potting soil that you use for a plant should break apart easily after you squeeze a moistened ball into a fist.

When you have umpteen houseplants to quench, your watering-can selection is critical. Mine is nothing fancy, but the spout is slender to achieve a direct hit without dribbling. Take aim and fire.

WATERING

All of gardening is interconnected. The way you water has everything to do with the type of soil you use. When I teach, my students always beg for a formula. "So, do you water every three days, or what?" they ask, pens poised. There are no formulas; there is no schedule. When I wake up in the morning, I stroll through the house visually checking my plants for dryness. All 300 of them. Some will be dry, others will not. If the weather has been cloudy and rainy, none will be thirsty. When it's sunny outside, several will need a drink. Sometimes the whole crew has to be quenched.

How do you know when a plant needs water? Don't wait for it to wilt. Withholding water until a plant slips into a faint is stressful, and stress makes a plant susceptible to insect infestations. Some people suggest "the weight test," the theory being that dry soils are lighter than their wet counterparts. With several hundred plants, the last thing I want to do is pick up each one to determine whether the soil is moist or dry. Instead, I just eyeball it. It works for me, and it'll work for you. Soil turns pale when it is dry, and that's when it's ready to be watered. Don't let the soil get to the parched stage, even with succulents. If it becomes too dry, the soil will not take up water properly or distribute moisture evenly.

Of course, if you are new to this, start by doing the "finger test." Insert your finger down an inch or so and feel the soil for dryness. With this method, you will gain a sense (literally) of what the soil looks like when it is dry. It's a good way to get a feel for it.

As for top dressing, I occasionally use sheet moss or river stones and sometimes even go the pinecone route. It adds another dimension to the look. But a top dressing can add to the guesswork when watering. The only wise counsel I can share is to wait until you have a feeling for how often a plant dries out before hiding the soil under top dressing. Or be prepared to dig a finger in periodically to sample the soil.

Depending on the weather, plants tend to need more water in the summer than in the winter. But during a summer rainy spell, you might not need to water at all for a week or more. And when the temperatures outdoors are frigid and the heat is running full blast both day and night, you might need to water daily. But, in general, plants dry out more frequently during the warmer and sunnier seasons of the year.

How much water should you deliver per serving? If you have potted your plant correctly, you will have space between the soil surface and the rim edge. Fill it up with water, then let it slowly seep down. There is no need to fill it several times at the same serving. When a plant is watered regularly, the water should penetrate slowly down to the roots and nourish them. If the water you have just served goes rushing down and out the drainage hole like a waterfall, something is wrong. When soils are too dry, they fail to moisten like a sponge. Instead, they just shed water—it's like stormwater runoff. The remedy is to soak the plant from the

bottom by adding water to the saucer and letting it draw up gradually. After you've remedied the emergency, go back to watering normally, and apply water more faithfully in the future.

Saucers are imperative for keeping your furniture and floors tidy. I select handsome ones because it's all about aesthetics for me. Cheap, clear plastic saucers aren't my speed. But there's nothing wrong with enlisting your plates or using copper trays. I don't own any expensive furniture, but I still don't want to mar the surfaces in my decor. Keep in mind that unglazed saucers can leave mildew marks on wood. It might be wise to add a cork trivet or tuck a tablecloth underneath a plant.

The main trick is to find a saucer that is wide enough to handle any overflow that might dribble out of the drainage hole. Even if you water a plant properly, there is bound to be a little excess that puddles out. You need

Top dressing isn't essential, but it's a nice touch. For an evergreen, pinecones seem apropos.

It's true that my furniture is mostly shabby chic, but every plant in my home sits on a saucer or a zinc tray. Fitting each pot with the right saucer size can keep surfaces from being ruined.

something capable of catching that runoff effectively. Because I'm caring for hundreds of plants, I do not empty each saucer after the water dribbles down. Everything does just fine nonetheless.

I have hard, mineral-rich water in my home. With this quantity of plants, I certainly don't purchase bottled water for them. And it isn't an issue. I've lived in towns with treated water, and the plants drank without problems. If you find your plants are suffering and suspect your water might be the culprit, try collecting rainwater or purchasing the bottled version.

I use a watering can to water and aim the spout strategically at the soil surface. I can't imagine watering a small potted plant with a "rose" sprinkling attachment on a watering can. Although

African violets are notorious for their dislike of water sprinkled on their foliage, they are not alone. In cloudy weather, especially in winter, make sure not to wet the leaves. My containers come in all shapes and sizes, varying from tiny on up, so I use a slender-spouted can that I can point precisely. It makes all the difference.

I water in the morning to let the plants drink all day long. It's a ritual, really. After watering, that wonderful smell of earth and moisture wafts into the air. My complexion loves it. It smells like home.

FEEDING

I think gardeners put too much emphasis on the need to feed houseplants, but I don't grow in a soil-less mix. My soil mixes have built-in nutrition, and the plants need not survive only from one meal to the next. Fertilizer isn't a life-or-death situation. When I worked in a retail nursery, we always told customers to feed with a balanced fertilizer with an even distribution of nitrogen, phosphorous, and potassium (N-P-K), such as 20-20-20, once every three weeks or so. Rather than a chemical fertilizer, I now use an organic fish emulsion at the same intervals—once every three weeks. Although it is not a balanced fertilizer, it works when combined with good potting soil underfoot.

One piece of advice remains the same. Do not fertilize during late autumn and winter, when light levels are low. There are exceptions. I'm always monitoring for houseplants with that lean and hungry look. And I find that gardenias, citrus, and stephanotis need a shot of fertilizer in February as soon as light levels begin to increase. If any plant begins to look starved, I serve up appetizers. It's the same old sensitivity refrain I've been harping on throughout this section. When you start fertilizing in spring, do it gradually, diluting the fertilizer a little more than the label directions suggest. Otherwise, faithfully follow the instructions. From a plant's point of view, more is not better, and gluttony can lead to problems down the road far more serious than mere obesity.

PRUNING

Not everyone loves to prune, but I do. My mother-in-law used to rant, "How would you feel if someone cut off all your fingers and toes?" after I went on a pruning spree. But when the begonias (or whatever) bristled with new growth, she beamed. I like to keep a tight ship. And I think pruning brings about a sharper picture in the long run.

I'm almost always brandishing pruning shears. Although the rampage against leggy limbs reaches its high point in spring, I hit shaggy appendages whenever they appear. In winter, plants often make stretchy growth because of diminished light. Away it goes. In autumn, when plants re-enter the house after their summer sojourn, they often become too large for their allotted space. Clip. And sometimes I just want to exercise control and encourage a plant to branch out during the summer or sprout fresh from the base in winter. Off with its head. I think good grooming spells the difference between an okay crowd of amateurs and a turned-out kick line of well-rehearsed performers.

When pruning plants, make your cut right above where the leaf blade juts out, and be sure there is a side sprout waiting in the wings to branch out. Some plants, like begonias and pelargoniums, have what we call "blind eyes" with no side shoots. They might sprout lower down or push another branch up from the base, but they will not branch just below the cut.

If pruning has you quaking in your boots, I can only say that I have never (or almost never) murdered a plant by pruning. I have ended up with some gawky specimens as a result of clueless cuts, but time healed the wounds. And I sometimes chopped too enthusiastically in winter and sent the plant into a temporary tailspin. But if you play it safe and prune in spring and make sure there are side sprouts, you are on fairly safe ground. Your plants will have more branches and increased bloom, and will form a handsomer picture. Why would you resist?

Cut right above the leaf node (in this case, we're working on a pelargonium) to encourage that side shoot to branch out.

Some plants, such as this acalypha, can become leggy, but make branches from the base. Cut away the old, woody growth and let the young, compact stems have their moment in the sun.

A truly yellow leaf (as opposed to one that is slightly chlorotic because of nutrient deficiencies) will never improve. Whisk it away.

GROOMING

When watering my plants, I come back to the faucet via the composting can clutching a handful of dead leaves and flowers to discard. Forever in the process of growth, plants are also continually shedding. But it's no worse than your cat. And most of the time, the cleanup is considerably less arduous.

I figure that a yellow leaf will probably never look prime again. I'm not talking about slightly pale green leaves, which can darken up if given fertilizer. But when a leaf is going south, what is the point in leaving it to tarnish the plant's image? Might as well clip it off. There is no hope for a brown leaf. It's gone. Same with spent flowers and flower stems. Take them away before they attract disease spores. The scene will look so much better.

Some plants make more of a mess than others. I adopted *Loropetalum chinense* this year, and I am beginning to regret it. Each flower is composed of many thread-like pink petals that look lovely while they are prime. But when their moment of glory passes, they shower all over the floor. Or, even worse, they shrivel up and cling to the branch like the Wicked Witch of the West's broom. You know the look. Same for the powder puff shrub, calliandra. It is divine while blossoming in autumn, but what a mess after the show is over.

Of course, shattered petals are not always an eyesore. I sort of like the way a camellia's petals float to the floor. Ditto for fuchsia blossoms. And not all plants are self-cleaning. For example, you have to snip off pelargonium flowers. But keep tabs on it. Basically, if it looks ugly, get rid of it. This is your home, after all. You make the rules.

INSECTS

Whenever I lecture or teach, the first question I hear from people on the verge of adopting houseplants has to do with insects. Are they a problem? Not in my house. That's the truth. I don't grow plants that are prone to insects. I keep my home temperatures cool, which really helps for limiting insect issues. I check the plants carefully for bugs before incorporating them into my home garden. I wish I had room to segregate them, but I don't, so I monitor them carefully. If a problem occurs with a plant, I usually just discard it. That's the way I deal with bugs.

My approach to pest control is to treat my plants very well. When a plant is healthy, insects rarely infect it. Watering regularly is key. If a plant is invaded by aphids (and that is generally the full extent of my issues), it is because I've somehow neglected it. Beyond watering, light levels also affect a plant's overall health. When a plant isn't getting sufficient light, it will suffer. I grow plants only where they have a good chance of thriving.

I grow organically in my home, so I don't spray. On the very rare occasions when I really, really want to keep a plant despite a problem, I start with very mild organic insecticides, such as insecticidal soap or neem oil. Ultra-fine horticultural oil is another option for most houseplants. If these remedies don't work, I discard the plant. Keep in mind that organic sprays must come in contact with the insect to be effective.

No matter what I am applying, I always spray outdoors and wear protective clothing. For all insecticides, even the organic formulas, always read, understand, and follow the manufacturer's recommendations and warnings. If a spray is not prescribed for a certain insect, do not apply it. My agricultural-extension agent warned that insecticidal soaps sometimes do not work with hard water. In addition, certain plants might be sensitive to soaps and oils. Ferns—especially maidenhair ferns (adiantums)—and some succulents (I have heard that

crassulas are sensitive) can react negatively. And be careful when you bring a plant back into the fold after applying any sort of treatment. Keep it away from pets and kids.

Watch out for insects. Needless to say, it is much easier to get a grip on a bug problem when it is fairly contained. When pest population numbers multiply, the nightmares begin. Your best method of patrol is to learn to identify the usual suspects. For the most part, houseplants tend to be pestered by aphids (clearly visible with the naked eye, they look like green, cream, or black many-legged critters about the size of a tiny water drop, usually found on the young leaves and flowers), spider mites (visible if you have great eyesight, these web-forming red bugs crawl on the undersides of leaves), mealy bugs (easily visible cottony masses often wedged in the juncture between leaf and stem), root mealy bugs (cottony masses in the root system and a pill to combat—just toss the plant), whiteflies (tiny but visible white flying insects that roost on leaf undersides and take wing when you disturb the leaf), and scale (easily visible little brown raised bumps on the leaf or stem surface). I occasionally get infestations of fungus gnats, especially when I am raising seedlings and watering them frequently (they dote on constantly moist soil surfaces). They are unsightly little flying bugs, but they don't bother me and I don't worry about them. Although some indoor growers have issues with slugs, they aren't one of my problems. Slug baits are available, but a simple diabolical beer trap of your favorite lager poured on a pie plate should do the trick.

Purchasing a hand lens or magnifier is a great idea when working with plants of any kind. Not all bumps and deposits on leaf surfaces are bugs. Some plants, like gardenias and passion flowers, have an exudate that forms on the leaf surface. It does no harm.

If you do opt to spray a plant for an insect problem, keep in mind that one spraying is probably not going to squelch the problem, especially when you are working with an organic method. After you identify the perpetrator, learn about the duration of its reproductive cycle and remember to keep up a regular regimen. Or try predatory insects, which work to keep a population in check. (But if your predator eats all of its prey, it will starve, so you will need a resupply.) I have not had to work with predators. I have a resident population of ladybugs that does a lot of patrolling. Unfortunately, Einstein has a vendetta against ladybugs, but he hasn't succeeded in decimating the population. Yet.

Needless to say, if you see a problem, immediately segregate the imperiled plant and its livestock. If at all possible, put it outside, away from the rest of the indoor-plant community. But don't assume that Mother Nature is going to step in and sort things out. When insects find a promising meal ticket, they tend to hang around the café and chow down. Intervene. Outdoor pests are rarely an issue when you put plants outside, except for slugs and snails can be a problem. Monitor for and remove them, especially when you bring a plant back inside.

DISEASES

Keeping a plant tidy and its foliage dry will go a long way toward limiting your disease issues. Again, a healthy, well-fed, unstressed plant should not have problems. But if you find a leaf that is mushy or has brown spots or browning edges, get rid of the offender. Don't wait for whatever has gone wrong with that leaf to infect the rest of the plant or its neighbors. Just take it away.

I very rarely have problems with diseases on plants. I steer away from sticky wickets. For example, I don't grow heliotrope in the winter because it tends to have issues: I can't provide sufficient sun for a heliotrope to thrive, so it is continually stressed. I have tried to recommend plants that are a good match for the average home. Nobody wants to watch a plant pout until it perishes. In that same spirit, I avoid certain plants because they have a tendency to develop powdery mildew. Mildew is my foremost bugaboo indoors. Although I have excellent air circulation in my house (old buildings tend to be drafty), the breezes are not sufficient to keep rex begonias from getting powdery mildew. I just avoid growing them. And again, always segregate a problem immediately. By all means, make that call to the extension agency to get a diagnosis for your problem. But in the meantime, put distance between the sick plant and the rest of your pack.

TROUBLESHOOTING

All these elements combine into one big care picture. Often, indoor gardeners panic and only make the situation worse. A better method might be to hold the status quo. If a plant is beginning to falter, drenching it with water is not going to remedy the problem. Ditto for throwing on the fertilizer when a plant is on its deathbed. Instead, keep up the slow-but-steady watering regimen that houseplants prefer and don't try to serve a feast to a plant when it's headed for the hospital. If your plant is on shaky ground, check out the root system. The roots should be healthy and slightly swollen, rather than shriveled or nonexistent. If the roots do not warrant more room, don't assume it needs a pot graduation. If the root system is insufficient, a wiser plan of action might be to demote the plant to a smaller container.

Moderation in all things isn't a bad approach to indoor gardening. Rather than reacting, think through the problem—and its remedy. Look for the source of the issue. Is the plant growing in soil that has good drainage? Are you watering properly? Does the plant have sufficient light? Make a mental checklist and do the detective work. Keep your finger on the pulse of your houseplants. The relationship will blossom.

FINALE

So that is what it's like in my home. This is my life. Yes, I had to juggle the plants around a little so you could see the forest for the trees when we were photographing. But the plants in these pages reside by my side day in and day out, season after season, throughout the years. And I've got to say that we've grown accustomed to each other, like family. The ctenanthe is used to getting whopped as I breeze by on the way into the kitchen, and the sedum that showers from its container has learned to take some gentle stomping as I move around the house.

The point is, we're intimate. I can't imagine an existence devoid of the plants that fill my life and living space. I couldn't survive in a world without green. And I'm not so very different from you. I'm hoping you will find it contagious. No, you don't have to do this with my level of fervor or fanaticism. But bring a few plants into your home and it will make all the difference. It will change your world, I promise.

Happiness is a healthy,
lush houseplant
 grinning in a window
near you.

SOURCES

Ballek's Garden Center
90 Maple Ave.
East Haddam, CT 06423
860-873-8878
balleksgardencenter.com

Brushwood Nursery
gardenvines.com

Campo de' Fiori
1815 North Main St.
Sheffield, MA 01257
413-528-1857
campodefiori.com

Gilbertie's Herb Gardens
7 Sylvan Lane
Westport, CT 06880
203-227-4175
gilbertiesherbs.com

Glasshouse Works
glasshouseworks.com

Goldner Walsh Nursery
559 Orchard Lake Rd.
Pontiac, MI 48341
248-332-6430
goldnerwalsh.com

Hollandia Nurseries
95 Stony Hill Rd.
Bethel, CT 06801
203-792-0268
ctgrown.com

J&L Orchids
20 Sherwood Rd.
Easton, CT 06612
203-261-3772
jlorchids.com

Kartuz Greenhouses
1408 Sunset Dr.
Vista, CA 92081
760-941-3613
kartuz.com

Lauray of Salisbury
432 Undermountain Rd.
Salisbury, CT 06068
860-435-2263
lauray.com

Logee's Tropical Plants
141 North St.
Danielson, CT 06239
888-330-8038
logees.com

Peckham's Greenhouse
200 West Main Rd.
Little Compton, RI 02837
401-635-4775
peckhamsgreenhouse.com

Pergola
7 East Shore Rd.
New Preston, CT 06777
860-868-4769
pergolahome.com

Terrain at Styer's
914 Baltimore Pike
Glen Mills, PA 19342
610-459-2400
shopterrain.com

Waldor Orchids
10 East Poplar Ave.
Linwood, NJ 08221
609-927-4126
waldor.com

Walker Farm
1190 US Rt. 5
East Dummerston, VT 05346
802-254-2051
walkerfarm.com

Alber, John I., and Delores M. Alber. 1987. *Baby-Safe Houseplants and Cut Flowers.* Highland, IL: Genus Books.

Alioto, Michele Driscoll. 2002. *Glorious Indoor Gardens.* New York: Stewart, Tabori and Chang.

Crockett, James Underwood. 1971. *Flowering House Plants.* New York: Time-Life Books.

Cruso, Thalassa. 1972. *Making Things Grow.* New York: Alfred A. Knopf.

Turner, Nancy, and Patrick von Aderkas. 2009. *Common Poisonous Plants and Mushrooms of North America.* Portland, OR: Timber Press.

Langer, Richard W. 1975. *Grow It Indoors.* New York: Saturday Review Press.

Loewer, Peter. 1974. *Bringing the Outdoors In.* Chicago: Contemporary Books.

Loewer, Peter. 1990. *The Indoor Window Garden.* Chicago: Contemporary Books.

Marston, Peter. 1998. *Garden Room Style.* New York: Rizzoli.

Martin, Byron E., and Laurelynn G. Martin. 2005. *Logee's Greenhouses Spectacular Container Plants.* Minocqua, WI: Willow Creek Press.

Martin, Laurelynn G., and Byron E. Martin. 2010. *Growing Tasty Tropical Plants.* North Adams, MA: Storey Publishing LLC.

Martin, Tovah. 1991. *The Essence of Paradise.* Boston: Houghton Mifflin.

Martin, Tovah. 2009. *The New Terrarium.* New York: Clarkson Potter.

Martin, Tovah. 1988. *Once Upon a Windowsill.* Portland, OR: Timber Press.

Martin, Tovah. 1994. *Well-Clad Windowsills.* New York: Macmillan.

McCreary, Rosemary. 2002. *Tabletop Gardens.* North Adams, MA: Storey Publishing LLC.

McDonald, Elvin. 1993. *The New Houseplant.* New York: Macmillan.

Peterson, Deborah. 2008. *Don't Throw It, Grow It!* North Adams, MA: Storey Publishing LLC.

Pleasant, Barbara. 2005. *The Complete Houseplant Survival Manual.* North Adams, MA: Storey Publishing LLC.

Toogood, Alan. 1986. *Indoor Gardens.* Topsfield, MA: Salem House Publishers.

INDEX

M

Madagascar jasmine, 125, 272
maidenhair ferns, 110, 313
Manadarin orange, 41
marantas / *Maranta leuconeura* / *Marantaceae*, 59, 60, 61, 62, 63
marjoram, 128, 131
Marrubium vulgare, 130
masdevallias, 143
mat moss, 157, 159
milkweed, 125
mints, 130
mosses, 156–159, 188
   'Frosty Fern' (*Selaginella kraussiana* 'Variegata'), 14
mother-in-law's tongue, 79
moth orchids, 143, 146
muscari, 115, 116, 117, 119

N

narcissus / *Narcissus*, 16, 115, 119, 123
neoregelia / *Neoregelia marmorata*, 131, 235, 236
nepenthes, 187
nephrolepis / *Nephrolepis*, 109, 110, 178
never-never plant, 63

O

olive, fragrant and sweet, 124
Oncidium cheirophorum × O. ornithorhynchum 'Twinkle', 142–143, 145
orange, 41
orchids, 91, 143–146, 229
oregano / *Origanum*, 127–131
ornamental grasses, 64–68
Ornithogalum thyrsoides and *longibracteatum*, 15, 166, 167
Orthophytum gurkenii, 234
Osmanthus fragrans, 121, 124
oxalis / *Oxalis*, 69–73

P

pachyphytums / *Pachyphytum*, 261, 263, 265
paperwhites, 123
Paphiopedilum, 86–87, 145, 148
   Maudiae, 178
Papver nudicaule, 201
papyrus, 67
parlor maples, 279, 280
parrot's beak, 271
parsley, 87, 130
passion flowers / *Passiflora*, 254–259, 314
   caerulea, 16, 254–255, 257–258
   citrina, 258
   jorullensis, 256
patchouli, 130
peace lilies, 153
peacock moss, 158, 159
peacock plant, 60

pelargoniums, 147–151, 312
pelican flower, 269
pelican's beak, 271
pennisetum / *Pennisetum setaceum*, 65, 68
peperomias / *Peperomia*, 152–155
perennials, 194–195
perlite, 305
Persian violet, 134
phalaenopsis, 143, 145, 146
philodendron, 150
Phormium, 64
Pilea involucrata, 153
pineapple lily, 241–243
pineapple plant, 233, 236
pitcher plant, 185, 188
plant(s)
   care, 302
   favorites, 277
   moving outside in summer, 227–228
   shade-tolerant, 27, 155, 229, 298
   sun-loving, 229
Platycerium species, 111, 112
plectranthus / *Plectranthus oertendahlii*, 24–25, 74–77
Pogostemon heyneanus, 130
poinsettia, 91, 133, 136
Polypodium formosanum, 86–87, 108–109, 110, 214
Ponderosa lemon, 39, 40
poppies, Icelandic, 201
pots / potting and repotting, 174, 175, 230, 302–303. *See also* containers
prayer plant, 63

INDEX

ABOUT THE AUTHOR

Tovah Martin emerged from 25 years working at Logee's Greenhouses with a serious houseplant addiction. Author of the classics *The New Terrarium* and *Tasha Tudor's Garden*, Tovah has written more than a dozen gardening books. She served as garden editor for *Victoria* magazine throughout its lifetime, and currently writes for a broad range of magazines and periodicals, including *Country Gardens*, *Garden Design*, *Coastal Home*, *Martha Stewart Living*, *House Beautiful*, *Connecticut magazine*, *Yankee*, *The Litchfield County Times*, and *The Daily Telegraph*. For two years, she served as segment producer and frequent guest on the PBS television series *Cultivating Life*, and she is a repeat guest on the CBS *Sunday Early Show*. Tovah teaches houseplant cultivation to Master Gardeners and lectures extensively throughout the country.

An accredited Organic Land Care Professional through NOFA, Tovah gardens fanatically and organically both indoors and throughout her seven-acre Connecticut garden. In addition to bestowing their Sarah Chapman Francis Medal for "outstanding literary achievement" on Tovah in 2008, The Garden Club of America and the Litchfield Garden Club awarded Tovah honorary memberships. *People, Places, Plants* magazine called her "one of the top 10 most influential educators in gardening" and the Massachusetts Horticultural Society honored her with their Gold Medal "for extraordinary service to horticulture, especially greenhouses and indoor plants." For those who might need more handholding with their houseplants, Tovah provides advice and troubleshooting via her blog at plantswise.com.

Kindra Clineff travels far and wide specializing in location photography for commercial and editorial clients. She regularly produces feature assignments for national magazines, and her images have appeared in numerous books. Kindra also collaborated with Tovah Martin on her recent book, *The New Terrarium*. When not chasing light, Kindra can be found cultivating heirloom vegetables and attempting to tame the perennial garden of her seventeenth-century home in Essex County, Massachusetts.